Thinking
Through the Body

GENDER AND CULTURE
Carolyn G. Heilbrun and Nancy K. Miller, *editors*

GENDER AND CULTURE
A Series of Columbia University Press
Edited by Carolyn G. Heilbrun and Nancy K. Miller

In Dora's Case: Freud, Hysteria, Feminism
   Edited by Charles Bernheimer and Claire Kahane

Breaking the Chain: Women, Theory, and French Realist Fiction
   Naomi Schor

Between Men: English Literature and Male Homosocial Desire
   Eve Kosofsky Sedgwick

Romantic Imprisonment: Women and Other Glorified Outcasts
   Nina Auerbach

The Poetics of Gender
   Edited by Nancy K. Miller

Reading Woman: Essays in Feminist Criticism
   Mary Jacobus

Honey-Mad Women: Emancipatory Strategies in Women's Writing
   Patricia Yaeger

Subject to Change: Reading Feminist Writing
   Nancy K. Miller

Gender and the Politics of History
   Joan Wallach Scott

Thinking Through the Body

Jane Gallop

Columbia University Press

NEW YORK 1988

Columbia University Press
New York   Guildford, Surrey
Copyright © 1988 Columbia University Press

LIBRARY OF CONGRESS

Gallop, Jane, 1952—
Thinking through the body / Jane Gallop.
p.   cm. — (Gender and culture)
Essays originally published 1977–1986.
Includes bibliographies and index.
ISBN 0-231-06610-4 (alk. paper)
1. Feminist literary criticism. 2. Body, Human, in literature.
3. Sex in literature. 4. Feminism and literature. 5. Feminism—
Philosophy. 6. Women—Psychology. I. Title. II. Series.
PN98.W64G35 1988   87-34927
801'.95—dc19   CIP

Book design by Jennifer Dossin
Printed in the United States of America
Hardback editions of Columbia University Press books are Smyth-sewn
and are printed on permanent and durable acid-free paper.

FOR MAX

Who as yet thinks only through the body.
May he never lose that.

Contents

Acknowledgments

I want to thank the following publishers for permission to reprint:

"The Bodily Enigma" includes parts of the article "B/S" published in *Visible Language* (1977), vol. 11, no. 4.

"The Seduction of an Analogy" was originally published in *Diacritics* (1979), vol. 9, no. 1.

"Why Does Freud Giggle When the Women Leave the Room?" was originally published in *Hecate* (1984), vol. 11, no. 1.

"The Student Body" was originally published as "The Immoral Teachers" in *Yale French Studies* (1982), no. 63.

A substantially abridged version of "Sade, Mothers, and Other Women" was published in *enclitic* (1980), vol. 4, no. 2.

A substantially abridged version of "Snatches of Conversation" was published in *Women and Language in Literature and Society* (New York: Praeger, 1980).

"Lip Service" was originally published as *"Quand nos lèvres s'écrivent:* Irigaray's Body Politic" in *The Romanic Review* (1983), vol. 74, no. 1.

"The Perverse Body" was originally published as "Feminist Criticism and the Pleasure of the Text" in *North Dakota Quarterly* (1986), vol. 54, no. 2.

"Beyond the *Jouissance* Principle" © 1984 by The Regents of the University of California was originally published in *Representations* (Summer 1984), no. 7, pp. 110–15.

"Phallus/Penis: Same Difference" was originally published in *Men by Women: Women and Literature* (New York: Holmes and Meier, 1981).

"A Good Lay" was originally published as "Psychoanalytic Criticism: Some Intimate Questions" in *Art in America* (1984), vol. 72, no. 10.

"The Prick of the Object" was originally published as "The Pleasure of the Phototext" in *Afterimage* (1985), vol. 12, no. 2.

"The Other Woman" was originally published as "Annie Leclerc Writing a Letter, with Vermeer" in *October* (1985), no. 33.

Thinking Through the Body

"I am really asking whether women cannot begin, at last, to *think through the body*, to connect what has been so cruelly disorganized." This passage is from Adrienne Rich's *Of Woman Born;* the emphasis is Rich's.[1] The subtitled, indexed subject of Rich's first book of prose is motherhood, but *Of Woman Born* is also about what the European philosophical tradition calls "the mind-body problem," which has in fact had everything to do with motherhood.

"To connect what has been *so cruelly* disorganized": for Rich, thinking through the body is not primarily a happy reunion, an idyllic picnic in nature's warm embrace. The phrase "mind-body split" connotes appropriately metaphysical abstraction, even though it poses the fundamental question of and to metaphysics. But Rich's "so cruelly" may remind us that if we think physically rather than metaphysically, if we think the mind-body split *through the body*, it becomes an image of shocking violence.

One image stands out from Rich's beautifully composed book, appearing in the first and reappearing in the last chapter. From chapter 1: "In a living room in 1975, I spend an evening with a group of women poets, some of whom had children. . . . We talked of poetry, and also of infanticide, of the case of a local woman, the mother of eight . . . who had recently murdered and decapitated her two youngest, on her suburban front lawn" (p. 24). The last chapter begins: "On June 11, 1974, 'the first hot day of summer,' Joanne Michulski, thirty-eight, the mother of eight children . . . took a butcher knife, decapitated and chopped up the bodies of her two youngest on the neatly kept lawn of the suburban house where the family lived outside Chicago" (pp. 256–57). So cruelly disorganized. Decapitation: the mind-body split.

A mother decapitates her own children. Michulski's act appears outside the bounds of civilized human behavior; we are scandalized, fascinated, horrified. Yet in a silent, fundamental way, our civilization—with its neatly kept lawns proudly demonstrating our domination of nature—has achieved a systemic mind-body split that is in fact killing our children. As Rich puts it, "Culture: pure spirit, mind . . . has . . . split itself off from life, becoming the death-culture of quantification, abstraction, and the will to power which has reached its most refined destructiveness in this century" (p. 285).

A mother brutally murders her babies, the youngest two months old. The act seems inhuman; the perpetrator a monster. Yet Rich tells us that, in 1975, "every woman in that room who had children . . . could identify with her. . . . We spoke of our own murderous anger at our children" (p. 24). *Of Woman Born* not only speaks the secret of common maternal anger but treats that anger as a surface eruption of an even darker, deeper violence that systematically constitutes motherhood as a patriarchal institution. The mind-body split makes the mother into an inhuman monster by dividing the human realm of culture, history, and politics from the realm of love and the body where mother carries, bears, and tends her children.

Accomplice to the mind-body split, in capitalist patriarchy, is the division between public and private. "When we think of the institution of motherhood," writes Rich, "no symbolic architecture comes to mind, no visible embodiment of authority, power, or of potential or actual violence. Motherhood calls to mind the home, and we like to believe that the home is a private place" (p. 274). The home is a haven of intimacy, protected from the public eye by the rights of privacy. Motherhood is immured in the home. The creation of residential suburbs separates "home" further from the city of man and the brokering of power. In American middle-class society, the suburbs function as a mothering ghetto. Joanne Michulski brought maternal violence—violence by and to the mother—out of the home and onto the lawn, into the public eye. Adrienne Rich brings Michulski's desperate act out of the suburbs and reinscribes it in the world of work and meaning, power and knowledge.

Of Woman Born was published in 1976; it took Rich four years to write. That same year I received a Ph.D., after four years of graduate school, for a dissertation on the works of the Marquis de Sade. In early 1977, when I visited a university to be interviewed for a job, a feminist assistant professor asked me—in the privacy of her car— how a feminist could work on Sade. I was unable to give a coherent or convincing answer.

Sade's writings present an alternation of philosophical harangue and graphic sexual scene. He called his philosophical dialogues—which include a long revolutionary tract—*Philosophy in the Bedroom;* the gesture brings public discourse, knowledge, and meaning into the intimate space of love and the body. Connecting body to mind, Sade generates images of incredible brutality. He locates this cruelty in the very heart of society's most revered institutions: the church, the court, the family. Sade lends coherent, rational discourse to his butchers, struggling to give meaning to their barbaric acts. I think he created monstrous characters to-be-identified-with, by their author, by his readers, who are to recognize in them the image of their own unspeakable, aggressive desires. Attempting to enlarge the boundaries of philosophy so as to include the body at its crudest, he was also loosening the definition of the human so as to include his monsters.

Sade calls his monsters "philosophers." The philosophers hate mothers. In Sade, women can be philosophers. Female "philosophers" prefer anal intercourse, are experts on contraception and abortion, practice infanticide; in Sade's books, a philosopher never becomes a mother. *Philosophy in the Bedroom* climaxes in a scene of torturing the mother. In her reading of *Philosophy in the Bedroom,* first published in 1976, Luce Irigaray concedes that it lays bare "the sexuality that underlies our social order."[2]

Joanne Michulski, mother of eight, certainly does not have the curriculum vitae of a Sadian philosopher/butcher. In fact, she fits the description of a prime Sadian victim. Yet if we accept the connection between her violence and the violence done to her, then Rich's mother and Sade's philosopher face each other in blind rage and incomprehension across the mind-body divide.

The present book is a collection of essays, written over a decade, from the mid-seventies to the mid-eighties. The oldest piece in the collection, "Sade, Mothers, and Other Women," is an attempt to work out Sade's relation to mothers, in his novels and his life. Written during the years when I was working to become a Doctor of Philosophy, it does not fully succeed in working through that relation. Five years later, I wrote "The Student Body," my reading of *Philosophy in the Bedroom* and my attempt to understand "the sexuality that underlies" my chosen profession.

The first essay in this collection—"The Bodily Enigma"—also discusses Sade. I chose to head off the collection with this piece because it explores the way thinking through the body can go and has gone wrong in a male European philosophical tradition. Rather than treat the body as a site of knowledge, a medium for thought, the more classic philosophical project has tried to render it transparent and get beyond it, to dominate it by reducing it to the mind's idealizing categories.

Sade's writing is undoubtedly an attempt to contain everything in the categories of logic. His corporeal encounter is, however, also unflinching enough to bear witness to the inevitable failure of such a project, teaching willy-nilly that the body always exceeds the mind's order. This cohabitation of both meanings of the phrase "thinking through the body" points to a difficulty at its heart, the impossibility in our cultural tradition of separating an earnest attempt to listen to the material from an agenda for better control.

In "The Bodily Enigma" Sade is joined by Roland Barthes, whose work also exemplifies these two different modes of intellection—attentive encounter and dominating project. Whereas his reading of Sade is a systematic reduction of everything to logical order, he eloquently recognizes the impossibility of intellectually mastering the body in *Roland Barthes par roland barthes*, the book which provided the phrase "The Bodily Enigma."

Published in 1975, that book is an unusual combination of theory and autobiography. On the crest of post-structuralism, the French literary critic crosses the line between scholar and writer, and at the same time blurs the boundary between public and private. The next year Adrienne Rich published *Of Woman Born;* it too is an extraordinary mix of autobiography and scholarship. In the heat of American radical feminist thought, the poet crosses over to scholarship and yet refuses to respect the separation between objectivity and subjectivity. Barthes and Rich: strange bedfellows? I presume that the two books were conceived and executed in ignorance of each other. But they appeared at the moment this American feminist pursuing French studies at the height of post-structuralism was dreaming of such an impossible couple.

The present book dates back to the moment of these two books. Both the poet trying to write documented nonfiction and the theorist trying to be a "writer" were rethinking the relation to the body. Both were challenging the split between public and private which keeps our lives out of our knowledge. In collecting my essays for this retrospective volume, I found myself adding autobiographical bits, not only, I hope, because I tend toward exhibitionism but, more important, because at times I think through autobiography: that is to say, the chain of associations that I am pursuing in my reading passes through things that happened to me.

At the age of eleven months I was strangled and left for dead by a woman who cared for me. I have no memory of the event, of course, but learned about it years later from a newspaper clipping my mother gave me to read.[3] Whereas decapitation actually severs head from body, strangling simply stops the life-giving flow between the two. Strangling may be a more accurate figure for the "cruel disorganization" that prevents us from thinking through the body.

The passage between theory and life story is paved by two non-aligned intellectual movements of the seventies—American feminism and French post-structuralism. *Of Woman Born* and *Roland Barthes par roland barthes* make that journey in the mid-seventies and bring us back riches. The present book takes its title from Rich. It is also a working through my intellectual filiation to Barthes. Two of his books, published while I was a graduate student, heartened me, gave me the courage to write. One was his "autobiography"; the other was *The Pleasure of the Text*, appearing two years earlier. In the seventies I was unable to write coherently about Barthes. "The Bodily Enigma" originated in the mid-seventies but has been radically revised for the present volume. The other essays on Barthes were written during a twelve-month period in 1983 and 1984. "The Perverse Body," "Beyond the *Jouissance* Principle," and "The Prick of the Object" all think through *The Pleasure of the Text*.

That 1973 book provides an interesting example of both modes of knowledge: categorizing and sensitivity to what is violated by such categories. Not only does it set up an opposition between pleasure and jouissance, but at the same time, it insists upon the inadequacy of any such opposition to account for the subtle relation between these two terms, which are sometimes opposed, sometimes united. The title "Beyond the *Jouissance* Principle" pokes fun at the neat distinction by substituting one for the other in its allusion to the title of a book by Freud, *Beyond the Pleasure Principle*.

Freud is the third thinker occasioning several essays in the present collection. He too worked at the juncture of the autobiographical and the theoretical, inventing a science by interpreting his own dreams and personal history in connection with his work with others. The chapter called "The Anal Body" contains two short essays on Freud from the late seventies. The essay "A Good Lay," found in the last chapter, dates from 1984. All three essays read Freud not so much for his knowledge of subjectivity as for the imprint of his own subjectivity upon his pursuit of knowledge.

Rich finds Freud disappointing, not so much—as one might suppose—as a feminist but, ultimately, as a poet. "Rereading Freud, and some Freudians . . . what finally leaves the strongest impression is a tone-deafness in the language. This may well result from the psychoanalysts' desire to feel that they are dealing with memory, dream, fantasy, on a 'scientific' level; that is, in the false sense of science as the opposite of poetry" (*Of Woman Born*, p. 201). Memories, dreams, and fantasies cannot be known outside the subject's accounts of them; they are not available for objective verification. Psychoanalysis, as the study of such suspect phenomena, a study that must pass through the mediation of subjectivity, is extremely anxious about its status as a science, since "classical science [is] rooted in the premise that the subject can and should be totally removed from our description of the object."[4]

In the preface to the first edition of his first solo book, *The Interpretation of Dreams*, Freud explains that he had no choice but to use his own dreams for constructing and demonstrating his theories. "But if I was to report my own dreams," he adds, "it inevitably followed that I should have to reveal to the public gaze more of the intimacies of my mental life than I liked, or than is normally necessary for any writer who is a man of science and not a poet."[5] For Freud, the scientist respects the division between private and public, whereas the poet "reveals the intimacies of [his] mental life to the public gaze." Freud finds in dreams the very sort of intimate violence that Joanne Michulski brought out onto the lawn. Rich tells us that "every poet could identify with [Michulski]" (p. 24).

Freud nevertheless does use his own dreams as the material for his book, apologizing and justifying throughout, repeatedly trying to defend its scientific status. Trained in classical nineteenth-century experimental science, Freud found himself, in his study of dreams, resembling a poet. Willy-nilly, he stumbled into a realm of knowledge where science is not clearly separate from poetry.

The first essay on Freud, "The Seduction of an Analogy," considers the option of reading Freud as a literary text, an option that can be justified by all those points throughout his work where Freud notes that his writing resembles a work of the imagination. This genre-change operation, reassigning Freud to the other side of the science-poetry divide, would ignore the way his work is located so as to call into question the neat distinction between science and poetry. Rich is disappointed because Freud seems too attached to the classic definition of science. She is too quick to assimilate Freud to "some Freudians" who have tried to protect the scientific status of psychoanalysis in an economy that privileges science and devalues poetry. I am heartened by the possibility of reading Freud in a way that challenges the neat opposition between science and poetry, objectivity and subjectivity, theory and intimacy.

The second essay in "The Anal Body," unlike the first, could be said to read Freud from a woman's point of view. A footnote to *Of Woman Born* suggests how woman would read Freud. "[W]oman-reading-Freud . . . has to ask herself, not merely 'What does my prior intellectual training tell me?' but 'What do my memories, my sexuality, my dreams?' " (p. 95 *n*). What Rich sees women bringing to their reading of Freud seems only appropriate. The founder of psychoanalysis could be said to have built his "science" out of Rich's two questions, combining his "prior intellectual training" with knowledge gained through his memories, sexuality, dreams.

If Freud, and Barthes, and Sade were all doing critical thinking connected to the body, then men too must be capable of crossing the divide. But lest this become a universal human issue, beyond gender, let us remember the ways in which it is both harder and easier for men. Harder because men have their masculine identity to gain by being estranged from their bodies and dominating the bodies of others. Easier because men are more able to venture into the realm of the body without being trapped there. Men who do find themselves in some way thinking through the body are more likely to be recognized as serious thinkers and heard. Women have first to prove that we are thinkers, which is easier when we conform to the protocol that deems serious thought separate from an embodied subject in history. Rich is asking women to enter the realms of critical thought and knowledge without becoming disembodied spirit, universal man. As a woman academic, I dared make connections between my work and "my memories, my sexuality, my dreams" only because of the example of men who had challenged the classic split in knowledge and were nonetheless influential thinkers.

Besides the pieces on Sade, Barthes, and Freud, this collection includes four essays on women who were rewriting the body in the mid-seventies. "Snatches of Conversation" is a reading of the 1976 *Hite Report*, showing it to be a classic attempt to dominate the body through ideas. My reading gets at the desire and fantasy under the white coat of an objective report, and closes with a provocative image of a "French feminist." The other essays are readings of what we Americans call "French feminists." In the seventies, I hoped French feminism to be the impossible marriage of Adrienne Rich and Roland Barthes.

"Phallus/Penis: Same Difference" looks at another 1976 book—*Partage des femmes* by a woman Lacanian analyst, Eugénie Lemoine-Luccioni—and finds there theory imbued with female heterosexual desire. The essay's title is meant to poke fun at the separation of phallus and penis in Lacanian theory, a division which exemplifies the

mind-body split, disembodying the phallus and rendering it transcendental. The disembodied phallus is the linchpin of the move that
raises maleness, a bodily attribute, to the realm of the spirit, leaving
femaleness mired in inert flesh.

The essay "Lip Service" is central to this entire collection. It is a
study of Luce Irigaray, who has frequently been accused of biological
essentialism. Concentrating on her 1977 volume *Ce Sexe qui n'en est
pas un*, I find she is not trapped in the body but uses anatomical
figures to renew thought, to move it out of its ideological ruts. The
tendency to dismiss Irigaray as trapped in biologism bespeaks the
split which makes us suspect that any sustained attention to the body
must fall outside the bounds of serious thought.

The last essay of the book, "The Other Woman," reads Annie
Leclerc's 1977 text "The Love Letter." It is an attempt to consider
class difference *through the body*. Thinking through the body may seem
most appropriate for reflecting on gender, but it is essential that we
not restrict our embodied intellection to sexual difference lest we
reinforce the split between women's issues (love, family, sexuality)
and "serious" subjects (military history, cultural imperialism, political economy), trapping feminist thinkers out in the suburbs of intellectual life.

The last essay begins and ends by thinking about book covers. For
the cover of the present collection I chose a photograph that shows
the head in the midst of the body. "Lip Service" comments that the
female genitals are "normally considered to be at the antipodes of
culture." I wanted to represent thinking there, to undo that opposition.

There was some question about the suitability of using this picture.
Some people find the picture gross. I wanted to put an image of the
body out on the front cover that was not already neatly placed, that
might still have some power to disturb. It was suggested that the
nurse be cropped out to make the photo easier to read. I like the en-
tanglement, the difficulty in sorting out one body from another. It
was feared that people would think it a book about obstetrics rather
than a book of theory. In thinking about Sade for this introduction,
I came to see the mind-body split as exemplified in an opposition
between philosophers and mothers.

Of course, that uncanny little head is surrounded by body for but
a brief pause in an irrepressible progress. Things will soon be sorted
out into their proper categories: mother, baby, doctor, nurse. At this
point in history, thinking that truly passes through the body only occurs in brief intervals, soon to be reabsorbed by the powerful nar-

ratives of mind over matter. Like the photograph, I want to catch and hold on to those moments when something else occurs.

Notes

1. Adrienne Rich, *Of Woman Born: Motherhood as Experience and Institution* (New York: Norton, 1976), p. 284.

2. Luce Irigaray, " 'Françaises,' ne faites plus un effort . . . ," in *Ce Sexe qui n'en est pas un* (Paris: Minuit, 1977), pp. 197–202. Translated by Catherine Porter as " 'Frenchwomen,' Stop Trying," in *This Sex Which Is Not One* (Ithaca: Cornell University Press, 1985), pp. 198–204.

3. "Hearing in Choking," *Duluth Herald*, March 31, 1953, sunset final, p. 1.

4. Evelyn Fox Keller, *Reflections on Gender and Science* (New Haven: Yale University Press, 1985), p. 84. Keller convincingly links the subject-object split to the patriarchal institution of motherhood and demonstrates how it deforms the pursuit of scientific knowledge.

5. Sigmund Freud, *The Interpretation of Dreams*, in *The Standard Edition of the Complete Psychological Works*, ed. James Strachey (London: Hogarth, 1953–74), 4:xxiii–xxiv.

1.

The Bodily Enigma

BS No More

In 1975, I wrote a dissertation chapter on Barthes's reading of Sade. Some months later I met with my dissertation director; we tore the chapter to shreds, while I laughed hysterically at the stupidity of my reading of Barthes. The chapter was not included in the dissertation. This was a turning point in that "book" project: I gave up my position of facile superiority—trying to show how every reader of Sade before me had been wrong—and entered into a more sympathetic and complex relation with the Sade readers I was studying.

Although the dissertation was far better for the loss of that chapter, I regretted not registering my reading of Barthes on Sade. When I was a graduate student, Barthes was the leading literary critic–theorist in French studies. He had already passed out of his scientific stance (structuralism) into something that seemed softer, more subjective, more bodily. The Barthes of the seventies authorized my own push out of objective, scholarly discourse into something more embodied. Comparing Barthes's reading of Sade to my own was a way of articulating my relation to the authorized form of embodied criticism.

In 1977 when I arrived at Miami University as an assistant professor, my new colleague Randolph Runyon told me about a "Barthes issue" of the journal *Visible Language* that was being prepared. I saw an opportunity to retool my discarded chapter and get it published. Since the context was *Visible Language*, I felt it needed a framing shtick about letters.

I quickly whipped up a piece I entitled "BS." At the time I thought it a clever, outrageous title—based on Barthes's *S/Z*—for an article concluding on the difference between the shape of the letter B and the shape of the letter S. "B, like S, is comprised of two half-circles which *do not* come together to form a circle. But in B, they face the same way, fragmentary but not in conflict; *and they are barred.* Rol and bar the S."[1] I see now that the title was also my way of commenting on the clever sort of disinvested intellectual play which I thought I needed to get published.

Not fundamentally interested in "letters," I was concerned with the body, but thought I could use a fashionable surface to dress my interest in the body and allow it to pass into publication. The result was one of my most alienated pieces of writing.

In 1986 when I collected my essays for this book, I included "BS," still not able to read what was writ large in the title. It was the only essay which the editors of the Gender and Culture Series thought should not be included. I nonetheless wanted to retain something of this effort to consider the relation between Barthes and Sade who, as critical authority and quasi-canonical author, were absolutely central figures authorizing my attempt to think through the body. I have tried to strip off the clever surface and salvage some of the ideas about the body and desire which were twice buried beneath the bullshit of intellectual gamesmanship.

The Bodily Enigma

In 1975, Roland Barthes, by then France's preeminent literary critic, published a book in the series "the writer by himself" called *Roland Barthes by roland barthes.* Although normally the "writers" in the series are dead, their books compiled by someone else, a critic, Barthes still alive places himself in this series, thus functioning as both writer and critic. The book bespeaks a fascination with self, but it is a self divided and doubled in the very title. Writing about himself as about another, Barthes embraces himself not in transparent self-possession but doubled, thus split, opaque, and beyond reach. The split of self into writer and critic, into subject and object of the book, moves not toward the all-encompassing whole of narcissistic fantasy, self-possession, self-sufficiency but toward the self as enigma.

In *Roland Barthes by roland barthes* the author displays a fascination with simple enumerations of his likes and dislikes in their irreducibility to any meaning. "Thus out of this anarchic foam of tastes and distastes, gradually emerges the outline of a bodily enigma."[2] Bedrock given, a priori to any subjectivity, the body calls out for interpretation, hermeneutic solutions to its being-as-riddle. The human being cannot help but try to make sense out of his own idiosyncratic body shape: tall or short, fat or thin, male or female, to name but a few of the least subtle morphological distinctions. Outside the theological model there is no possibility of verifying an interpretation: no author to have intended a sense in composing such a body. No guaranteed sense, but still there is a particular shape, intimating associations, molding and containing the "anarchic foam." A shape which by being distinct and diacritically *not another shape* (tall, not short) is a signifier, the signifier as enigma, teasing allusion to a signification to-be-guessed, yet without a puzzle-master to pronounce the verdict of "correct divination."

Not just the physical envelope, but other puzzling and irreducible givens, arising from the "body" if that word means all that in the organism which exceeds and antedates consciousness or reason or interpretation. By "body" I mean here: perceivable givens that the human being knows as "hers" without knowing their significance to her. In such a way a taste for a certain food or a certain color, a distaste for another, are pieces of the bodily enigma. We can, a posteriori, form an esthetic, consistent system of values (rules for Good Taste) to rationalize our insistent, idiosyncratic tastes. But the system is a guess at the puzzle, a response to the inscrutable given. A taste for women, or men, little children, decrepit invalids; a predilection for legs, breasts, asses, hands, feet, panties; a repulsion for spiders, worms, blood: we can (and do) theorize endlessly about the peculiarities of individual taste/distaste. But the theorizing is precisely endless, an eternal reading of the "body" as authorless text, full of tempting, persuasive significance, but lacking a final guarantee of intended meaning.

One way to make sense of, rationalize, aestheticize our bodily givens, our embarrassing shapes and insistent tastes is to transform them into a consistent style. Barthes theorizes this opposition between consistent style and the insistent. In the preface to *Sade, Fourier, Loyola* he specifies that, as opposed to the "consistency" implied by style, "writing, to borrow Lacanian terminology, knows only *insistances*."[3] An "insistance" is a "symptom," an unconscious message that persists in manifesting itself despite its nonsense or inconsistency.

Sade, Fourier, Loyola contains four critical essays—the first and last on Sade, the second on Loyola, the third on Fourier. After the four essays, there is a nine-page Life of Sade and a two-page Life of Fourier; Loyola has no Life. Instead of a Life of Loyola, we have only the single remark in the preface that what grabs Barthes from the Jesuit's life is, exclusively, "his beautiful eyes always slightly filled with tears." In the article on Loyola we learn that in Loyola's *Spiritual Journal* there is a graphic code for tears: "A = tears before mass (*antes*); L = tears during mass (*lacrima*); D = tears after mass (*despues*); L– = sparse tears, etc." (p. 79 *n*). These notations in the *Journal* are Loyola's inscription of his bodily enigma.

To be sure, Ignatius de Loyola gives full credence to the theological model of knowledge. Reading his body with Barthesian fascination, he wishes to interpret God's intention. Yet he cannot know God's meaning. The solution to his body-as-enigma is a question of faith. As a mortal bereft of total immediate communion with the Godhead, he cannot be certain.

So his journal simply marks down the brute facts; the scribe copies God's text, ignorant of its sense. Loyola's writing does not theorize or interpret but simply notes, faithfully, the unexplained, irreducible phenomenon of tears. The Jesuit's transcription of the bodily enigma is both the mark of physical passion, of the prelogical flow of corporal fluid, and a monument to God's silence, God's refusal to resolve the enigma, which can only be traced, not interpreted.

My insistence on the mark of an enigmatic silence (sign of an impossible transcendence) in *Sade, Fourier, Loyola* contradicts the explicit thesis of Barthes's book. According to the preface, Sade, Fourier, and Loyola are juxtaposed in order to dismiss their transcendent ideologies (which they do not share): sadism, revolution, religion. This reunion would rather emphasize their similar practices of writing ("same erotics of classification, same enumerative obsession," p. 7). Barthes reads the three as "Logothetes," founders of languages, and thus producers of fortified, closed systems: "the reconstitution of a whole, for them, can only be an addition of intelligibles: nothing unspeakable, no irreducible quality of ecstasy, happiness, communication: nothing that is not Spoken" (p. 9). In these obsessional, fortified systems of defense,[4] the articulation and the order work to keep out the pain, despair, and chaos caused by transcendent ineffables.

Whereas the last essay in the book, Sade II, is fragmentary, choppy, composed of unabashed sharp breaks, Sade I, the first essay, is continuous, organized around a thesis, a logical argument leading to a verdict. At the conclusion of Sade I, Barthes declares that "the function of discourse . . . is to conceive the inconceivable, that is, to leave nothing outside words and to allow the world no ineffables: this, it seems, is the keynote which repeats through the Sadian world, from the Bastille, where Sade existed only through words, to Silling Castle, not a sanctuary of debauchery but of the 'story'" (p. 42). The "story" reigns supreme in the Sadian world. Narrative consistency contains enigmatic, disruptive "insistances." Or does it?

The only illustration in *Sade, Fourier, Loyola* is a rendering of the amphitheater which is the center of Silling Castle, scene of Sade's novel *120 Days of Sodom*. Daily, in that amphitheater, a prostitute/storyteller recounts five scenes of criminal/sexual pleasure in lurid detail. The four libertine friends who have arranged this for their own greater pleasure are surrounded by various categories of objects for their desire: pretty young girls and boys; extraordinarily well-endowed young men; decrepit old women; the friends' own wives and daughters. When moved by a story, a libertine can reenact it using any of the objects he chooses.

Barthes presents this amphitheater as the emblem of Sadian writing: a universe enclosed within the safe boundaries of the "story." "Practice follows the word and is absolutely determined by it: what is done has been said" (p. 40). Yet in the preface to this scene of supposed adequation of word to act ("absolutely determined by it"), the narrator confesses, "it is certain that these gentlemen, behind-the-scenes and before it was quite exactly permitted, indulged in things which had not yet been recounted to them, and in that they were in violation of the conventions they had established."[5] Having established conventions specifically for the regulation of violations, they turned around and violated those regulations. The narrator makes confessions similar to this over half a dozen times in the course of *120 Days of Sodom*, and at the end of the existing manuscript (which is but a first draft), in his notes for revision, Sade chides himself: "Above all never have the four friends do anything that has not been narrated; you were not careful about that" (p. 526).

In order to emphasize his point about the absolute determination of action by story, Barthes adds a footnote: "Crime has exactly the same 'dimensions' as the word: when the storytellers reach the murderous passions, the harem will empty out" (p. 40 *n*). The four libertines do wait until the fourth month (month of narrated murders) before they kill any of their victims. However, this deferral is a difficult sacrifice. On two separate occasions a couple of the libertines, carried away by passion (that is, inspired by something outside the daily storytelling) appeal for the right to annihilate a victim before that fourth month (see p. 448 and pp. 472–73). The order imposed by the story is not absolutely secure; these disruptions bespeak the force of what is suppressed. And although the libertines manage to kill no one until the fourth month, they actually kill only a small number of their victims during that fourth month; and none of the murders follow the blueprints offered in the storyteller-of-the-month's examples (cf. Barthes: "Practice follows the word and is absolutely determined by it"). In fact, the majority of victims are killed after the 120th day, when the storytelling structure itself has disappeared. In exuberant excess of the framing "story" called *120 Days of Sodom*, the libertines stay a fifth month, until the snow melts.

Even when a libertine does faithfully reenact a "passion" recounted by the storyteller, the fact that certain stories move him and others do not as well as the choice of particular "objects" for his performance reflect some taste or preference beyond the closed circuit of story (acting-out recounted by the novel) repeating story (prostitutes' narration). The predilection indicates a bodily enigma; it points to an outside—beyond/before language.

The last paragraph of Sade II presents a hierarchized alternative of two ways of reading Sade: "Of course, Sade can be read according to a project of violence; but he can also be read (and this is what he recommends we do) according to a principle of delicacy" (p. 174). Barthes chooses not to read Sade according to a "project of violence." Yet Sadian violence is not simply crimes of mutilation and violation. The really disconcerting violence in Sade disrupts the Sadian system itself. Sade's text is scarred by breaks in its obsessive structures, chinks in the fortifications that enclose this world and render it stable and orderly. The real, untamed violence in Sade is the persistence of a bodily enigma which never can be definitively interpreted. As Barthes says in the preface to *Sade, Fourier, and Loyola:* "as style [consistency] becomes absorbed by writing [insistances], the system unravels into systematics" (p. 11). Sade's work is obsessively systematic but never settles into a totally closed system.

As an emblem for this other Sadian violence ("in violation of the conventions they had established"), I would propose the heroine's breaking out of the convent at Sainte-Marie-des-Bois in the novel *Justine.* That convent is the ultimate closure: everyone and everything is arranged in categories. The convent is isolated, impregnable, surrounded by seven walls. We are even told that the seven walls are gratuitous since it is already impossible for a victim to get out of the building. Yet the obsessive proliferation of defensive structures is only the inadequate response to the inevitable although impossible escape of Justine. Sade creates an inescapable closed system and a character who breaks out.

Barthes sees in Sade only the violence encompassed by the system—ordered, arranged violent acts. He ignores the violations to the system, thus dismissing Sadian violence as contained, consistent, and uninteresting.

In the reading of Fourier which is part of Barthes's book on Sade (libraries classify *Sade, Fourier, Loyola* in the Sade section), Barthes writes: "Fourierist pleasure is free from evil: it does not include vexation, in the Sadian manner, but on the contrary dissipates it; his discourse is one of 'general well-being': for example, in the war of love (game and theater), out of delicacy, so as not to upset, the flags and leaders are not captured" (p. 187). Fourierist pleasure is camped under the banner of delicacy rather than that of violence. So when Barthes chooses to read Sade "according to a principle of delicacy" rather than a "project of violence," he gives Sade a Fourierist reading. In fact, the very last sentence of the book (where the conclusion might be), which is actually the last item in the Life of Fourier, is "Fourier had read Sade" (p. 188).

Barthes's exposition of the Fourierist view of violence continues: "What if someone has a taste for vexation? Must he be allowed to do it? Pleasure in vexation is due to a congestion; so Harmony [Fourier's Utopia] will decongest the passions and sadism will be reabsorbed." Violence here is domesticated, and ultimately cured as a contingent malfunction. Fourier's Utopia, where no pleasure will be looked at askance, excludes sadism, denies it any status as a passion. If admitted, violence would threaten the entire stable system of Harmony. Echoing this Fourierist reduction of violence, in his final entry in the Life of Sade, remarking on the fact that the marquis in prison was denied both writing and exercise, Barthes declares that "with neither stroll nor pen, Sade *becomes congested*" (p. 186, emphasis Barthes's).

Fourier "reabsorbs" Sadian violence into Harmony. Fourier serves Barthes as a way of dominating what is most disquieting in Sade, a violence that opens onto some radical exteriority. Contradiction in Sade retains its intensity as disturbing conflict, as a rift in the mind's logical domination of the world. Sade is distressed over his transgressions of his own self-imposed order in writing *120 Days of Sodom*. "You were not careful about that," he tells himself. In order to tell himself, he uses a second person pronoun. The split is between a "you" that violated the system and an "I" (implied first person of second person usage) who is anxious to secure that system.

Barthes has a theory of contradictions to calm him. He chooses to write fragments, opts for ruptures and inconsistencies, and supports this choice with an ideology of writing (insistances) as opposed to style (consistency). Convinced that contradiction is inevitable, that fractured writing is "truer," more "authentic" than attempts to cloak the bodily enigma in meaning, rather than being vexed by persistent contradiction, Barthes can feel gratified at this verification of his theory.

Barthes's celebration of the fragmentary, of "writing," is simply the latest ruse of style, the formulation of a style that is consistent with the inevitability of discontinuity. *Choosing* fragmentation is a strategy to recontain the violence of contradiction by means of an overarching theory of inconsistency, creating a work in which inconsistency would not be out of place, putting inconsistency in its place just as Sade would put violence in its place. Yet in order to do that Barthes must posit the absolute consistency, closure, and adequation of Sade's writing. This allows it to appear to be a question of choice between closure and inconsistency. To choose fragmentation as a style is to erect a consistent defense against the body as insubordinate to man-made meaning.

Sade's project was to contain the body at its most violently passionate within the categories of logic; and so is Barthes's. Sade did his utmost, and failed. Barthes does not recognize Sade's failure. The body is enigmatic because it is not a creation of the mind.

Afterthoughts

In graduate school I read Rousseau's *Julie*, noting in the margin each time I cried. I imagined that some day I could do a reading based on understanding when I cried and why. This fantasy was kin to the project of writing on Sade, a text which moved me to masturbate. I wanted to think through these physical responses to reading.

The connection between these two productions of bodily fluids— tears and arousal—points to a similarity between the sentimental (coded as feminine) and the pornographic (coded as masculine). In Sade, the difference between libertines and victims is that, in the same situation, libertines get aroused whereas victims cry.

The Fourierist dismissal of sadism from the socialist sexual utopia finds a striking echo in the contemporary feminist rejection of lesbian sadomasochism.[6] Both see the desire for violence as a sickness that must be excluded from the utopic space of Harmony. In both cases, what is at stake is the attempt to contain the body within discourse, to make desire consistent with political discourse. The really disturbing violence is not physical violence but the physical as it violates the rational categories that would contain and dominate it. Defensive suppression is another form of violent domination, but one which if successful passes under the guise of calm and order rather than violence.[7] Sade insisted that one must distinguish between the explicitly eroticized acting-out of domination and real political domination.[8] Contemporary lesbian feminist sadomasochists are making the same claim.[9]

The closed world of discourse—"nothing outside words"—is the structuralist version of the modernist doctrine of the autonomy of the work of art. Now it is not just Poetry, not just Art, but all language, discourse that is a closed world. Feminists attacked modernism/formalism for raising defensive barriers that protected literature from worldly concerns: history, politics, ideology, life. Barthes's structuralist closure likewise defends against something outside language, outside logic, against a body that is not already rationalized and subordinated to discourse.

The sense of superiority over old-fashioned closure and style is a modernist gesture. Barthes's "writing" is the latest style, truer and more adequate than what precedes it. It is a modernist defense against the realization that the body will never be totally dominated by man-made meaning.

Barthes's inscription of himself into a series of dead writers has an interesting relation to his banner phrase "the death of the author." Having encountered that idea which at its most radical undercuts any writer's ability to control and dominate his writing, Barthes's strategy is to choose to be a dead author, thus making what undercuts the will appear to be a matter we can will. Death is a key part of the bodily enigma, perhaps the most violent sign that we live in a nonsensical body which limits the powers of our will and consciousness. Yet the doctrine of the death of the author ironically became a way of separating the text from any human who might have lived in a body, the last gesture of formalist autonomy defending against any body outside language, outside discourse. "Ironically" because the literal death of the author is a mark that the author is mortal, that is, embodied. This irony, this contradiction, bespeaks the way the death of the author, like the choice of "writing" over style, is the latest defense strategy against the realizations of death, contradiction, and embodiment which can never totally be dominated by some autonomous mind, art, or discourse.

Barthes moves from the classic domination of scientific structuralism to the cleverer and more subtle mechanisms which characterize a certain post-structuralist embrace of what undercuts mastery as the last hope of some masterful position in a world in which the sons of Descartes, the sons of a certain Western European tradition of subjugating the secondary body to a disembodied consciousness, are less and less able to maintain that domination, a domination which historically depended on other sexes, classes, and races to embody the body as well as care for the Master's body so he would not have to be concerned with it, so he could consider himself disembodied, autonomous, and free to will.

Notes

1. Jane Gallop, "BS," *Visible Language* (1977), 11(4):386.
2. *Roland Barthes par roland barthes* (Paris: Seuil, 1975), p. 121. All translations mine.
3. Roland Barthes, *Sade, Fourier, Loyola* (Paris: Seuil, 1971).
4. In reference to both Loyola and Sade, Barthes mentions a "defensive redan" (pp. 66 and 183). A "redan" is a firmly resilient, defensive wall fortified by joining wall sections at salient angles.
5. D.A.F. de Sade, *120 Journées de Sodome* (Paris: Pauvert, 1972).
6. See Robin Linden et al., eds., *Against Sadomasochism* (California: Frog in the Well, 1982).
7. For an insightful articulation of these three kinds of violence, see Jacques Derrida, *Of Grammatology*, trans. Gayatri Chakravorty Spivak (Baltimore: Johns Hopkins University Press, 1976), p. 112.
8. D.A.F. de Sade, *Le Philosophie dans le boudoir*, in *Oeuvres complètes* (Paris: Pauvert, 1970), 25:283n.
9. See Members of Samois, ed., *Coming to Power* (Boston: Alyson, 1982).

2.
The Anal Body

Premeditation on a Seduction

In October 1977, Naomi Schor asked me to replace a well-known critic who had backed out of her upcoming MLA session. Although the convention was only two months away, as a first-semester assistant professor I jumped at the chance to speak in a session called "Freud as Literary Text." I felt like the understudy who gets her chance to go on stage. My wish to captivate the audience probably occasioned the metaphor of seduction.

Called in to replace a successful older male critic, I wanted to make it possible for me to be in the father's place. In wishful identification with Freud, I put him in the position of seducee. Freud is seduced through his desire to be in the father's place; so am I. Yet I can only accede to the father's place by first unveiling his femininity. In this piece I demonstrate that Freud is a "whore."

My desire to be an academic, intellectual speaker is a desire to speak from the father's place. Yet the spiritual father's place (ideologically, the place of the academic who was originally a cleric) demands separation of ideas from desire, a disembodied mind. I want to expose the father's desire so that I could take his place but as a sexed subject. If the intellectual, the cleric, epitomizes the life of the mind, woman epitomizes the life of the body. To be a woman intellectual necessitated an attack on the supposed objectivity and transcendence of the thinker. If Freud admitted being seduceable, then a woman too could speak as a thinker.

The Seduction of an Analogy

Psychoanalytic criticism of literature has been condemned as reductive by champions of the complexity and plurality of the literary text. Critics who want to respect this textuality of literature and yet are nonetheless drawn to Freud are attempting a reverse operation. Rather than a psychoanalytic reading of a literary text, we can do a "literary reading" of a psychoanalytic text.

For example, we can turn our reading expertise on Freud. Thus we are liberated from the awesome figure of Freud's scientific, therapeutic discoveries and can indulge in the pleasures afforded by the marvelous prose he wrote but could not and does not control. Freud's text, as literary text, can be read with the attentive respect we have learned for literature, a respect for the tissue of literary language which precludes any reduction, for practical purposes, to some single, intended sense.

Annexing Freud's writing to the realm of the literary transgresses the boundary between literary and nonliterary texts. In place of a difference between genres, we have a difference between two kinds of reading: literary and nonliterary. Literary reading here implies painstaking regard for a plurality of signification; nonliterary reading demands reduction to a manipulable sense in the service of efficient use.

That opposition between painstaking regard and efficient use is not only a highly moralized issue in literary theory; it also poses a conflict for Freud. In a short article of 1937 called "Constructions in Analysis," Freud writes: "I am aware that it is of small service to handle so important a subject in the cursory fashion that I have employed. But nonetheless I have not been able to resist the seduction of an analogy."[1] Freud's generally reiterated commitment to attentive appreciation for details makes it rather unsavory to "handle a subject in [a] cursory fashion." Analogy leads him to compromise his attention and go too far too fast. He knows he ought to resist, but despite his principles, Freud always was a sucker for a juicy analogy. After slow, careful exposition of the workings of one facet of analytic technique, Freud's article suddenly leaps headlong, in hot pursuit of analogy, first into indecorous speculation about delusions in general and then, going all the way, to a totally unsubstantiated declaration about religion's relation to mankind.

Noticing the same tendency to sacrifice caution for speed at the lure of an analogy, Roland Barthes terms this leap forth onto shaky grounds "The Galloping Induction."[2] Unable to resist a fault which has, so to speak, my name on it, I would like to venture an analogy: the reader who would reduce writing to some manipulable signification for the sake of utility is like the analyst who would seek a way to shorten the duration of analysis.

In another 1937 article called "Analysis Terminable and Interminable," where Freud considers this question of foreshortening analytic therapy, the possibility of speedy analysis seems to be attended by an insistent notion of "prosperity." The word "prosperity" appears twice in salient English in the original German version of the article. Freud dismisses Otto Rank's experiment in speeding up analysis as an effect of "the haste of American life," which is the correlate of "prosperity." Haste, Rank, and prosperity are soon dispatched since, in 1937, as Freud says, American prosperity is "a thing of the past."

Yet the cohesion of haste and prosperity survives an abrupt shift in perspective, a turn toward the Russian rather than the American horizon. Freud himself had tried to speed up analytic treatment in the care of a young Russian, who was, according to Freud, "a man spoilt by wealth." The prosperity of this young Russian (famous to us as the Wolfman) is like America's: that is, a thing of the past. When the young man later returned from the war, destitute, it was necessary to continue his therapy, thus belying Freud's attempt at an efficient treatment. A few pages further on in this article, Freud introduces a woman who, following her recovery through analytic therapy, suffered financial losses. As opposed to such a case of poverty following upon cure, Freud remarks in *An Outline of Psychoanalysis*, spontaneous remission often follows real, worldly misfortune.

In any case, one must pay for cure. Effectiveness is bought through reduction: in one's wealth, in the wealth of plurivalent material. Putting resources, language, money into use means spending them, diminishing them, rather than respecting their irreducible inequivalency, rather than fetishizing them.

Of his own experiment with foreshortening analysis, Freud comments: "In this predicament I resorted to the heroic measure of fixing a time-limit for the analysis" (p. 217). The hero accomplishes things; he is effective, violently so. "A hero," according to *Moses and Monotheism*, "is someone who has had the courage to rebel against his father and has in the end victoriously overcome him" (p. 12). To act heroically is to effect a change in spite of the necessity for guilty, forceful action. The hero assumes responsibility . . . and he is willing to be in the wrong. Freud's heroic measure with the young Russian failed.

To return to my analyst-reader analogy, the heroic measure would be to reduce violently the undecidable plurality of Freud's text and simply use it as a steppingstone in some practical pursuit. To read Freud as literary text is not courageous; it is simply right, theoretically correct, just as analysis is theoretically interminable, although its termination, the 1937 article says, is a practical matter.

Analogy is not the only temptation in Freud's steep path. "The patient," Freud writes in *An Outline of Psychoanalysis*, "is not satisfied with regarding the analyst in the light of reality as a helper and advisor who, moreover, is remunerated for the trouble he takes and who would himself be content with some such role as that of a guide on a difficult mountain climb" (p. 174). If the patient would only be reasonable, if he weren't so *neurotic*, the analyst would be content merely to do his difficult, but humble, job for money, just a working man trying to make an honest wage. But the patient is not satisfied. Like a John trying really to seduce the whore, he wants the analyst to do it for love, not money. And somehow when we switch from a money to a love transaction, things get a bit sticky. Rather than following his hired guide, the patient, in full transference, might just lead the analyst astray.

Freud cautions of the need for self-discipline in the face of this enticement. "However much the analyst may be tempted to become a teacher, model and ideal for other people and to create men in his own image, he should not forget that that is not his task in the analytic relationship, and indeed that he will be disloyal to his task if he allows himself to be led on by his inclinations" (p. 175). The analyst is to serve as guide, yet he must take care not to be himself led on/guided by his own inclinations. The guide may go first, but must remain the employee; the remuneration ensures that the analyst does not lead where he wishes to go. By doing it for money, not love, by prostituting himself, the analyst buys his innocence.

The temptation is to create men in his own image, play God, author of the world. Were Freud to succumb to this temptation he would rival in guilt his own Moses, the one Freud created in the book he called at first *The Man Moses: A Historical Novel*. The founder of psychoanalysis would be nearly as guilty as the irascible founder of Judaism who, according to Freud's construction, created God, the vengeful Jewish God, in his own angry image. In Freud's tale, Moses took on the transference of the Children of Israel, and the negative transference was so powerful it killed him. According to Freud, the Jews revolted and repeated the murder of the primal father by murdering Moses. Moses led the Children of Israel where he wanted them to go. Freud must resist that temptation, must guide as mere hireling. But can this simple working man resist the patient, soft and malleable, just asking for it?

A few sentences after the statement about it being disloyal to be led on by one's inclinations to be teacher, model, and ideal, Freud writes: "Some neurotics have remained so infantile that in analysis too they can only be treated as children" (p. 175). Moses treated the Jews like children, he brought the law down from the mountain rather than guiding them up the mountain. To treat patients in analysis like children is to fall for the fiction of the transference, to believe in it and try to embody it, to repeat the parents, and like the parents, try to mold the child/patient in one's own image.

In "Constructions in Analysis" Freud tries to defend psychoanalysis against the frequently voiced accusation that the analyst "is always in the right against the poor helpless wretch [*hilflose arme Person*] whom he is analyzing, no matter how the patient may respond to what the analyst puts forward" (p. 257). The damning force of this accusation, that which Freud must defend against, resides in this image of the analyst as capricious power and the analysand as a "poor helpless wretch." If the patient were helpless, like a child, and without wealth—"poor" retains this sense from the German *arme* it translates—then the analyst could not be construed as an innocent hired guide. The guilt of the analyst derives from his great influence over a helpless person.

After describing this image of the "hilflose arme Person" at the beginning of the article, Freud strenuously pleads his innocence, carefully asserting in various ways that "no damage is done if we make a mistake . . . and offer the patient a wrong construction" (p. 261). Freud is on the defensive until the end of the second of the three sections of the article, where he builds to a crescendo and claims: "we do not pretend that an individual construction is anything more than a conjecture. . . . We claim no authority for it. . . . In short, we conduct ourselves on the model of a familiar figure in one of Nestroy's farces—the manservant who has a single answer on his lips to every question or objection: 'It will all become clear in the course of future developments'" (p. 265). Freud wishes to claim no authority. In fact rather than trying to serve as model for his patients (the temptation he spoke of in *An Outline of Psychoanalysis*), he is himself merely following a model, a literary model, a humble model, a mere servant.

Freud slips from guilty author of his imaginative constructions, from powerful authority over his helpless patients, to faithful follower of a model, to powerless servant whose words are authored by another (Nestroy in this case) and who merely repeats his line. Freud is thus doubly relieved of responsibility.

And at precisely this point in the article Freud ceases to defend himself. Having gotten to a point of liberation from responsibility, immediately after the Nestroy quotation, he begins the last of the three sections by stating that it is "hardly worth describing the way in which a conjecture of ours is transformed into the patient's conviction" (p. 265). Yet that is the very piece necessary to hold together the case for the defense. Although Freud has written the first two-thirds of this article as answer to criticisms of psychoanalysis, now he no longer deems it worthwhile to continue to respond to the accusations. He desists from further defense even though the accusations to which he has been speaking bear precisely on the process of transformation from analyst's conjecture to patient's conviction. Having donned the role of manservant, Freud feels free to forget responsibility and allows himself to be seduced by an analogy. "The delusions of patients appear to be the equivalents of the constructions we build up in the course of an analytic treatment" (p. 268). At this point in the article, Freud leaves behind analytic therapy, the locus of the task, where questions of disloyalty are possible ("the analyst will be disloyal to his task if he allows himself to be led on by his inclinations"). Analogy leads him down the path of wild, tantalizing conjecture as he gladly casts his authority aside.

In fact, the analogy between hallucinations and constructions functions quite effectively in a certain implicit plea for the defense, since it suggests that the analyst, far from a powerful authority who has obligations for his poor childish patients, is himself sick, deluded, himself a poor wretch. Freud actually refers to the analyst as der Ärmste (the poorest one) in "Analysis Terminable and Interminable" (p. 248), when he considers there the question of resisting the temptation to model patients in one's own image. The analyst himself is a poor wretch seduced by his weak inclinations.

The irresistible analogy, seeming fanciful flight far from the reality of defending psychoanalysis, actually picks up and draws out an underlying tone in the early part of the article, part of the argument for the defense which is likely to play on the sympathies of the jury. In direct answer to his critics, Freud has written: "the danger of our leading a patient astray by suggestion . . . has been enormously exaggerated. An analyst would have had to behave very incorrectly before such misfortune could overtake him" (p. 262). Note the passive construction at the end of this dismissal: an analyst guilty of an abuse of power is, in the rhetoric of this plea, an innocent prey of misfortune. Let us here recall the remark from *An Outline of Psychoanalysis* to the effect that cure often followed misfortune. A release occurs after a loss of fortune, loss of authority, loss of power, a delivery from guilt, from loyalty to the task. The analyst would be content to be a simple mountain guide, a servant in a farce. "We have no authority." Is not the choice of a powerless position, whether by analyst or by literary critic, an effective ruse to elicit leniency from the jury, to get away with one's crimes, to have underhanded, unacknowledged, unauthorized influence?

In "Analysis Terminable and Interminable" Freud considers the possibility of having godlike power, the absolute authority of the primal father which patients in transference and detractors of psychoanalysis alike ascribe to the analyst. The context for embarking on this fantasy of absolute power is a discussion in which Freud asks if the analyst, in order to determine whether the patient is thoroughly cured and thus immune to further outbreaks of neurosis, should "bring about a situation in reality in which a latent conflict becomes currently active" (p. 231). In this scene once again we find the patient as "arme hilflose Person" as opposed to the powerful analyst; and once again Freud, the analyst, projects accusation all around him. "We should receive admonitions from all sides against the presumption of vying with fate in subjecting poor human creatures [*arme Menschenkinder*, literally poor human children] to such cruel experiments. . . . Could we, for purposes of prophylaxis, take the responsibility of destroying a satisfactory marriage, or causing a patient to give up a post upon which his livelihood depends?" (p. 232). "Could we take the responsibility of destroying?"—in other words, "Can we take heroic measures?" and through prophylactic action risk destroying the helpless child? Can we act courageously, heroically, violently to effect change, in full guilty responsibility for our actions? Will Freud be the hero, will he be the great man Moses inflicting his will upon the poor Jewish slaves he takes from the land of plenty into the desert?

Freud answers, or more properly avoids, this question with a great sigh of relief, once again escaping the trap of reenacting the primal father, the all-powerful tragic character Freud created in *Totem and Taboo*, whose actions Moses repeats in the historical novel *Moses and Monotheism*. "Fortunately," Freud writes, "we never find ourselves in the position of having to consider whether such interventions in the patient's real life are justified; we do not possess the plenary powers which they will necessitate" (p. 232). Fortunately (*zum Glück*) we don't have full, absolute power (*Machtvollkommenheit*); luckily we are not the primal father, not God, the transference is a fiction, and we have no authority. Fortunately the shrink too is a poor human creature (*armes Menschenkind*) whom Freud later in this article terms *der Ärmste*, the poorest one.

Another analogy beckons, or the same one slightly altered, made up or dressed differently, just enough to renew our imprudent desire, as if, perhaps, seduction always operated by means of an incompletely disclosed analogy, the merest glimmer of a similarity hidden in an apparent disparity.

Fortunately, misfortune overtakes us; luckily we are poor servants, without plenary powers. What makes misfortune fortune? What do we gain when we lose the world? In *Moses and Monotheism*, Freud writes: "the nation of Israel's political misfortune taught it to value at its true worth the one possession that remained to it—its literature" (p. 115).

Israel had no power, a nation without land, and, as Freud marvels with a hint of pride, it survived whereas all the prosperous nations around it, to which it continuously fell victim, are no longer with us. As was the case with Rank's America and the Russian young man, prosperity is necessarily a thing of the past, a thing passing, terminable. Fortunately, the Jews were unfortunate.

This interminable (which is to say, in the terms of our ever-shifting analogy, powerless and theoretically correct) realm of the Jews and other poor wretches such as impractical, speculative psychoanalysts, is literature. According to *Moses and Monotheism*, "immediately after the destruction of the Temple in Jerusalem by Titus, the Rabbi Jochanan ben Zakkai asked permission to open the first Torah school in Jabneh. From that time on, the Holy Writ & intellectual concern with it were what held the scattered people together" (p. 115).

In place of the destroyed temple, that concrete proof of Israel's political power and the priest's authority, is literature and scholarship. Although Jewish literature predates the destruction of the temple, its value is its ability to fill in that lack. Destroyed temples attract archaeologists, which leads us, by way of one of Freud's favorite analogies, back into analysis. "The analyst's 'work of construction' or, if it is preferred, of reconstruction, resembles to a great extent an archaeologist's excavation of some ancient edifice that has been destroyed and buried" ("Constructions in Analysis," p. 259). The analyst's conjectures, speculations, delusions even, according to the end of the article, are mostly called constructions by Freud, or maybe reconstructions. This process of imagination becomes, by analogy, one of building, even restoration, restoration of the destroyed temple, reconstruction. "What then is [the analyst's] task? His task is to make out what has been forgotten from the traces which it has left behind or, more correctly, to construct it" (pp. 258–59). According to *An Outline of Psychoanalysis*, this construction, this act which provokes the accusation that the analyst is taking unfair advantage of his poor helpless patient, is for the filling-in of gaps in the patient's perception.

Moses and Monotheism is erected in response to the tantalizing analogy between the early history of a people (in this case, the Jews) and the latency period in individual development. And parallel to the filling-in of gaps (*Ausfüllung der Lücke*) which *An Outline of Psychoanalysis* states as the analyst's job in therapy, Freud finds some very attractive gaps being filled in, in a rather more creative, less practical context. "If all that is left of the past are the incomplete and blurred memories which we call tradition, this offers an artist a peculiar attraction, for, in that case he is free to fill in the gaps [*die Lücken auszufüllen*] in memory according to the desire of his imagination and to picture the period which he wishes to reproduce according to his intentions. One might almost say that the vaguer a tradition has become the more serviceable it becomes for a poet" (p. 71).

Were I to be seduced by the latency period–early history analogy Freud erects, I might suppose that the analyst's constructions are not merely, as Freud suggests by analogy, hallucinations; but that they are poetic creations, that is, that the analyst produces literary texts "according to the desire of his imagination." And I doubt I can resist that analogy.

That means that not only did Freud produce a historical novel, filling in the gaps in the early history of the Jews with his constructions, but that the somewhat suspicious business of psychoanalysts would be to produce, following their inclinations, works of fiction designed to replace destroyed temples. Such an enterprise would be incredibly unethical, were not analysts, unlike priests, like poets, able to claim that they have no authority.

Now, after having given myself over to this analogy, I feel a little ashamed, a little cheapened. It was all too easy to prove Freud merely literary, to mirror our avoidance of scientific, humanistic, therapeutic responsibility in Freud's escape from loyalty to the task. In Freud there is ever present a tension: the choice to read as literary text is always a bracketing of something practical which cannot be forgotten. Analysis must be terminated. Perhaps we wish to get Freud, by using our expertise as readers, to reduce the power of his science with our deconstructive tricks, but did we not turn to him, did we not turn on him, precisely because we want that science, want to understand the psyche, to cure our neuroses, quiet our desire with truth, and no longer be such easy prey for any handsome analogy that might come along?

Impure Thoughts

Although introduced into this text as a second temptation, falling for the fiction of the transference is in fact also falling for an analogy. Transference puts the doctor in a position analogous to a parent. When the doctor acts as if he really were a parent he has been taken in by the analogy.

In this text I had stumbled onto the function of money and worldly power as antidotes to a transferential view of power. Freud is not the all-powerful father because he is literally in the employ of the patient. Since I was writing out (of) my desire to be in the place of the "powerful" male literary critic, I was unable to see clearly the significance of the psychoanalyst's/critic's lack of power. Mostly I saw a guilty denial of power. It seems Freud too is not at all sure that he isn't enormously powerful. He both claims innocence and guiltily fantasizes *Machtvollkommenheit*.

Far off on the barely perceptible horizon of this piece is the question of the politics of criticism. Are we critics powerful or powerless? Are we of use to society or "fortunately" do we have no effect? Behind the phenomenon of "Freud as Literary Text" is the more general deconstructive gesture of the generalized text. The generalized text extends the idea we have of literature to include all writing and, even beyond that, the whole world. We have been taught that, in reading a *literary* text, form matters, that we must attend to the surface play of the signifier rather than go beyond the linguistic surface to some transparent meaning. The idea of the generalized text means we must read *everything* that way. What is the politics of that gesture? Does it make nothing matter? it is all discourse; there is no reality. Or does it assault the border that would contain the literary in a purely aesthetic and therefore purely innocent realm, uncontaminated by practicality?

In actually reading Freud as a literary text, I wanted to make explicit the psychopolitics behind that move. The generalized text is most powerful when it means that everything must be *read*—in the strong sense—*and* that everything is also a practical question. No pure realms: no pure aesthetic/formalist autonomy; no pure theory; no pure spirit.

Freud is one of the great disturbers of purity. By not limiting the psychical to consciousness, the Freudian model of the mind is shot through with impurities: sex, nonsense, unintended meaning, infantile desire. In the Freudian model, the impure manifests itself not in some other space but as a disruption to any pure realm.

One of the major goals of feminist criticism has been the demolition of formalist ideology which separates the aesthetic from politics, life, the world. Freud as literary text might function to fray the boundary that cordons off the aesthetic but only if it does not function as a gesture to aestheticize an even larger realm, implying that Freud too is only a tissue of signifiers, not a practical attempt to understand and affect people and the world.

At its best, reading Freud as a literary text might return us to some preformalist understanding of reading: that reading for pleasure (stylistic appreciation) and reading for knowledge (practical use) are both inevitably at odds and yet inseparable as joint, conflicting aspects of reading. Formalism was an attempt to resolve that conflict by neatly separating the two: we would read "literature" for stylistic appreciation and everything else for practical use.

Pursuing the analogy between Freud and the literary critic, we might see that when the critic cordons off an aesthetic realm which is powerless, that claim of powerlessness is simply the negative transferential obverse of believing in a guilty fantasy of omnipotence (*Machtvollkommenheit*). Freeing ourselves from the seductions of that position might mean speaking with a sense that the critic is neither enormously powerful nor totally without effect on the world and might facilitate appraisal and use of whatever power to affect the world we might actually have.

The Triangle of the Base

Although not written until my second year of teaching at Miami (January 1979), "Why Does Freud Giggle" had its origin in my relation to two men who were centrally important to me in graduate school. One of those men is acclaimed as source in this paper, the other wholly denied. This paper takes off from an article by Jeffrey Mehlman which focused on the scene of the genesis of the sexual joke in order to pursue an analogy between Freud's joke theory and his sexual theory.

Mehlman was my dissertation director, the teacher who had the single most profound influence on me, the teacher who (intro)(se)duced me into the world of Lacan, French post-structuralist theory, and Freud. He had written his article while I was working with him; I had read it sometime around 1973 or 1974. As a source it is clearly marked in the original, published version of my paper, if anything, marked too clearly and awkwardly. But behind that clearly marked influence, another source is suppressed.

In the spring of 1978 Alex Argyros told me about a lecture he had given on the scene in Freud's jokebook where the men tell a joke when the woman leaves the room. A few weeks later Nancy Miller asked me to give a paper in a Northeast MLA Session on Women and Humor. I gave her the present title, planning to work out Argyros' idea. There is no mention of Argyros in the present text.

Argyros had been a student with me in graduate school; Mehlman was also his dissertation director. Argyros and I had lived together as best friends and lovers. Structurally, Argyros was my brother, Mehlman our father. I excluded Argyros to be textually alone with the father, out of my sense and fear that everything conspired to exclude me and to reinforce the academic father-son relation. This is not a commentary on the real men Mehlman and Argyros—both of whom took me quite seriously as a scholar, neither of whom seemed to want me to leave the room—but upon a structure which threatened to exclude me despite my having gotten myself into the room, despite any man's intentions toward me. As a child I witnessed my father's enormous pleasure in my brother's company, my father who never was alone with me.

In 1979 I wrote: "besides the familiar Oedipus, every *child* also has the desire to murder his mother and marry his father." I have now revised that to "every boy." Of course Freud makes the classic gesture of universalizing the male position as the human position. If I unquestioningly repeat Freud's error in this essay explicitly written for a feminist context, it is because my parapraxis expresses the fantasy of being the son, my wish that any child, male or female, could be in the same relation, the relation of sames, to the father. In my family, in the academy, in patriarchal society, it is the son who gets the father's love. If the son fears that makes him into a woman, what would I, already a woman, have to fear.

A few months after writing this essay I started working on *The Daughter's Seduction*, writing the chapter called "The Father's Seduction." At that point my oedipal desire and its relation to my intellectual work became visible to me. Until then it was manifesting itself unbeknownst to me. It was not that I was unaware of my desire for teacher/father figures, but I could not read the inscription of that desire *in my writing*.

Why Does Freud Giggle When the Women Leave the Room?

There is something funny going on in Freud's work *Jokes and Their Relation to the Unconscious.*[3] In Freud's milieu ("higher social levels," "society of a more refined education" pp. 99–100) dirty jokes are not told in the presence of women. Freud nonetheless posits that this exchange between men has its origin in smut uttered by a man in order to seduce a woman. If the woman resists seduction, the sexually exciting speech itself becomes the aim. Freud writes that "the *ideal case* of a resistance of this kind . . . occurs if *another man is present* at the same time—a third person" (emphasis added). This third person (specified by Freud as another man, not another woman) becomes of "the greatest importance" (p. 99). The joke is addressed to the other man, and can even go on quite well in the woman's absence. This marginally derived case ("can go on in the woman's absence") returns us to precisely the context of sexual jokes as Freud knows them. In fact, not only are sexual jokes not told to women at the "higher social levels," but what goes on at lower levels is elsewhere characterized by Freud as smut or jests, and not jokes proper. So the sexual joke which originates in a mythical scene between a man and a woman, never takes place except between two men.

In an article called "How to Read Freud on Jokes," Jeffrey Mehlman reads this "ideal" triangle in Freud's text as oedipal.[4] Like the oedipal drama, this mythical scene also moves from a man alone with a woman to the intrusive and yet enabling presence of another man. In the oedipal moment the boy gives up possession of the mother and gains identification with the father. According to a structuralist, Lacanian reading, the boy loses the imaginary dyadic relation and is inserted into the symbolic order, into the circuits of exchange which constitute (male) society. Lacan's symbolic order is based upon Lévi-Strauss' understanding of the incest taboo which exposes the supposedly heterosexual institution of marriage as actually an exchange for the purpose of creating and strengthening bonds between men.

At the end of Mehlman's article, there is a fleeting moment of regret for a certain lost object: "For it will be seen that the further we pursued our analysis of [*Jokes*], the more did the apparent object of Freud's analysis—jokes—disappear. Like the woman—the second person—in Freud's paradigm of the joke. I *confess* that this *homology* between Freud's model and our own undertaking strikes me as *sufficient consolation* for the loss" (emphasis added).

The woman is lost, but the man consoled. Rather than a woman he has a homology. The second person, the other sex, has been irretrievably lost. But no matter, it was worth it to gain a sameness, to find an identification (with the father, with Freud). The Oedipus is good: one loses the mother but gains entry into the world, into the exchange between men—Lévi-Strauss' exchange of women, Freud's exchange of dirty jokes. The Oedipus is good, for the man. He escapes from his difference with the resistant, other sex into the world of homologies; man's economy.[5]

Mehlman is not the only one in pursuit of an analogy. Freud's articulation of the mechanisms of jokes is based on an analogy (*Analogie*) he discovers between jokework and dreamwork. There seems to be some guilty pleasure in this analogical gratification, homological acquisition. For Freud, analogy is dangerously seductive: "Shall we not *yield to the temptation* to construct [the formation of a joke] on the analogy of the formation of a dream?" (p. 195, emphasis added). He repeatedly defends himself against the imagined complaint that "under the influence of the model" he is abusing the material, "looking only for techniques of joking which fitted in with it, while others would have proved that this conformity (*Übereinstimmung*) is not invariably present" (p. 167). Freud works to fend off the suspicion that he excludes otherness, difference, in pursuit of an analogy, a conformity.

In speaking of the similarity between the jokework and the dreamwork, he alternates between the two terms *Analogie* and *Übereinstimmung*. The latter term reappears in the explanation of how the teller of the joke (the first person) can give pleasure to the hearer (always referred to as the third person, although he corresponds to the grammatical second person, whereas the joke's second person is generally absent). In order for the joke to work there must be psychical accord (*Übereinstimmung*) between the first and third person. Rather than tell a joke to a woman, who would resist, not be in agreement (*Übereinstimmung*), not be analogous, the man tells it to another man.

Analogy (in this case a translation of *Gleichnis*, from *gleich* meaning same, equal) is the last technique considered in the chapter on the technique of jokes (chapter 2). The section on analogies begins with an apology; Freud is not certain that *analogies* ever are really jokes, rather than merely comic. But he nonetheless pursues this dubious section, citing various uncertain examples of joking analogies. The last one is a lengthy quotation which Freud attributes to Heinrich Heine's *Bäder von Lucca* (*The Baths of Lucca*). After that analogy, he declares, "In the face of this . . . example, we can no longer dispute the fact that an analogy can in itself possess the characteristic of being a joke" (p. 87). Analogy (elsewhere seductive and guilty, here dubious and equivocal) has been justified, doubt dispelled. However . . . the paragraph Freud quotes is not to be found in *The Baths of Lucca*.

This doubtful Heine analogy ends chapter 2, which many, many jokes earlier began with another joke from *The Baths of Lucca* (this one correctly attributed). Hirsch-Hyacinth, a character in *The Baths of Lucca*, says: "I sat beside Salomon Rothschild and he treated me quite as his equal, quite famillionairely" (*ganz wie seinesgleichen, ganz familionar*—"equal" here translates the word *gleich*, as in *Gleichnis*).[6] Freud "reduces" this joke to the meaning: "Rothschild treated me quite as an equal, quite familiarly, that is, so far as a millionaire can." This joke about an apparent equality, an apparent analogy between two men with undertones of humiliation for one of them allows Freud to explain the process of condensation in jokes. Because there are similarities between "familiar" and "millionaire," because there is conformity, an entire thought—"that is, so far as a millionaire can"— is reduced to a small change in a word, an addition of one syllable. The joke about a certain humiliation underlying the relation between likes (*gleichen*) reveals itself as a condensation, a technique in which one thought can be subordinated by another (humiliated, so to speak) because of a conformity.

The famillionairely joke is capital in this book. It is the first joke of the book, the only example in the first chapter. Freud makes his first return to this joke in chapter 2, where he begins: "Let us follow up a lead presented us by chance" (p. 16)—chance translates the word *Zufall*. There follows the lengthy explanation of the mechanism of this joke, summarized above. Freud returns to the joke again in chapter 5: "It is a remarkable coincidence that precisely the example of the joke on which we began our investigations of the technique of jokes also gives us a glimpse into the subjective determinants of jokes" (p. 140). "It is a remarkable coincidence" translates "ganz zufällig trifft es sich"—*zufällig* is the adjectival form of *Zufall*, the word for "chance" in chapter 2. The emphasis on chance seems to deny any responsibility for the importance of this joke, treating it as if it just kept coming up without being solicited.

The analogy-joke from *The Baths of Lucca* is not to be found there. The Rothschild joke is, but is treated as uncanny, as if its repeated appearances were surprising coincidences. A third mention of *The Baths of Lucca* is found in chapter 2, in the section on allusion as a joke technique. Freud praises Heine's ingenious use of allusions for polemical purposes. The polemic is against Count Platen, a homosexual poet who wrote a satirical work on the romantic movement. According to Freud, *The Baths of Lucca* contains frequent remarks alluding to anal and homosexual concerns, providing an insistent subtext until finally those themes are made explicit. Freud and Heine treat anal and homosexual as, for all intents and purposes, interchangeable; the two constitute one theme. Freud is indeed right about the pervasiveness of this closet thematic; *The Baths of Lucca* fairly reeks of the anal and the homosexual.

Hirsch-Hyacinth, the hero of the famillionairely anecdote, is the servant of the Marquis Christophoro di Gumpelino. In the chapter after the Rothschild joke, Gumpelino gets a letter from his lady-love, a married woman with a watchdog brother-in-law. The letter says that tonight the brother-in-law will be gone and Gumpelino can finally consummate his love, but in the morning the lady must leave Lucca for good. However, just before the letter arrives, because his master is depressed about the possibilities of satisfaction in his love affair, Hyacinth gives him Glauber salts, a tremendously powerful laxative. So when the letter comes, Gumpelino cannot go, because he "has to go." He cannot satisfy his desire for the lady and instead must spend the night on the pot. It is hard to resist the reductive Freudian reading of this as regressive substitution of anal satisfaction for genital.

In the morning, the lover is no longer sad. The lady is gone forever, but Gumpelino has found consolation (Heine's translator uses that word). Mehlman's "consolation" was a homology, Freud's an analogy. Gumpelino's consolation is an anal orgy and a book of Count Platen's homosexual poetry which he reads all night on the toilet— a book so fine Gumpelino tells Heine that, although sorely tempted, he never used a page to wipe his ass. Heine remarks that Gumpelino is not the first to be thus tempted.

Freud uses another joke from *The Baths of Lucca* in chapter 2, but this time he does not name the work, but merely writes: "Heine said of a satirical comedy: 'This satire would not have been so biting if its author had had more to bite'" (p. 37). The line is from the *Baths'* last chapter, and refers to the satire which Platen wrote against the romantic poets. Freud makes a small mistake in his quotation; he uses the word *Dichter* for author, whereas Heine had used *Verfasser*. Condensing *Dichter* and *Verfasser*, we might reach *Verdichter*, a word meaning "condenser." *Verdichtung* (condensation) is precisely what leads Freud to the seductive, guilty analogy between dreams and jokes.

Condensation and the famillionairely joke share a structure of humiliation or subordination between similars (*gleichen*). That is precisely Freud's view of male homosexuality: one of two equals (*gleichen*) is debased, humiliated, castrated.

What is the name of this satire, occasion for such a rich network of slips, truly "Freudian" slips? Platen called his satire of the romantics *King Oedipus*. Oedipus is not mentioned in Freud's jokebook, but Mehlman's reading has unveiled its operation there.

Heine suggests that Platen's play might have been better if "instead of Oedipus murdering his father Laius, and marrying his mother Jocasta, on the contrary, Oedipus should murder his mother and marry his father." Thus here, in *The Baths of Lucca* that manifests itself so uncannily, functioning like the unconscious of Freud's jokebook, we can read what Freud would only postulate much later, what Freud would someday call the negative Oedipus. Freud was to find that besides the familiar Oedipus, every boy also has the desire to murder his mother and marry his father.

The negative Oedipus never was fully integrated into the Oedipus complex. It merely disturbs the calm homologies of the structural Oedipus. Should we return to the mythic origin of the sexual joke, we might see another sense of Freud's statement that "the ideal case" is when there is another man present, and especially when the woman is absent.

Mehlman's Freud writes the myth (that is, the fantasy) of heterosexuality in an economy of homology, analogy. Men exchange women for heterosexual purposes, but the real intercourse is that exchange between men. The heterosexual object is irretrievably lost in the circuits, and the man is consoled by the homology. But the pleasure in the joke, in the homology, the temptation of the analogy points to the homosexual, the anal. Freud's Heine points to Freud's heinie.

A Posteriori

I described the structure of condensation and of the famillionairely joke as two "likes" being debased; yet, in the joke at least, it is clear that only one of the two is debased, precisely by being treated as "not like." Unable or unwilling to read anal intercourse as humiliating only the penetrated, I misread in the direction of an egalitarian view of humiliation in which both participants are reduced to the level of the anal. If anal intercourse (or the boy's desire for the father) is debasing inasmuch as the passive male is treated like a woman, equalizing the position attempts to assert sexual equality within this homosexual model. Aspiring to the son's position in relation to the father, I could only see that position as superior to the daughter's by being more equal, could not imagine the son's fears and anxieties, the son's humiliation. In the fantasy of being a son buggered by the father, our perverse debauch would make us equal, bringing the father down to the son's humble level. Whether that phantasmatic reading of negative male oedipal desire be correct or simply wishful, it led to an unquestionable misreading of the class-based humiliation between Rothschild and the servant.

The Rothschild joke makes the issue of class distinction quite explicit. If Rothschild treats Hirsch-Hyacinth as his *gleichen*, his analogue, but only so far as a millionaire can, then we see how class difference renders impossible an analogical relation between men.

For Freud, the joke is something that goes on not just between men but between ruling-class men. Smut which is still sexual, not properly sublimated as are jokes, occurs in a heterosexual situation or among members of the working class. In Freud's genesis of the sexual joke, both the lower classes and the presence of women are linked to an origin, which for Freud is always infantile. Freud's work is shot through with the ideology of the working class as more infantile. Like the ideological notion of the immaturity of women, this idea justifies ruling them. The realm of the homosocial contract is not just that of men but that of ruling-class men. It probably has more to do with rule than with masculinity or homosexuality. Given a certain analogy functioning in bourgeois ideology between women and the working class, the only purely sublimated, only truly ruling-class situation had to be men only.[7]

Whereas the homosocial is the realm identified with the father, the realm of power, the homosexual is associated not with power but with humiliation. Identification with the father equals patriarchal power; desire for the father equals castration, humiliation. The Rothschild joke thus can be read as a slippage from the homosocial (treated as an equal) to the homosexual (humiliated). Exposing the homosexual desire hidden behind the homological identification may operate in the psychosexual realm like exposing the class exploitation hidden beneath the ideology of equality and democracy.

Notes

1. All quotations from Freud in this section are taken from *The Standard Edition of the Complete Psychological Works*, ed. James Strachey (London: Hogarth Press, 1953–74), vol. 23.

2. *Roland Barthes par roland barthes* (Paris: Seuil, 1975).

3. Freud, *Jokes and Their Relation to the Unconscious*, in *Standard Edition*, vol. 8.

4. Jeffrey Mehlman, "How to Read Freud on Jokes: The Critic as Schadchen," *New Literary History* (1975), 6(2):439–61.

5. This analysis of the male homosexual economy that underlies Freud's theory as well as our supposedly heterosexual cultural institutions and that insists in the form of homology is based on the work of Luce Irigaray. See especially *Speculum de l'autre femme* (Paris: Minuit, 1974).

6. Freud, *Jokes*, p. 16. Quoted from Heinrich Heine, "The Baths of Lucca," in *Pictures of Travel*, trans. Charles Godfrey Leland (New York: Appleton, 1898), p. 296. Leland translates the condensed adverb as "famillionaire."

7. For a related connection between male homosexuality and the turn-of-the-century European ruling class, see Jane Marcus, "Liberty, Sorority, Misogyny," in *The Representation of Women in Fiction*, ed. Carolyn G. Heilbrun and Margaret R. Higgonet (Baltimore: Johns Hopkins University Press, 1983), pp. 60–97.

3.

The Student Body

Prelims

This paper was originally published with the dedication "Aux hommes de trente-six ans." I had had a series of affairs with thirty-six-year-old men (at the time I was in my mid-twenties). Not a dedication to an appropriate intellectual figure or to a friend or family member, it was the mark of my history as a desiring subject. Unlike the rest of the article, the dedication was in French, removing and mediating its unseemly personal nature. The thirty-six-year-olds were all "unavailable" men, some married, some otherwise unavailable—a certain oedipal insistence which this paper interprets.

The series began while I was in graduate school. The first member was a professor on whom I developed a crush. Tempted toward a mystical, numerological explanation of the repetition, my analysis of Sade's insistence on ages gives those numbers not only an oedipal but a specifically pedagogical interpretation. I wrote "The Student Body" while working on *The Daughter's Seduction*; it is another version of thinking through daughter-father desire, but specifically located here in the student-teacher relation, the real locus of seduction of the daughter intellectual. This paper tries to think through the place of the female student in the pederastic institution.

The eighteenth century was a time preoccupied with the education of girls. Formal education was spreading to the middle classes and to women. The pedagogical model for a classical education arose in schools with male students and male teachers. Schooling for girls posed the problem of relating the model to sexual difference. By the twentieth century girl pupils and female teachers are a matter of course. But the female coed, more so the female graduate student, and even more so the female professor are now the locus of a paradigm shift. If at the age of 14 I did not encounter a pederastic institution, in graduate school, in my professional adolescence, I did. Although French departments in the early seventies were full of female students, the faculty was predominantly male, the powerful professors were nearly all male, and it was the male graduate students who were treated and took themselves to be "professional," who were being groomed to take the place of the faculty.

Do I identify as student or teacher in this text? Although literally in my third year as an assistant professor, this text seems to locate me somewhere in between the two positions: no longer 15, not yet 36. In "The Student Body" "the reader" is generically female, "the teacher" generically male. I identify "my body, my self" as a reader, but my identity as a teacher is still mediated through male identification.

When the present book is published I will be 36.

> I'm just wild about fourteen.
> —Donovan, "Mellow Yellow"

The Student Body

The Marquis de Sade's *Philosophy in the Bedroom* is a group of dialogues staging the sexual/philosophical initiation of a young girl. Also published under the title "The Immoral Teachers," this book can be read as Sade's major consideration of the pleasures and dangers of pedagogy. Certain structural details from *Philosophy* are repeated in other instances of immoral instruction in Sade's fiction, giving the sense of preoccupations which continue to demand working out. Beyond the literal scenes of instruction, one might treat the entirety of Sade's writings as a meditation on teaching, in that what is continually, repeatedly represented is a confrontation between ignorance as innocence and knowledge as power—a confrontation constitutive of the classroom dialectic. What insists in Sade's writing is the drive to "teach someone a lesson."

Philosophy in the Bedroom has been the pretext for essays by both Jacques Lacan and Luce Irigaray.[1] The essays discuss widely divergent aspects of the text, making very different points. But there is one point that both Lacan and Irigaray make. Both the "master" of the Freudian school of Paris and the teacher dismissed from the Lacanian department at Vincennes point out that Sade's dialogues lay bare an institutional structure that is usually covered over. According to Lacan, Sade exposes the "anal-sadistic" in education; according to Irigaray, what is exhibited is "the sexuality that subtends our social order." Taking my cue from this, I propose to examine what is laid bare. Such an examination is a classic Sadian scene: the object is stripped and her or his body carefully examined and commented upon before any intercourse with it.

One of Sade's contributions to pedagogical technique may be the institution, alongside the traditional oral examination, of an anal examination. The Sadian libertines have a technical term for such an examination; they use the verb *socratiser* (to socratize), meaning to stick a finger up the anus. This association between the great philosopher/teacher and this form of anal penetration recalls the Greek link between pedagogy and pederasty. A first glance at the sexuality Sade exposes behind the pedagogical institution could certainly suggest pederasty. The "master" in *Philosophy in the Bedroom*, Dolmancé, is an advocate of buggery, who indeed refuses on principle "normal" penile-vaginal intercourse. The only schoolmaster by profession in Sade's fiction, Rodin, who appears in *Justine* and *The New Justine*, likewise will only penetrate asses. Both Rodin and Dolmancé are 36 years old[2] and have anal intercourse with their students who are just pubescent, between 12 and 16 years of age.

Pederasty is undoubtedly a useful paradigm for classic European pedagogy. A greater man penetrates a lesser man with his knowledge. The student is empty, a receptacle for the phallus; the teacher is the phallic fullness of knowledge. The fact that teacher and student are traditionally of the same sex but of different ages contributes to the interpretation that the student has no otherness, nothing different from the teacher, simply less.

This structure and its sexual dynamic become explicit in Sade. The student is an innocent, empty receptacle, lacking his own desires, having desires "introduced" into him by the teacher. If the phallus is a sign of desire, then the student has no phallus of his own, no desires, is originally innocent. The loss of innocence, the loss of ignorance, the process of teaching, is the introduction of desire from without into the student, is the "introduction" of the teacher's desire. From the first dialogue of Sade's *Philosophy*: "we will place in this pretty little head all the principles of the most unbridled libertinage, we will inflame it with *our fires* . . . we will inspire in it *our desires*" (emphasis added).[3]

Although in many ways Sade's scenes literally do lay bare the pederasty behind pedagogy, at the same time they disturb the paradigm by testing it against sexual difference. *Philosophy in the Bedroom* stages the education of a young girl, not a young boy. By engaging a man to teach a girl, Sade dramatizes a contradiction in terms, which I will call heterosexual pederasty.

Not only is the pupil female, but the instruction *in the bedroom* is also an example of coeducational team-teaching: Eugénie (the ingénue of *Philosophy*) has two teachers, Dolmancé and Mme de Saint-Ange. Although in *Justine* Rodin is the only teacher at his school, in *The New Justine* he is joined by his sister. The sister's first name is Célestine, which seems to put her in the same orbit as Saint-Ange. Mlle Rodin, we are told, has replaced Rodin's late wife in *all* her wifely duties. A brother-sister incest, thus, underlies this example of team-teaching. Although Dolmancé and Saint-Ange are not related, Dolmancé is seconded by the Chevalier who is Saint-Ange's brother. The two siblings in *Philosophy*, like the two Rodin siblings, have long engaged in a pleasurable incest.

The first dialogue of *Philosophy in the Bedroom* is a conversation between Saint-Ange and her brother, in which they set up the whole scene, the whole "education." Saint-Ange (26) supplies the 15-year-old girl; her brother (20) brings the 36-year-old man. In this case, the heterosexual pederastic structure stems from and in a sense replaces brother-sister incest.

It seems worthwhile to examine the relations between these two sexual models. Brother-sister incest plays out, in a purified form, the question of sexual difference. Both partners are of the same generation and the same origin, so they can paradigmatically be thought to differ only by sex. The pederastic structure, as I see it, ignores sexual difference and concentrates on age difference, difference of generations. It would seem that the move from brother-sister incest to pederasty is a move away from sexual distinction and into classification by age.

The Chevalier, Saint-Ange's brother/lover, prefers vaginal penetration, whereas Dolmancé shuns that feminine orifice. The Chevalier has a larger penis than Dolmancé; but Dolmancé is older and more libertine (that is, less innocent). If phallic power were organized around sexual difference, the Chevalier would be more phallic. But it is Dolmancé who is more phallic, more powerful, more masterly. He is the schoolmaster and director of the scenes. The Chevalier, when he tries to voice his ideas, is told to shut up and stick to his cocksmanship. He obeys meekly and at the end of the dialogues is dismissed. That Dolmancé should be more phallic with explicitly less penis is the mark that phallic power is attached to questions of knowledge, experience, and age, rather than to the sexual distinction. Thus the move from the brother-sister couple at the beginning of the dialogues to the pederast-ingénue couple is a move away from sexual difference, despite the fact, perhaps intentionally *to spite the fact*, that the ingénue is female.

Age difference, in Sade, seems to function as another form of sexual difference, another mode of the distinction phallus/receptacle. *Philosophy in the Bedroom* begins with the invocation, "Voluptuaries of all ages and of all sexes. . . ." Sade meticulously finds a way (even in the dialogues where there is no narrator) to inform the reader of every character's age. This is perhaps best understood in relation to the importance of pedagogy as a structuring model for Sade's fictional world. It is in school that one is classed by age group. The persistence of classification by age group throughout Sade makes even nonpedagogical institutions resemble schools—for example, the Convent of Saint Mary of the Woods in the various versions of Justine's story and Silling Castle in *120 Days of Sodom*. When pederasty substitutes age difference for sexual difference, age becomes the determining sign for the distinction knowledge/innocence, which is to say phallus/receptacle. When the model of age difference replaces the model of sexual difference, ages come to occupy the place of sex organs. So in the Sadian school, ages fascinate and tantalize; the numbers become erogenous zones.

All these digits strewn through Sade's pages recall the digits that socratize. Those penetrating fingers might seem to be phallic substitutes, but their bodily specificity and marginality as well as their multiplicity deflate the model, belie the phallic expectation. Likewise, if one considers the phallus to be a centrally organized meaningful structure (reproductive genital sexuality rather than polymorphous perversity), the digits always promise some revelation of a centralized meaning, promise the erection of some system; but the promise is merely a tease, is never fulfilled. All the ages in Sade's book seem to be on the verge of organizing into a meaningful structure. For example: the fact that Dolmancé and Rodin (as well as Eugénie's father) are both 36; the fact that Eugénie is 15, which would allow her to attend Rodin's school where the pupils are between 12 and 16. But the ages never seem to fall into neat categories, as if the attempt to organize and divide the world scholastically were continually failing. The reader, to the extent that she wants to make sense of this text and its numbers, is drawn into the role of sadistic schoolmaster, trying to whip the unruly objects into shape and order, into neat rows and classes.

In *Justine*, we are told that Rodin has 14 pupils of each sex. He never admits any younger than 12 years old, and he dismisses them at 16. Prompted by a desire for order and symmetry, I at first read that the pupils ranged from 12 to 16. Certainly those are the numbers which appear in the text. This range makes 14 the median age, reinforcing the emphasis on that number, since there are 14 girls and 14 boys. But paying closer attention, I realized my assumption was incorrect. If the students are sent away at 16, there are no 16-year-old students. They range from 12 to 15, and 14 is not the center of the structure. My inattention to this detail, my misreading, was prompted by a desire, solicited by the text, for all these cute little "numbers" to line up.

When Rodin reappears in *The New Justine*, Sade in fact alters the school's age policy so that in the later version the pupils are sent away at 17. In *The New Justine*, Rodin's pupils do indeed range from 12 to 16, centering the institution on 14. But it is too late, for in this expanded version of the novel, there are a hundred pupils of each sex, rather than 14. This appearance "too late" of the necessary piece to the pattern seems emblematic of the way Sade's numbers constantly seem about to reveal their significance, but then there is always something else, something new that necessitates another attempt at classification.

A more striking example of the ways Sade's text arouses and frustrates the reader's urge for order can be found in the scene in *Justine* of Rodin's punishing his disobedient pupils. The first student punished is a 14-year-old girl. She is followed by a 15-year-old boy, who is in turn succeeded by a 13-year-old girl. It appears that Rodin is alternating sexes, as well as centering the structure on 14, balancing out the 15 by following it with a 13. The 13-year-old girl is followed by a boy and then another girl. Ages for these two are not specified, but the sexual alternation continues. Rodin whips 9 students altogether, 5 boys and 4 girls, the last victim being a boy of 14. Ending with a 14-year-old boy seems to bear out the importance of 14 and to balance out the fact of beginning with a girl. The alternation of sexes bespeaks an impartiality on Rodin's part, a position of mastery beyond sexual difference, an indifference. Such an alternation thus follows the model of pederastic power, a model that ought to be equally applicable to male or female student, since the student's own sex is unimportant, either is but a blank, empty receptacle for Rodin's phallic mastery.

The reader is led to assume an orderly, elegant alternation of the sexes of Rodin's victims, because those mentioned separately do alternate. But this is a hasty interpretation, a premature presumption of the pederastic paradigm. Only 6 of the 9 victims are listed separately—the first 5 and the last 1. But if Rodin whipped 5 boys and 4 girls and began with a girl and ended with a boy, he must somewhere (in the undisclosed, in the veiled part of the scene) have done two boys in a row. This graphic, detailed text does not list all the victims' sexes separately, does not show the point where the symmetry, the order breaks down. This concealed break in the order marks Rodin's subjectivity, his desire, his loss of mastery. The truly masterful libertine would have no preferences, treat all the objects of his passions equally. Rodin's slight preference for boys—not the preference for boys he expresses in his pederastic discourse, but the one nearly covered over by a narration which gives the reader the quick impression that this is an orderly structure of alternation—is not the ideal, phallic pederasty of the teacher, but his specific, irrational, disorderly desire.

Thus this stock scene of corporal punishment is not reducible to the simple thesis that the teacher gets sadistic, sexual pleasure from his corrections. Not only does Rodin's nonmasterful, nonmastered desire leave its mark, but the scene arouses and frustrates (arouses by frustrating?) the reader's drive for mastery. The disorderly detail elicits the reader's urge to reduce that detail to some thesis, some meaningful system, in other words, to class it. Is the reader's desire for orderly classes so different from the impulse behind the teacher's corrections of the disorderly students?

The tension between a desire for neat order and the specific details that seem outside any order enacts one of the central Sadian conflicts: the conflict between rational order, that is, "philosophy" and irrational bodily materiality. Sade's work seems to be a long, concerted effort to bring Philosophy into the Bedroom, that is, to subsume the body, sexuality, desire, disorder into the categories of philosophy, of thought. But there is always some disorderly specific which exceeds the systematizing discourse, thus always necessitating another philosophical harangue.

The same contradiction is also at the heart of pedagogy. The position of teacher implies a mastery over knowledge, a mastery only possible by mastering desire, by an ascesis transcending one's subjective position. "Sex education," especially one that chooses to join practice to theory, cannot help but make painfully evident the teacher's subjectivity, his desire, his inability to impose an impassive, orderly classification. Yet to exclude sex from education is to leave something powerful outside the teacher's mastery, outside the teacher's knowledge, thus giving him a limited, which is to say, a subjective, position.

In Sade's text, the teacher's desire is not to be located in the explicit thematics of sex, in the schoolmaster's planned and directed sexual activities with their philosophical justifications and explanations, but in the little details that exceed the vast enterprise of categorization and systematization characteristic of the libertine philosopher. It is those details in Sade that are truly sexy, which is to say disorderly and disconcerting.

With all this philosophizing about classes and specificity, smoothing over the asperities of paragraphs full of digits, I have left behind a certain number, insistent in its particularity. What of the number 14? What can the reader make of its near centrality? It is in Rodin's school that the number 14 prevails, and Rodin has a 14-year-old daughter named Rosalie, his only child. Is Rosalie in some way the center of her father's scholastic institution, the father-daughter relation the heart, the meaning of this pederastic structure? Almost, but not quite. The relation between Rodin and his daughter is an incest, but one always consummated by anal intercourse. Here again is the structure I have called heterosexual pederasty, a structure situated at the intersection of heterosexuality (privileging sexual difference over other differences) and pederasty (privileging age difference). Heterosexual pederasty is not, however, a third alternative, another stable paradigm; rather, the full force of this oxymoron persists as a tension, a conflict that never quite stabilizes into either of these two conventional ways of representing, modeling, and thus guaranteeing phallic specular opposition.

Rosalie is 14; her father/lover is 36 (or 35 or 40). In Sade's short story "Eugénie de Franval," the ingénue Eugénie is 14 when her father becomes her lover. Franval is explicitly his daughter's schoolmaster, having sole control of her education, and designing her curriculum. The name Eugénie suggests analogies with the ingénue heroine of *Philosophy in the Bedroom*. The latter work, of course, does not contain a father-daughter incest. In those dialogues Eugénie's father M. de Mistival and her teacher Dolmancé are in fact both 36, would thus both be in the same class. And the father authorizes this education of his daughter and plans someday to take advantage of it. "I am glad to allow you the first harvest," he writes to her teacher, "but be assured nonetheless that you will have in part been working for me" (p. 291).

Rodin begins his punishment scene with a 14-year-old girl (same category as his daughter), but he and the scene climax with a 14-year-old boy. So it seems that his profession allows him to veer away from his incest with his daughter, in a pederastic direction through digital displacement (Rosalie = 14; 14 = 14, Rosalie's specificity and sexual difference are effaced). In *Philosophy in the Bedroom*, Eugénie's father is replaced by the bugger Dolmancé. Again one finds a displacement of father-daughter incest in the direction of pederasty. It is only in the short story "Eugénie de Franval," from the collection *Crimes of Love*, that the pedagogical relation coincides with father-daughter incest. It is worth noting that in this story the consummation is not anal intercourse.

How does the ingénue of the *Crimes of Love* story, Eugénie de Franval, compare with the pupil of the philosophical dialogues, Eugénie de Mistival? Nominally, the difference between them can be located in the contrast between *fran(c)* and *m(y)sti*,[4] a contrast between two sorts of *vals*, two sorts of vales, of hollows, of receptacles. The vale in *Philosophy in the Bedroom* is misty, mysterious, mystical; in the short story, the vale is *franc*, frank, straightforward, open. If, as Lacan says, "the phallus can only play its role when veiled,"[5] then a misty vale is a better receptacle for the phallus than a frank vale.

And so it would seem. Franval, who had always been libertine and inconstant, falls hopelessly in love with his daughter Eugénie. He refuses his patriarchal power which is the power to exchange her: he cannot bear to pass her on to any other man. If he cannot exchange her, he does not really possess her, and instead finds himself possessed by her. The story is a tragedy: this very powerful man loses everything out of passionate love for this eighteenth-century Lolita. But in this case, it is not on account of her cruelty, for Eugénie loves her father unreservedly. Tragedy seems to result merely from the father's loss of patriarchal power, loss of the power to exchange his daughter.

No wonder Mistival allows someone else to gather the first harvests. Not only is the initiation to the mysteries displaced from Mistival to Dolmancé, but Dolmancé likewise refuses her prémices, her first fruits, her virginity, and hands them over to the Chevalier. This passing from hand to hand, from man to man, protects the phallus, veils it in mystery, vales it in mist. *Philosophy in the Bedroom* has a happy ending.

But there is another difference between the two Eugénies, one more difficult to speculate upon, to arrange neatly into a specular opposition, like frank/mysterious. Eugénie de Franval is 14, but Eugénie de Mistival is 15. This digital difference lacks the neat symmetry of the nominal opposition, but it is not without associations, hints, and clues bearing the promise of some philosophical explanation in the Sadian context.

In *The New Justine*, Justine and her sister Juliette are respectively 14 and 15 at the moment that their parents' death sends them out into the world. Justine, like the 14-year-old Eugénie de Franval, lives a tragedy. Juliette, like the 15-year-old Eugénie de Mistival, has a fortunate existence. This story of two sisters so occupied Sade that he wrote it at least three times, the last time covering three thousand pages with it. The fascination of this story of two sisters lies in the puzzling difference between two members of the same sex, with the same origin (from the same parents), of the same generation, and nearly the same age. In the two earlier versions of their story (*The Misfortunes of Virtue* and *Justine*), Justine is 12, not 14, when the story begins. That the difference between 12 and 15 should be reduced to the barely perceptible difference between 14 and 15 in the final, least restrained, most excessive, most violent version of the story implies an attempt to strip their enigmatic difference of any possible garb of rational explanation by categories. That such specularly opposite roles should hang upon the difference between 14 and 15 moves us into a world derisive of structures of meaningful opposition, whether the structure of sexual difference or difference of age group. All the mysterious difference between Juliette's libertinage and Justine's innocence, the entire structure knowledge/innocence—that is, as we have said, phallus/receptacle—hinges upon making a cut between 14 and 15.

It is Rodin who makes that cut. At the end of the Rodin episode in both *Justine* and *The New Justine*, the daughter Rosalie is locked up in the cellar while Rodin and his friend Rombeau (why all these *ro*'s?) plan to do experiments on her in the following terms: "Anatomy, says Rodin, will never reach its final degree of perfection until the examination of the vessels [vaginal canal] is performed on a child of 14 or 15, who expired from a cruel death."[6] Here, at 14 or 15, in the zone between those numbers, Sade makes another addition to the pedagogical battery: to complement the oral and anal examination, Rodin adds the vaginal "examination."

Rosalie, who is 14 when Justine first meets her, is 15 by the time of her "examination." Rodin's school, the only actual school visited in all Justine's adventures, is narrated in the space between a 14-year-old daughter and a 15-year-old daughter. The whole process of pedagogy, the confrontation between knowledge and innocence, can be situated in the slice between 14 and 15. In that way Rodin's literal, surgical slice can be read as an emblem of his pedagogical activity.

Rodin has two professions: he is not just a teacher; like so many of us, he also does "research." In his case it is surgical research. That the only teacher Justine meets should also be a surgeon leads one to ponder the relation between the two professions. One articulation might be the "examination." After all, Dolmancé's socratizing introduction of a finger itself resembles common medical procedure. The academic examination is an effort to discover what the pupil knows: that is, what is inside her head, what of the teacher's discourse has penetrated and made an impression. The medical examination is an attempt to find out what is inside the patient's body. The two examinations have in common the penetration of an interiority (psychical/figurative, in one instance; physical/literal, in the other). Sade's pedagogical battery makes physical/literal the exam as a penetration of interiority. Certainly the easiest path to the inside is through one of the orifices. But Rodin's double profession carries the penetration one sadistic step further. The surgeon does not need a natural orifice; he can enter the body wherever he likes by cutting an opening.

Sadian pedagogy depends upon the pupil's virginity. The two Eugénies are virgins at the beginning of their educations/initiations, as are all Rodin's pupils including his daughter. Rodin's and Dolmancé's preferred practices even leave the pupil's virginity intact. If the pupil is virginal, never before penetrated, she is a blank, empty receptacle, and examination will be exact, revealing nothing but what the teacher puts there ("We will inspire her with *our desires*").

Rodin's surgical research seems equally concerned with virginity for the exactitude of the examinations. To Rodin's plan to examine the "vessels" of a 14- or 15-year-old, Rombeau adds: "It is the same with the membrane that assures virginity; a young girl is absolutely necessary for this *examination*. What can one observe in the age of puberty? nothing; the menses tear the hymen, and *all research is inexact*" (*Justine*, p. 152, emphasis added). Irigaray, in her reading of *Philosophy in the Bedroom*, suggests that Sadian libertines like only the blood they cause to flow. Like menstruation, defloration includes bleeding, but in the latter blood is a sign of some penetration of interiority from without, while in the former it flows from interior to exterior without the necessity of a penetrating agent. Just as pedagogical tests seek to draw out from the student what was implanted there by the teacher; so the Sadian surgeon wishes to examine an interiority devoid of any sexuality, any carnal knowledge originating within.

Both "examine" and "exact" come from the same Latin word *exigere*, itself derived from *ex* (out, from) and *agere* (to lead, to drive).

The examination "leads out," "drives out" what was cloistered within. For the examination to be exact there must be some external agent, some researcher, some surgeon to "lead" or "drive" the interior stuff out into the light. Menstrual blood does not wait for a leader or driver to exact it; so it renders the examination inexact.

Hidden in this supposedly scientific discussion between two surgeons is a rather unscientific confusion between puberty and defloration. To be sure, both can represent some kind of break between girlhood and womanhood, but in this discussion puberty is assimilated to the model of defloration. "The menses tear the hymen," asserts Rombeau. But a surgeon would know that this is false. Defloration is the tearing of the hymen by a force which goes from outside to inside. In this mythic model, puberty would consist in a tearing of the hymen by a force moving from inside to outside. This myth of puberty sets up a specular relation between the two different sorts of passages from innocent child to sexual adult. It works to assimilate both to one model, like Dolmancé/Rodin's attempt to assimilate heterosexuality to pederasty.

In the zone of 14 or 15, in the space between Justine the virgin and Juliette the whore, lies the mysterious break between innocence/ignorance/virginity and experience/knowledge/sexuality. The hymen is the emblematic wall partitioning these two realms. What we have here is the Sadian version of the *coupure épistémologique*. That term from contemporary French philosophy refers to a discontinuity in thought, dividing it into a before and an after, into classification by ages. The word *coupure* literally means "cut." Prefiguring mid-twentieth-century philosophical modes, Rodin enacts a physical/literal epistemological *coupure*.

Rodin's *coupure*, his surgical cut into the virgin, his examination of the hymen, is an examination of the distinction knowledge/innocence, is epistemological research, which is to say research into the origin and nature of knowledge.

Rombeau says of their victim that although 15, she is not yet *réglée*. *Réglée* can usually be translated as "regulated," but it has a peculiar sense meaning "having begun to menstruate," from *règles*, the usual term for a woman's "period." The pedagogical examination which attempts to regulate the student on the basis of external rules, of the teacher's rules, is messed up by the *règles*, the rules, flowing from within. The bodily, fluid, material, feminine sense of *règles* undermines the Sadian pederastic pedagogue's attempt at exact examination, at subjugation of the pupil to his rational, masterful rules.

Yet, like pederasty, the woman's bloody "rules" suggest numerical regulation. 14 or 15 is not usually considered the age of female puberty. In fact, the first version of Justine's story, *The Misfortunes of Virtue*, places the age of Rombeau/Rodin's victim at 12 or 13. Perhaps 14–15 insists, not because it is the age of puberty but because those numbers constitute the center of the 28 to 30-day menstrual cycle. The zone between 14 and 15 would thus be the scene, not of the origin of knowledge, but of another mysterious origin.

Having circulated the manuscript of the foregoing text among a small number of readers, I learned—to my surprise—that what I had posited as "the reader's desire" to line the numbers up, to do arithmetic, was not shared by many readers. The numbers that fascinate me could leave another reader cold. What I assumed was a general desire, a "normal" attraction to these numbers, turns out to be my peculiar tendency, my perversion. My original attraction to Sade is to a site of perversions. Yet Sade's text makes the recognizably perverse readings appropriate and normal. To fix on the numbers is perhaps a way of recovering the thrill originally sought from Sade.

Finally, it does not seem inappropriate that an arithmetic perversion should arise in a discussion of pedagogy. School presents us with a world of numbers: grades, curves, credit hours, course numbers, class hours, and room numbers. I suppose not all teachers experience as I do a diffuse yet unmistakable pleasure when calculating grades at the end of the term.

Traces

Sade's sense that menstruation threatens the pederastic order of our educational institution finds its uncanny reply in Adrienne Rich's statement: "the scholar reading denies at her peril the blood on the tampon."[7] Rich's sentence stuck in my craw. It is easy to celebrate female desire, motherhood, fluidity, or any number of other revalorized images of female sexuality. But how could "the blood on the tampon" possibly be raised to the level of theory?

"Her own peril" rings melodramatic. Yet in *Justine* we see a literalization of the female scholar's "peril," based precisely in her innocence of menstrual blood. Sade's surgeon's desire for exactness, which the menses would mess up, is philosophical kin to the quest for the perfect tampon. Shortly after Rich published that sentence in 1976, the toxic shock syndrome made graphic the peril of neatness.

"Rely" tampons were the most absorbent tampon ever invented. The ideally absorbent tampon kills.

Irigaray has pointed out that Sadian libertines cannot tolerate menstrual blood.[8] She considers Sade valuable inasmuch as his work lays bare "the sexuality that subtends our social order." Subtending our pedagogy and our research, underlying the pursuit of knowledge in our society, is a drive for order, a drive to subordinate the disorderly body to man's categories.[9] Menstrual blood cannot immediately be absorbed into the category of female sexuality as phallic turn-on, phallic receptacle, or the category of maternity as carrier of phallic products, reproductions of the phallus. Thus it remains an embarrassment for either classic feminine representation: the mother or the whore. How much more of an embarrassment to the scholar who is trying to prove her ability to arrange into categories. Of course, a woman can be a scholar too. Sade's work is precisely an attempt to think coeducation. But the woman scholar must not mess up the categories which already exist. And so she denies, absorbs, and is absorbed. At her own peril.

Notes

1. Jacques Lacan, "Kant avec Sade," in *Ecrits* (Paris: Seuil, 1966); Luce Irigaray, " 'Françaises,' ne faites plus un effort . . . ," in *Ce Sexe qui n'en est pas un* (Paris: Minuit, 1977). These two articles are the subject of the chapter "Impertinent Questions" in my book *The Daughter's Seduction* (Ithaca: Cornell, 1982).

2. Actually, it is only in *The New Justine* that Rodin is 36. In *Justine*, he is 40 and in *The Misfortunes of Virtue* he is 35. All of these fall within the same "age group," but the fact that Sade bothered to revise the age with each version points to the puzzle of ages which I take up later in this paper.

3. D. A. F de Sade, *La Philosophie dans le boudoir*, in *Oeuvres complètes* (Paris: Pauvert, 1970), 25:19. All translations mine.

4. In French, there is no difference in the pronunciation of *fran* and *franc*, nor between *mysti* and *misti*.

5. Jacques Lacan, "La Signification du phallus," in *Ecrits*, p. 692.

6. D. A. F de Sade, *Justine ou les malheurs de la vertu*, in *Oeuvres complètes* (Paris: Cercle du livre précieux, 1966), 3:150–51. In the original French it is not specified what "vessels" are meant. In Richard Seaver and Austryn Wainhouse's excellent English translation (New York: Grove Press, 1966, p. 551) this is rendered as "vaginal canal," which seems most likely from the context. The same passage occurs in *La Nouvelle Justine*, in *Oeuvres complètes* (Cercle du livre précieux), 6:262.

7. Adrienne Rich, *Of Woman Born: Motherhood as Experience and Institution* (New York: Norton, 1976), p. 285.

8. Irigaray, " 'Françaises,' ne faites plus un effort . . . ," p. 199.

9. For a fascinating rendition of this story see Susan Griffin, *Woman and Nature: The Roaring Inside Her* (New York: Harper and Row, 1978).

4.

The Female Body

Nero played a superior Oedipus.
—Sade, The New Justine

Sade, Mothers, and Other Women

On the surface, the work of the Marquis de Sade appears to be a systematic transgression of every interdiction weighing upon civilized man. The anthropologist Claude Lévi-Strauss posits the incest taboo as the fundamental interdiction, the primal taboo which founds society.[1] Not surprisingly, incest is prevalent in Sade's novels. In *The New Justine*, Verneuil, whose entire household is allied through multiple incests, argues in defense of his pet crime: "Let a father, a brother, idolizing his daughter or his sister, descend to the bottom of his soul and interrogate himself scrupulously about what he feels: he will see if that pious tenderness is anything other than the desire to fuck."[2] As represented by Verneuil, incest is the passion underlying the relation between brother and sister or father and daughter. Likewise for Lévi-Strauss, it is intercourse with the sister or the daughter that must be abandoned so the brother or father can partake in the generalized exchange of women constitutive of society.

Whereas for Sadian libertine and structuralist anthropologist, incest means father-daughter or brother-sister sex, for Freud, the central configuration of incest—figured by the oedipal myth—is between son and mother. In the vast tableau of forbidden passions making up Sade's opus, mother-son incest is sorely underrepresented. And in all but one case of its occurrence it is consummated through anal intercourse, thus avoiding contact with the locus constitutive of the mother as mother.

Still, the mother is not absent from Sadian libertine activity. She is a privileged victim: many libertines start their life of crime by killing their mother; others view the murder of their mother as their greatest accomplishment. In fact, Minski, the only character who successfully accomplishes incest with his mother, combines the incest with murder "on the same day" (21:299).

In point of fact, the reader cannot be positive that Minski actually penetrates the maternal vagina. In this exceptional instance Sade simply uses the verb *violer* (violate, rape), thus not specifying, as he usually does, the orifice. In the Sadian context the verb becomes ambiguous, thus leaving a final veil of uncertainty as to whether any character ever makes it into his mother's vagina. Since in most contexts *violer* implies vaginal penetration, the reader infers as much. But the fact that the sole case of successful mother-son incest should be accompanied by an ambiguity about the orifice gives some sense of the extent to which Sade's text avoids contact with a specifically maternal organ.

In the novel *120 Days of Sodom*, prostitutes recount sexual acts to libertines who are then moved to reenact them with their victims. The storytellers are to recount "all the passions,"[3] a task they normally execute without showing personal taste or distaste—as the accomplished prostitutes they are. The first narrator nonetheless displays her lack of esteem for the seventh passion: "A young man whose mania, *although hardly libertine in my opinion*, was nonetheless singular enough. . . . His cock seemed paltry to me and his entire person rather puny, and his discharge was as mild as his operation" (p. 143, emphasis added). In the universe of this novel to call a passion "hardly libertine" is the ultimate put-down. This young man's perversion consists in sucking the milk from a wet-nurse and discharging between her thighs. *120 Days* includes the narration of six hundred "passions" and is full of shit-eating and murder. Yet this enactment of mother-son incest, this attempt to repeat the primary satisfaction of suckling at the breast, is the sole occasion in the entire book when a storyteller expresses her disapproval.

This supposed tableau of "all the passions" has elicited from Sade's devoted biographer, Gilbert Lély, the remark that "we must nevertheless note that a dominant error comes to compromise in many a place the didactic value of such a work: we mean the monstrously exaggerated place that the author devotes to the coprolagnic aberration carried to its final excesses."[4] I would add to Lély's observation that not only is there an overemphasis on shit-eating in this supposedly encyclopedic work, but there is a shocking dirth of obsessions with breasts, menstruation, and female genitalia. To Lély's disappointment, far from being didactic and encyclopedic, *120 Days* bears the imprint of a living subject's desire rather than issuing from the omniscient position of impartial observer.

Although seldom objects of desire, breasts and vaginas are favorite focuses of torture, just as mothers are favorite victims. Yet just as Minski raped *and* murdered his mother, throughout Sade's works a tight knot links lover and tormentor. Sade's text is haunted by the figure of Nero, in praise of whom, Clairwil exclaims: "He had been very taken with Agrippina. Suetonius assures us that he had often jerked off for her . . . And he kills her" (23:273–74). The ellipsis here is Sade's. Oedipus did not just marry his mother; he killed his father. Yet in Sade's classical myth, Nero expresses his desire for his mother by killing *her.*

Of all Sade's characters, Bressac most nearly repeats Nero's story. In the first two versions of Justine's adventures (*Les Infortunes de la vertu* and *Justine*), Bressac is a confirmed woman-hater and devotee of sodomy who murders his mother. The link between Bressac's misogynistic homosexuality and his desire to kill his mother is presented as merely contingent: Bressac's mother disapproves of his sodomistic activities and controls the fortune which Bressac wishes to squander on his passion. In the second version (*Justine*) she is actually an aunt but is otherwise identical to the first and third versions. Perhaps this revision is another strategy to avoid contact with the mother.

In the third and last version (*The New Justine*)—as if through repetition Sade gets closer to something he is trying to say—Bressac buggers his mother before he kills her. This is the only woman his member has ever penetrated. It is specified in this third version that in his sodomistic acts Bressac "was always the woman" (15:148). Banished from his sexual life, woman returns in the guise of Bressac's mimicry. Bressac says to Justine: "There is not one of your [women's] pleasures that is not known to us, not one we cannot enjoy" (15:164). By consummating the oedipal incest in the anus, Bressac is denying that his mother, that woman, has any pleasure "that is not known to us." However, this parodic attempt to deny her femininity is not sufficient; he must kill her, for her maternity, her otherness, remains inviolate, inappropriable.

According to Clairwil's story of Nero and his mother Agrippina: "he had often jerked off for her . . . And he kills her." Bressac repeats the Roman emperor's legendary bravado, filling in the ellipsis in Clairwil's account with a violation of the maternal anus. Bressac's representation of Suetonius' "he had often jerked off for her" is more

elaborate than the original. Bressac faces his mother and mastur-
bates at her while one of his "men" anally penetrates him. Before
enacting this "scene," Bressac explains to his mother what will happen: "[While I am being fucked] you will be soaked with my cum,
madame you will be inundated; that will remind you of the happy
times when my esteemed father would smear your navel with it"
(15:200). At once playing "the whore"—an epithet he applies equally
to himself as buggered and to his detested mother—and representing
his father, Bressac figures as the complete conjugal couple. In an attempt to transcend his subjective place as male child, Bressac figures
as his own father and mother, thus denying his issue from the fact
of sexual difference. It is not enough to combine the pleasure known
to women and that known to men into a "delicious union" (15:164)
which sets him above either men or women. He must recreate the
past and erase sexual difference as it preceded his individual existence and free himself from his inscription into a series where father
and mother are mutually exclusive alternatives. This attempt fails. A
few days later he buggers his mother (not only his first sexual act
with a woman, but his first active role) and then kills her.

Bressac's scenario is a compromise between the oedipal myth and
the Neronic myth. The ellipsis in Clairwil's version of the Neronic
myth has been occupied by the dead father. First the masturbation
is supplemented both by a man in the "background" and by an accompanying fantasy in which the dead father is invoked to mediate
the son-mother relation ("that will remind you of the happy times
when my esteemed father would smear your navel with it"). Then in
the space of the ellipsis Bressac undergoes a transformation from
mother-identified to father-identified, from buggered to bugger. Finally, returning to Clairwil's Neronic script, he kills her.

In the Neronic complex the mother-son relation remains dual, with
no mention of a father-term, and this leap from masturbatory desire
to murder is pure. The father is not simply dead; his name is missing.
Only an ellipsis marks the locus of the absence of the name of the
father.

A scenario which resembles the Neronic myth can be found in Freud's
work. However, it is not the story of a boy and his mother. In 1925
Freud wrote "Some Psychical Consequences of the Anatomical Distinction Between the Sexes"[5] to remedy the lack of girls in his theory.
Freud finds that the oedipal complex in girls (desire for the father,
hatred of the mother) is a secondary formation. The girl, like the boy,
has a preoedipal object in her mother. However, there is a discontinuity between that early mother-daughter attachment and the oedi-

pal complex in which the daughter hates her mother as a rival. Between the two falls the so-called "discovery of castration," of something missing, an ellipsis.

In Freud's story of the little boy the preoedipal attachment to the mother flows smoothly into the Oedipus complex where the father becomes the hated rival, and only then does the castration complex intercede, cutting off the little boy's potential for being his mother's lover, just as Oedipus himself succeeds in marrying his mother and *only later* discovers the facts of the situation. *Then* he loses his mother and is blinded (castrated). For the boy the ellipsis comes after the Oedipus complex as the anxious possibility that an ellipsis might intervene, that something will some day be missing. Nero's ellipsis is in the place of the girl's, not the boy's, castration complex.

One mode of reception for the girl's discovery of the ellipsis, of "castration," is denial, which leads into what Freud calls a "masculinity complex." Bressac has anal intercourse with his mother, denying the vagina, denying the mother's "castration," in order to fill the ellipsis between masturbatory fantasy (preoedipal, bisexual wholeness) and killing the mother. So too between the little girl's preoedipal desire for the mother and her oedipal hatred of her intervenes a denial in which the girl refuses to accept what Freud calls "the fact of being castrated" (19:253).

In "Female Sexuality" (1931) Freud once again takes up the question of the difference between the Oedipus/castration complex as it appears in the boy and in the girl. Freud tries to fill in the girl's ellipsis, to investigate what transpires between the girl's desire for the mother and her hatred of her. Considering the different reasons for the girl's hatred of the mother, he finds that it stems from experiences common to both sexes. He flirts with an assertion of "the ambivalence of emotional cathexes" as "a universally valid psychological law"[6] but then dismisses that as, albeit primitively true, not functioning in most adult emotional life. Freud then goes on to suggest that "boys are able to deal with their ambivalent feelings towards their mother by directing all their hostility on to the father." In trying to figure out *the girl's* hostility toward the mother, Freud comes up against *the boy's* hostility toward her, something Freud was ever loath to touch. He veers away, first gesturing toward the classic oedipal structure, and then the whole investigation leaves off with an air of mystery: "we have as yet no clear understanding of these processes with which we have only just become acquainted."

At the beginning of the same article Freud writes: "we can extend the content of the Oedipus complex to include all the child's relations to both parents" (21:226). "All the child's relations to both parents" includes not only the daughter's love of the mother and hostility toward the father but also the son's hostility toward the mother and love of the father. The simplicity of the "positive" Oedipus complex (boy loves Mom, hates Dad) will not hold. But Freud goes on to study only the details of the girl's penis envy, shying away from the intersection where the male and female positive and negative Oedipus complexes cross.

Universal ambivalence toward the mother is made up of a universal primary attachment to the mother as nurturer and universal disappointment in the mother. That universal disappointment has two sources: (1) "Childhood love is boundless; it demands exclusive possession, it is not content with less than all. . . . it has, in point of fact, no aim and is incapable of obtaining complete satisfaction" (21:231); and (2) discovery of the absence of the maternal phallus causes a devaluation of the mother who is thus considered incomplete, mutilated. In Freud's oedipal myth the ambivalent emotional cathexis is divided into a positive feeling fixed onto the mother and a negative feeling directed onto the father. In Sade's Neronic myth the ambivalence is kept intact and focused entirely on the mother. The ellipsis in Nero's story is the place of the absent father who reappears in Bressac's interpretation of the script.

This universal ambivalence toward the mother is reflected in the Sadian libertine's attitude toward Mother Nature, model and source of all crime. In Sadian philosophical discourses there are two Natures. Nature vanquished includes ideological notions of what is natural: for example, normal sexuality and procreation. Nature triumphant is anything that actually occurs in nature, which includes all sorts of monstrosities. The libertines transgress the first Nature, but the second Nature they can only imitate—their petty, contingent crimes but paltry images of Nature's universal, eternal destruction. Any violation of the weak Nature leaves the criminal with an all-encompassing strong Nature, whose agent he must be in any violation. Any possible transcendence of Nature has already been coopted and inscribed within the domain of the impervious, complete Mother Nature: "Convince yourself completely . . . that were you to trouble and disturb the order of nature in every possible sense, you would never have done anything but use the faculties she gave you for that" (21:126).

The first Nature is the Mother after the discovery of her lack of phallus. This castrated, incomplete Nature cannot encompass the universe of crime which the Sadian libertine aspires to. Nature triumphant is the preoedipal phallic mother, omniscient and omnipotent, whose ways are still dark mystery to the curious child. It is precisely the mystery, as yet impervious to the child's curiosity, which constitutes the maternal phallus.

Jacques Lacan locates the phallus as that which is interpreted as missing in the discovery of the fact of sexual difference which, according to Lacan, both sexes live as the discovery of the *mother's* "castration." Lacan writes that "the phallus can only play its role veiled, that is, as itself the sign of the latency which strikes each signifiable, as soon as it is raised to the function of signifier."[7] When the subject has access to knowledge (discovery of sexual difference), the phallus is the sign of the still-latent "signifiable" (that which is mystery), the sign of what is lost once the veil is removed, once knowledge is revealed: once the mother is *known*, she is *known as* "castrated." The (veiled) phallus functions as the sign of what she potentially (latently) has, what she has as potential, when it is not known what she has—when she potentially has any/everything.

In *The New Justine* we meet Almani, who as chemist is the curious child trying to learn what is under Nature's skirts. Nature as phallic mother causes Almani to despair that "the whore [Nature] mocked me. . . . In offering me only her effects, she veiled from me all her causes" (17:69–70). In the traditional theistic schema, only the knowable effects are attributed to Nature; the veiled causes constitute God, whose being is mystery. However, in an atheist schema based upon the negation of God, "it is a misprision of nature to suppose she has an author; . . . God is nothing but nature" (21:230–31). The existence of the Father is denied in favor of a Mother with a veiled phallus. Almani lives the Neronic rather than the oedipal myth.

Faced with phallic Mother Nature, the libertine is not subject to the disappointment which follows the discovery of the mother's "castration." He does not disparage her, but only hates her all the more for the older, preoedipal reason for hating mothers: "Childhood love is boundless; it demands exclusive possession, it is not content with less than all. . . . it has, in point of fact, no aim and is incapable of obtaining complete satisfaction." The libertine hates Nature and wants to be her tormentor, for he is not able to be her lover. Nature is a tease. She arouses desires, just as the mother who cares for her child and then doesn't "put out." In "Female Sexuality," Freud writes; "The part played in starting [masturbation] by nursery hygiene is reflected in the very common phantasy which makes the mother or nurse into a seducer" (21:232). The frustration caused by the teasing calls for revenge ("he had often jerked off for her . . . And he kills her").

In *Juliette*, the Pope, tired of always being Mother Nature's pawn, craves to violate her omnipotence, craves to unmask the maternal phallus which only exists as masked. Preserving a phallic mother necessitates an eternal desire to castrate her. The Sadian libertine despises the weak castrated Nature, yet can be satisfied by nothing less than castrating the strong phallic Nature: "When I will have exterminated on this earth all the creatures that cover it, I will be far indeed from my goal, since I will have served you . . . stepmother! . . . and I only aspire to avenge myself for your stupidity, or the wickedness you inflict on men"(21:310; Sade's ellipsis).

"Stepmother" is the epithet thrown at nature in anger and frustration. The "stepmother" usurps the loved mother's position, frustrating the child through "stupidity" or "wickedness." The negative component of the ambivalence felt for the mother is distilled into the evil stepmother. Just as in the oedipal myth the original ambivalence is divided into love for the mother and hatred for the father; so the Neronic myth (killing the beloved mother) degenerates into love for the good mother, hatred for the "stepmother."

The pure tension of passionate ambivalence cannot be maintained. Clairwil's Nero, Minski, and the third version of Bressac are rare moments in Sade's work. Usually the elements of the Neronic myth are separated, thus appearing either in a positive Oedipus complex (desire to be the mother's lover) or a negative Oedipus complex (desire to be the mother's killer). That split seems to run along the line dividing Sade's tame from his scandalous writings. Sade not only wrote graphic, obscene texts. He wrote many works which remain within the bounds of proper, decent discourse. Mothers are often literally and graphically killed, but (except in the limit-instances where the penetration is accompanied by murder) incest with the mother is represented in veiled, that is, decent terms.

The principal representative of the good mother in Sade's work is Mme de Blamont in *Aline et Valcour*, one of his "decent" novels. Aline loves Mme de Blamont, her mother, more than she loves her lover Valcour. Valcour considers Mme de Blamont as his own mother. In the course of the novel, two total strangers, on separate occasions, wind up at Mme de Blamont's summer retreat, and both these young women turn out to be her daughters. To disregard these chance meetings as the extravagances of a baroque novel is to obscure the point that Mme de Blamont is everyone's mother. An observer describes her funeral: "one would have said that everything there was attached to her by some tie . . . it seemed they were all her children, everyone mourned her as a mother."[8] Like Nature herself, Mme de Blamont is "the common mother of us all." But unlike Mother Nature who inspires a Neronic ambivalence, Aline's mother receives only the positive component of that ambivalence.

Most of all, Aline loves Mme de Blamont. In a startling moment very early in the novel—long before the unweaving of M. de Blamont's treachery gives the book a fatal, somber air—Mme de Blamont speaks to Aline of a projected bequest upon the former's death. Aline, unable to bear the possibility of separation from her mother, throws herself into her mother's arms. Then they swear to love each other and to die together: a lover's vow (1:66).

At the end of the novel, when Mme de Blamont is in fact dying, the two reenact primordial mother-daughter union: "the doctor allowed Mme de Blamont to take a bit of creamed rice that she seemed to desire. Aline . . . shared this last food, pressed to the very breast (*sein*) of her mother" (2:444–45). After Aline partakes of the milky food at her mother's breast, the mother dies and Aline faints. The pair here comes close to merging (the vow to die together). An observer describes the scene: "[Aline] was bent over her. Alas: it is difficult to know which of the two still lived" (2:447).

The hated father then arrives to tear Aline away from the preoedipal paradise, and offer her virginity up to his friend. In this oedipal variation, where the mother is unambivalently loved and the father hated as him who frustrates the ultimate union between daughter and mother, Aline triumphs by killing herself and being laid to rest with her mother in her mother's tomb, preserving her preoedipal "innocence" through a denial of the father and patriarchal society constituted by the exchange of women between men.

Aline's wish to lie in her mother's tomb repeats a wish Sade expresses in a letter to his mother-in-law upon his imprisonment in Vincennes: "From the depths of her grave, my unhappy mother calls me: it seems I see her open once more her *sein* to me and invite me to return there as to the only asylum I have left. It is for me a satisfaction to follow her so closely and I ask you as a last request, Madame, to have me put next to her" (letter to the Présidente de Montreuil, February 1777).[9] In fact, like Aline, the marquis is swept away from the side of his dead mother and imprisoned. *Sein* has the double meaning of breast and womb, so that to return to the maternal *sein* is to return both to the womb and to the breast. Aline's meal "pressed to the very breast [*sein*] of her mother," the wet-nurse perversion in *120 Days*, and Sade's and Aline's wishes to be buried with their mother where she will "open once more her *sein* and invite me to return there" all bespeak the phantasmatically closed dyad of mother and child.

That fantasy combines preoedipal "innocence," ignorance of sexual differentiation, with the "crime" of penetrating the mother's womb, of being the mother's lover. Any "return" to the womb is a penetration from outside, a repetition of the father's penetration which placed the child in the womb in the first place. Ignorance of sexual difference supports a belief in parthenogenesis, but the discovery of sexual difference is the revelation of how babies are made. The "original" mother-child intimacy is predicated upon a prior violation of that interior space by a third term.

In the same letter to Mme de Montreuil Sade writes "I asked you . . . if it was a second mother or a tyrant that I would find in you." Sade's mother has just died, and his mother-in-law would thus take her place, be a second mother. In fact his mother-in-law has had him imprisoned by *lettre de cachet.* The second mother usurps the good mother's place. That usurpation, the very fact of being the *second* mother, the "stepmother," is sufficient to constitute Mme de Montreuil as "tyrant." In this scenario the Neronic ambivalence toward the mother has been divided into love for the first mother and hatred for the second.

Mme de Montreuil is indeed primordially omnipotent for Sade. Paul Bourdin, editor of a volume of Sade's correspondence, writes that Sade "plunges like a child into the conviction that everything that happened corresponds to the plans of Mme de Montreuil."[10] Sade "plunges like a child into the conviction" that Mme de Montreuil is the phallic Mother, a belief which only exists in the mode of childish conviction. This conviction is based on a denial of Sade's more powerful enemies, of the third term outside the mother-son dyad. One of Sade's friends writes that "the dear présidente was not as guilty as we thought. [Sade] has earned enemies stronger still."[11] Sade believes every jailer and official he comes into contact with to be the agent of Mme de Montreuil. He is convinced that his entire universe is subjugated to her, his every thought suggested by her, just as the Sadian libertine's universe is ruled and encompassed by Mother Nature, just as the infant's world seems to be ruled by the early mother.

Like his characters, Sade craves revenge. In a letter addressed "to the stupid scoundrels who torment me," Sade writes: "here is the hundred eleventh torture that I invent for [Mme de Montreuil]. This morning, while suffering, I saw her, the bitch, I saw her skinned alive, dragged over thistles, and then thrown into a vat of vinegar" (Vincennes, 1783).

The Neronic complex has been divided into love for the mother (wish to return to her womb/tomb) and hatred for the second mother (wish to be the torturer of the stepmother). This same split is expressed in a divergence in Sade's discourse. The wish to join the mother is cloaked in decent language; the wish to torment his mother-in-law is expressed in the graphic detail typical of *120 Days*. Yet the most powerful cloak of decency in Aline's and Sade's wish to lie with the mother is the prerequisite of the mother's death. If the mother is not to be despised, she must be "phallic." But the phallic mother is hated for her omnipotence. Nero kills his mother so he can continue to masturbate for her. Alive, she must elicit his hatred, for she disproves her (his) unlimited potential by being knowable. The phallus disappears when the mystery is unveiled. By entering the realm of death the mother enters the domain of mystery, of the unknowable. The living mother, as unfallen, uncastrated mother, cannot be possessed understood, uncovered. Desire for the phallic mother is frustrated unless the mother is killed. The ambivalence of the Neronic myth is not some external marriage of love and hate, desire to possess (know) and desire to kill. The ambivalence is inescapable at that extreme of passion: the desire to know carried to its greatest intensity *must* kill. The existence of a real mother outside Nero's masturbatory fantasy is a threat to the integrity of that fantasy, and to Nero's feeling of mastery.

The dizzying precipices of this inextricable ambivalence are uninhabitable. Sade turns away after expressing his wish to lie with his dead mother, unable to bear the unassimilable knowledge of the truth of his desire: "One thing only stops me; it is a weakness, I admit, but I must confess it, I would want to see my children" (letter to the Présidente de Montreuil, February 1771). The fatal knowledge is obscured by hope (for the future). Sade is diverted from attempting to fulfill the desire for his mother by an interest in his children.

A similar turning-away occurs in Freud's story of the little girl. Trying to explain how the little girl's libido switches from mother to father (how the feeling for the mother turns from love to hate), Freud writes: "now the girl's libido slips into a new position along the line— there is no other way of putting it—of the equation 'penis-child.' She gives up her wish for a penis and puts in place of it a wish for a child: and *with that purpose in view* she takes her father as a love-object" (19:256). Although it appears that the child is a substitute for the penis, following Lacan's reading of Freud we find that both penis and child are equally inadequate substitutes for the always missing maternal phallus. Thus the Oedipus complex in girls which follows upon the knowledge of sexual difference is a denial of the phallus as always necessarily latent (never present) and an attempt to elect the child to the place of phallus, the locus signifying unlimited potential. Fulfillment through possession of the mother (maternal phallus), once it is accepted as impossible, is abandoned in favor of an attempt at satisfaction through the child. The child, like the phallus, "can only play its role veiled," as potential child. Sade wishes to *see* the children his imprisonment hides from his sight. The child wished for by Freud's little girl is a signifiable not yet signified, unlimited potential.

Freud renders the substitution child for penis explicit only in the story of the little girl. Yet he himself mentions, in a relaxed moment (within a parenthesis) that "It is easy to see how the suppressed megalomania of fathers is transferred in their thoughts on to their children, and it seems quite probable that this is one of the ways in which the suppression of that feeling, which becomes necessary in actual life, is carried out."[12] The substitution is equally applicable to the boy's history, to Sade who turns away from the union with his mother so as to see his children. The replacement of precastration complex mother-love by child-love as an (inadequate) substitute for the desire to have (and be) the phallus (Freud's "megalomania") is at play in both sexes.

The fact that incest with the mother and perversions centered on the breasts and female organs are underrepresented in the Sadian tableau of "all passions" is symptomatic of the turning-away from the Neronic myth, from the unbearable ambivalent intimacy with the mother. The mother returns—a mutilated, exposed, "castrated" mother—as object of tenacious hatred, the obsessive hatred which stems from an uncovered deception. The phallic mother returns in Nature-as-stepmother, hated for her mystery and potency, for her ability to have and be the phallus that is lacking to any living subject but also, and at the same time, admired and imitated as everything the Sadian libertine aspires to be.

Sade's text is filled with a staggering multiplicity of passions: variations, repetitions, and substitutions, none sufficient to compensate for the missing phallus, the unfulfilled mother-child union. The attempt to replace the eternal concentration on one object with a multiplicity of crimes and objects is represented in Clairwil's discourse: "Replace the voluptuous idea that fills your head, this idea of a prolonged torture of the same object, replace it with a greater abundance of murders: don't kill the same individual for a longer time, which is impossible, but murder many others, which is very feasible" (20:317). In their number and their diversity, the passions present themselves as all-inclusive, masking the underrepresented center.

Clairwil in her pragmatism ignores the attraction of the impossibility of impossible crime. Yet throughout Sade's text some libertine will bemoan the petty contingency of any possible crime. The only crimes worth doing are universal, eternal, the domain of Mother Nature. Curval in *120 Days* laments: "How many times, damn it, have I not desired that one could attack the sun, deprive the universe of it, or use it to set fire to the world, those would be crimes and not these little faults we devote ourselves to that do no more than transform in the course of a year a dozen creatures into lumps of earth" (p. 207).

Throughout Sade's work, the most wicked, most successful libertines utter this pathetic plea: why are my crimes individual, not universal? The most masterful and most powerful Sadian characters are despondent over the emptiness of their innumerable crimes. Yet apart from all these sad winners stands Juliette, whose story has a "happy ending." Juliette never bemoans her lack of omnipotence, never envies Mother Nature her phallus. Juliette expresses only positive feelings toward Nature, and finds a happy union with a mysterious, maternal woman named Durand who knows Nature's inner secrets. When Juliette and Durand travel together as lovers, Durand says to her, "I must pass for your mother" (24:71). Durand is old enough to be Juliette's mother, but if she is a mother, she is a parody of a phallic mother. Her vagina is literally blocked, impenetrable. Thus her lack of phallus is permanently hidden, inaccessible. Durand must be penetrated anally: anal intercourse being the act preferred by Bressac and most other Sadian libertines for its denial of sexual difference. When Juliette first meets Durand, the latter is presented as a sorceress whose effects are seen, but whose causes, like Almani's Nature, are veiled. Durand herself says to Juliette at this first meeting that "all nature is at my command" (21:226). She is omnipotent; she is Mother Nature's concealed cause; she is the (maternal) phallus.

Durand displays a remarkable ability to be resurrected. Twice in the novel she is believed dead—she is actually seen hanged—but she later shows up to everyone's astonishment. Durand's name sounds like the present participle *durant*, which means "enduring." Like Mother Nature she remains unaffected by creation and destruction, life and death. They are but phases for her: she is alternately dead and alive in this book. The phallus can be distinguished from the penis by being that which is inalienable, that which endures. The penis is a detachable object, not an intrinsic property. To be phallic is to be immune to the threat of castration (death). The phallus is not subject to the ups and downs of contingency, as the penis is. To discover the mother's "castration" is to discover she *never had* a phallus. To believe the mother phallic is to be ignorant of the possibility of castration.

Juliette (whose story is subtitled "the prosperities of vice") ends up happily with Durand, the mysterious phallic mother. Like Aline who commits suicide to join her mother, Juliette says to Durand what she says to no one else: "I like the idea of putting my life in your hands" (24:70). At the end of *Juliette*, with the "mother" and "daughter" reunited, a veil is thrown over their lives. The narrator insists that nothing more can be known about Juliette except that she dies ten years later. Her story ends like Aline's with the daughter triumphant in her union with her mother. Juliette's "mother" does not have to die—as is necessary with Aline's, Bressac's, Nero's and Sade's mother— she already possesses that mystery. So Juliette's story, which is composed of a plurality of passions and the principle of unmasking any prejudice that privileges one passion above another, can have an "ending," a closure, fulfillment. Yet the "happy ending" necessitates the ruse of a mysterious Durand, whose secrets are left concealed as the unique exception to the graphic detail that pervades a book in which the heroine's last line is "Philosophy should say everything" (24:337).

If the chemist tries to look up Nature's skirts to learn her hidden causes, the philosopher, who must say everything, is committed to the task of undressing Nature for all to see. Juliette's final remark is made in defense of the project of publishing the story she has just recounted, *The Story of Juliette*. Philosophy here means novel-writing. In "Ideas on Novels" Sade writes:

> don't lose sight of the fact that the novelist is nature's man; she created him to be her painter: if he does not become his mother's lover as soon as she gives birth to him, let him never write, we will not read him; but if he feels that ardent thirst to paint all, if trembling he opens up nature's *sein*, . . . that is whom we will read.[13]

The novelist as would-be lover of Mother Nature, by his very project to "paint all" would also be Nature's tormentor. The writer in his "ardent thirst" to paint all of nature, to know (possess) all of nature, "opens up nature's *sein*." In Sade's fantasy of a return to the mother's womb, it is the *dead* mother who "opens once more her *sein* and invites [him] to return there." Opening the mother's breast/womb and describing all that is found there is performing an autopsy. The penetration of the womb, the telling of all Nature's secrets, is the uncovering of the Mother's "castration." If the philosopher/novelist could say all, he would castrate/kill Mother Nature.

Durand's womb is blocked, inaccessible. No novelist or philosopher can open it in order to depict all her secrets. Juliette can find happiness through this impasse, behind which is hidden the impossibility of saying all, the impossibility of being the phallic mother's lover, of possessing the (maternal) phallus. This impossibility means that either the mother is phallic (mysterious), and the child is a mere pawn; or the child possesses the mother, thereby discovering her incompleteness and winding up empty-handed. These two alternatives correspond in Freud's story of the little girl to the choice between the acceptance of femininity with its correlative passivity, its diminution of libido, and the blind denial of fact, the futile activity of the "masculinity complex," as reactions to the discovery of the mother's "castration." In the Sadian text these alternatives are universalized, presenting themselves equally to both sexes. From the feminine position, the subject admits that he does not have the potential/potency to fulfill his impossible desires. This is the position of Justine, the lucid victim who believes her fate is written by God (out of her power), as well as of any libertine who has "broken all restraints" and knows that, whatever he does, Nature has circumscribed his possibilities so that he can do no more than serve her will. The second alternative is the masculine position, which is characterized by denial of the impossibility of having and being the phallus. This alternative is represented in Sade's text by those libertines of either sex who heap crime upon crime, always repeating the violation of the mother (the discovery of the mother's "castration"), deluded by the diversity of their crimes and their victims into believing that what is lacking for their satisfaction is quantitative not qualitative. This is Clairwil's position when she suggests replacing the impossible crime with an abundance of possible crimes. The masculine position means trying to prove that what one has (the penis or clitoris, the castrated mother) is the phallus.

Sade's text bears the imprint of the intimate ambivalence that constitutes the relation of the human subject to the phallic mother/maternal phallus. In that relation the feminine as well as the masculine position can be filled by either sex, both roles being equally unsatisfactory. Most of Sade's characters oscillate between the two positions: alternating between frustration/lucidity and hope/delusion. The phallic mother is neither male nor female but the impossible merging of all possibilities (of both sexes), thus equally impossible for either sex to be or to have.

Thinking the Join

Sade wrote the same story, the story of Justine the victim and her libertine sister Juliette, three times. The first two versions are narrated by Justine, who never gets aroused; the last by Juliette, who always gets aroused. Why does Sade write the story three times? Why does he switch from Justine to Juliette as narrator? Using Justine to narrate all this sexual activity might be an attempt to tell the story objectively, through an impartial observer. If sexuality is to be objectively known, the observer must be free of desire. For his last rendition of the tale, Sade switches to the desiring subject as narrator, perhaps because the truth of sexuality can only be known by one who perceives it sexually, who experiences desire.

"Sade, Mothers, and Other Women" was written in 1975 while I was working on my dissertation. "Snatches of Conversation" was written two years later, after I had finished graduate school but before I went to Miami as an assistant professor. Both papers unveil the subjective investment in apparently objective works: Sade's subjectivity distorting the encyclopedic project; Shere Hite's fantasies shaping her scientific report. At the beginning of my academic writing, I am unmasking others' subjective investments, in order to clear a place for my subjectivity in serious discourse.

Late twentieth-century feminist science seemed too imbued with nineteenth-century scientific ideology. One way to think about that scientific project is to go back and look at its origin in the Enlightenment. If twentieth-century epistemology is both trying to get out of and somehow still within the scientistic ideology of the nineteenth century, it may be helpful to look at that position's infancy in the eighteenth century. The paper on Sade shows desire as the ruin of the encyclopedic project. "Snatches" turns to Diderot, the editor of the Encyclopedia who also wrote the novel Les Bijoux indiscrets, which exposes the subjective, desiring base of the encyclopedic project and illustrates its problems. In Sade and Diderot we can read the intrication of the project to bring everything to light, to know all, with sexual desire and subjectivity.

Both the papers in this chapter are about the join between theory and practice. In Sade's books, theories are immediately put into sexual practice. In my reading of twentieth-century female sexology, I look for an opening onto practice. Although on the link between philosophy and practice, my writing in the 1975 paper is objective and not sexy. Serving my academic apprenticeship, although attracted to nonserious models, I write with "scholarly seriousness." Written after the dissertation, "Snatches" experiments with a seductive writing practice, not only examining the libidinal fantasies behind feminist science but embodying the theory in my own relation to the reader.

"Sade, Mothers, and Other Women" is written from an identification with Sade, with the man with a negative Oedipus complex. Its stance is, in a way, typical of the feminist androgyny position of the early seventies. The stance of the 1977 piece is in a way the opposite. Not only do I explicitly identify with Diderot's heroine Mirzoza, with a traditional feminine position, but I attack another woman, Hite, for identifying with men. The vehemence of my attack can be understood as a refusal of the position I had so recently embraced; I am attacking my own former identification with men. This passage from an androgynous identification with men to a revalorization of the traditionally feminine is fairly typical of the movement of American academic feminist criticism from the early to the late seventies.

In the texts of the present chapter, the switch from male- to female-identified corresponds to a passage from graduate student to someone authorized by virtue of her doctorate. In 1975, I looked in at a homoerotic world, trying to imagine my future place. How would I pass? In 1977, having "passed," I was trying to imagine being an academic speaker *as a woman.*

Snatches of Conversation

In the ideology of our culture women are objects described, not speaking subjects. Women as women, as incarnations of the myth of Woman, do not produce culture. Woman was never considered to be actually nonspeaking. Talking constantly, women emitted chatter, gossip, and foolishness.

Naïve men were ensnared by the siren's song, because they took the woman at her word, taking that word out of the context of its unending protean flow. So women were called liars, and their speech, not conforming to male rules of logic, clarity, consistency, deemed nonsense.[14]

Smart men knew better. They paid women no mind. So women became the silent sex, by dint of not being heard.

Thus the dealings of men-as-men with women-as-women (which are, after all, sexual relations) had to be predicated upon the body of knowledge compiled by men (the compilers of knowledge, speakers of sense) about Woman. Although this lore was inadequate and often in disagreement with women's utterances about themselves, there was nothing to be done. Women could not be trusted to tell the truth about themselves. Women's statements about their sexuality were notoriously subject to the distortions of flirtatious modesty and manipulative docility. Knowledge, to be useful, must transcend intersubjective dynamics. It was impractical to listen to women's chatter, for it offered no information that could be processed and reliably applied in some quest for greater power. Theories of women's sexuality necessarily remained inadequate.

Feminism, recognizing the mechanism by which women's talk was dismissed as idle chatter, demanded that women be heard. And so women came to speak their sexuality, not in the old private way: highly charged exchanges between confidantes or conversations between lovers. Out of feminism arose public female discourse on women's sexuality.

The most serious and sophisticated product of this speaking out is *The Hite Report*,[15] whose very title declares the scientific credentials of the work. To prove that women are capable of being logical, consistent, disinterested about their sexuality, Shere Hite gives her book the trappings of science; long methodological introduction, voluminous appended charts full of numbers. Hite places herself in the tradition of male sexologists (the Kinsey Reports, the fictional Chapman Report), yet would keep her special status as a woman. The contradiction inherent in this position is important and vexatious. It is the problem of "public female discourse": how to gain the logic and authority of science without losing the authenticity of confession.

In an attempt to analyze this contradiction, we will look at a less illustrious example of women making their sexuality public—Nancy Friday's *My Secret Garden*.[16] The title here is sexy (vaginal even), rather than drily scientific. The book sells through the titillation of confession; nonetheless, the author's explicit intention, borne out by the format, is to break women's silence and aid in their liberation.

Our two representatives of public female discourse focus, as one might expect from the divergent tones of their titles, upon different aspects of female sexuality. Hite prefers the sheer mechanics of sex, thus reporting a level-headed female sexuality, one of control and scientifically predictable results. *My Secret Garden* presents the fantasies which supplement mechanics, inviting us into the lush, irrational world of passion. Yet both books share the conviction that sense can be made from women's eroticism, that light and order can be brought to the murky tangles of the female genitalia/mind.

Their common fantasy is no bold new dream, no virginal daughter of Modern Feminism or the Sexual Revolution. This fantasy has long been part of Western male culture: the dream of imposing order upon mute, dark confusion, of channeling female gush into logical categories, of bringing woman's hidden powers into the open where they might be harnessed.

Perhaps the most graphic example of this traditional fantasy is Denis

Diderot's *Les Bijoux indiscrets* (The Indiscreet Jewels).[17] The hero of that novel, the monarch Mangogul, asks a genie for the power to learn the truth about women's sexual adventures. He wants this power because one cannot trust what women say, because in their conventional pretense of chastity, women dissimulate. The genie gives him a ring which when directed toward a woman causes her to speak clearly and distinctly, not from her mouth, but from her "jewel," her nether parts. These "snatches of conversation" seem to fulfill the desire for the unmediated word of the thing itself. The nether parts no longer are a dark mystery, but speak frankly and articulately. The novel presents a mixture of the jewels' confessions and reactions to and theorizing about this "chatterbox" phenomenon.

Just as a dream within a dream is often closer to "reality,"[18] so in this fantasy world the insatiably curious monarch has a dream which might be said to lay bare the philosophical underpinnings of the tale. The dream is found in chapter 32, a chapter entitled, "Perhaps the best and least read of this story." In this chapter, Mangogul dreams he is walking about in a highly unstable building full of undernourished cripples in rags. Despite the obvious lacks in both building and men, he is forced to acknowledge they have a certain beauty. The dreamer learns that he is in the "region of hypotheses" and that these people are "systematics" (which is to say, they arrange diversity into systematic worlds by means of hypotheses). Then Mangogul sees a child approach who grows with each step until it reaches colossal proportions. This child, he is told, is Experience, whose arrival causes the edifice of hypotheses to shake and crumble. Informed by Plato (the healthiest of the systematics) that "this edifice has but a moment left" (p. 117), Mangogul flees. The child arrives; the building falls; and Mangogul wakes up.

Dreaming of the triumph of empiricism over a priori hypothesis, Mangogul's sexual investigations can be seen as a rejection of all the lovely, faulty hypotheses about women, an empiricist's effort to learn the facts, to gather unprejudiced data. This is precisely the philosophy behind *The Hite Report:* "what should be done is to look at what women are *actually experiencing* and then draw conclusions. In other words, researchers must stop telling women what they should feel sexually, and start asking them what they do feel sexually" (p. 60, emphasis added).

Traditional sexology begins with a theory of "natural" female sexuality: woman's sexual fulfillment should be found in coitus, since that is *the sex act*, necessary for reproduction. Starting with this hypothesis, the scientist will inevitably label as dysfunction the inability to orgasm in intercourse, a dysfunction that is the condition of 70 percent of all women. Hite, on the other hand, would first gather the data, and only then create, a posteriori, a "new theory of female sexuality" (p. 11).

The new theory advocates that women take control of their own stimulation, have power over their own bodies. In the place of reproductive coitus as the basic sexual paradigm, Hite posits masturbation. The truth of woman's sexuality can be found in what the woman does when she is alone, when, unswayed by interpersonal dynamics and cultural pressures, woman can follow her "natural instincts" (pp. 59 and 243). Dropping the impartial mask of the researcher, Hite becomes a sex counselor, as she advises: "don't wait for the Right Man to be dependent on [in finding fulfilling sex], but create your own good situation—which can include yourself as being the Princess Charming" (p. 255).

The liberated woman, heroine of this new theory of female sexuality, would be in frank and lucid communication with her genitalia. Her hidden parts would speak sensibly to her, and she would know their secrets, so that she (that is, her rational self) might control them and her destiny, rather than being overpowered by a passionate loss of self. As Peggy Kamuf commented, "Woman masturbating is to her own sexuality (in control of it, mastering it—masterbating) what the Sultan is to female sexuality."[19]

Mangogul's mistress Mirzoza feared the cruel potential of his magic ring. "She knew the sultan's curiosity, and she hadn't sufficient confidence in the promise of a man who was less in love than he was tyrannical to be free from worry" (p. 15). The curious imperialist, with his ravenous will to power through knowledge, would use his charm over women not to love them or give them (or even himself) pleasure, but to strip them of their powers; dissimulation, coquetry, baffling inconsistency.

I am distinguishing here between two different sorts of "power(s)." Mangogul possesses a certain worldly power (command, control) which he can expand through knowledge (reason, logic). This is in contrast to Mirzoza's "powers." The first, expressed in the singular, is a monolithic authority which would subjugate everything to its unified rule. The second, expressed in the plural, consists of various abilities and charms that can be used strategically to influence other people's actions. Drawing upon traditional ideology, I characterize consolidated/consolidating power as male, and plural, tactical powers as female, although I realize that both real men and real women desire, strive for, and attain (to a certain extent) "power" and both men and women turn their persuasive "powers" (charms) to the manipulation of others. The central difference is that power (which is always a dream of power, a fantasy never quite achieved) would be an absolute attribute of a monadic self, not contingent upon situation; whereas (feminine, strategic) powers are always powers over others, dependent upon a given intersubjective dynamic.

Like Mangogul, Hite would banish all mystery which stands in the way of self-determination and control (monadic power). Masturbation is chosen as the primary model of female sexuality because it is the most efficient method of attaining orgasm. Orgasm, the calming teleology of sexual arousal, is the most important factor in *The Hite Report*. The new theory of female sexuality can be judged superior to the old because its application will produce more (and better) orgasms: "There is no great mystery about why a woman has an orgasm. It happens with the right stimulation, quickly, pleasurably, and reliably" (p. 270). In this scientific, nonmystic, nonecstatic sexuality, pleasure is allowed (it is, after all, a reasonable goal), but there is a premium on efficiency ("quickly") and predictable causality ("reliably").

Although from time to time *The Report* concedes that orgasm might be overemphasized at the expense of emotion and interpersonal relations, the privileged position of orgasm is unavoidable, given the empiricist dream behind the new theory. This dream sexology would gather its data without having to deal with the psyche and its irritating tendency to cloud facts with opinions, desires, and fantasies. In an extreme moment, the book betrays this white-coat fantasy when in defense of masturbation as the paradigm of female sexuality, it gratuitously mentions that "as a matter of fact, the highest cardiac rates of all the orgasms . . . studied occurred during female masturbation" (p. 192). "As a matter of fact" not only indicates this as a secondary argument whose purpose is impressive reinforcement rather than logical persuasion, but also that here we have a matter of *fact*, something solid, measurable, something to found a science upon.

Taken out of context, it seems absurd that the goal of sexual activity should be the sheer height of cardiac rate. Yet within the dream of a logical eroticism, an eroticism of control and power, striving in the spirit of Scientific Progress and the Technological Revolution toward the bigger and the better, there is nothing more desirable than that which can be measured by instruments rather than judged by a subject.

Predictably, a mathematical fantasy also makes an appearance in *Les Bijoux indiscrets*, in the account of a journey to an uncharted isle (chapter 17). In this fantasy-within-a-fantasy, people have genitals of various geometric shapes. Before two people can marry they are examined to ensure that they possess interlocking parts. Besides the morphological criterion, sexual temperature must match. Special thermometers measure "temperament" (an eighteenth-century word for passion which etymologically suggests measurable heat). Thus sexual compatibility is mathematically assured. The myriad individual manifestations of sexuality are civilized and categorized by geometry and arithmetic. Yet we are told in the novel that even these extreme "measures" are not sufficient to squelch infidelity. Sexual desire stubbornly resists even the most elaborate of logical confines.[20]

Although I turned to *Les Bijoux indiscrets* in an attempt to delineate the empiricist fantasy that structures recent attempts to make women speak their sexuality, the novel is much more than such a univocal reading would make it. It includes not just that dream but a criticism of it. Such is the effect of a mathematical allusion in the very title of the novel. *Discret* in French means not only "discreet" but also "discrete"—that is, separable into parts, countable. If the jewels are "indiscrete" they are not countable, and are the derision of the mathematical fantasy. When the sultan reads the report of mathematically arranged unions in the uncharted isle, Mirzoza leaves the room offended. My criticism of Hite's white-coat fantasy repeats Mirzoza's opposition to Mangogul's imperialism. In this way, the present text reenacts Diderot's novel.

More than a collection of forced confessions "straight from the source," more even than a philosophical allegory, *Les Bijoux indiscrets* is the history of a love affair, of the power struggle between two lovers, of each one's fight not to be totally overwhelmed by the other. Mangogul might strike out alone to wrest sexual secrets from the women of his kingdom, but it is always in order to bring back a report to Mirzoza, to score a victory in their private and well-matched battle of the sexes.

Mirzoza is an exceptionally accomplished storyteller, a Scheherazade who regaled her royal lover with the sexual adventures of the town until one day she ran dry. We are told in one breath both that she ran out of stories and that she had "little temperament" (p. 6). Mangogul and Mirzoza have reached an impasse: she is no longer putting out either verbal or vaginal enchantments. Testing his love, she suggests he look elsewhere in the court for entertainment. He gallantly counters that no one tells stories as well as she. Not won over from her suspicions and fears so easily, she replies that, regardless, he'll "more than make up in content what he may lose in form," that is, he might prefer her, but all the variety will certainly make up for the inadequacy of any particular woman/storyteller. She may be testing him out of jealous fear, but in his own insecurity he reads this as her indifference. So he goes to a genie to enlist aid in gaining access to (the truth about) all the women in his kingdom.

Although the explicit plot has Mangogul merely in search of tales of the ladies' romantic dalliances, he asks for access to the truth about these women in the most equivocal terms: saying he would like to "procure some pleasures at the expense of the women of my court." The genie thinks Mangogul wants to have sexual commerce with all these women, but Mangogul assures him that he only wishes to know their adventures, "that's all." So he is given the ring.

Immediately upon possession of this new power, the sultan goes to try it on his mistress. Yet as he is about to attain full possession of his love's secret interiority (and discover why she no longer "puts out"), he becomes frightened of what he might learn and in his agitation awakens her so that she forbids him (under penalty of loss of her love) to use it on her. Afraid to find out that she is not faithful, Mangogul causes his first attempt to founder. With all his power to force entry to any vagina, the man is powerless before someone whose love he wants.

The sultan continually requests Mirzoza's permission to make her genitals respond. She is ever fearful of being compromised, distrusting his love, for she sees his thirst for command. Having slept through his initial moment of anxiety, Mirzoza does not know that her lover is as afraid as she to put their love to the test of truth. Unaware of his doubts, she is unaware of the value he places upon her love for him. She therefore does not trust him sufficiently to leave herself vulnerable by proving her love to him. Thus he can play the cocky, carefree aggressor, and she must play the cautious, fearful prude.

At the close of the novel Mangogul finally does make Mirzoza's "jewel" speak. He takes advantage of her when she is in a swoon. The story has a happy ending: her vagina tells her love for him, so he has no more use for the ring and returns it to the genie. The entire baroque path of the novel is but a deferral of this confrontation with the voice of the loved woman's desire.

The sexual/scientific imperialism of Les Bijoux indiscrets is thus no simple, successful subjugation of woman's resistant mystery to light, truth, and worldly authority. All Mangogul's conquests go to even the score against Mirzoza, the beguiling storyteller who silently closes up. The fantasy of sexual expertise (domination of alterity by a monadic power) is belied by the intricacies of desire which include a need to hear the voice of the loved one's desire.

Of course Diderot's book is a novel, so it is no wonder that sexual research is given emotional motivation. Yet we find that Nancy Friday offers us a similar pretext for her nonfiction study of women's fantasies. Discourse about sexuality is apparently not very far removed from its context. Like sexuality, it is always bound up in emotional situations, intersubjectivity. It is only the white-coat fantasy that allows us to imagine that either sexual activity or discourse about sexuality could ever be purified of subjective content. It is this same white-coat fantasy that subtends the belief that there can be a discourse about sexuality that is not sexual talk, a scientific discourse that is not vulgar but clean and sterile. (Mangogul pointed his ring at women's vaginas from a distance; he did not have to get his hands dirty.)

My Secret Garden opens with a long, explicit, unprefaced sexual fantasy which the reader supposes to be an example of the subject matter collected by Friday. The fantasy reaches its climax, and the reader is shocked, in the afterglow of this very sexy scenario, to read the following " 'Tell me what you are thinking about,' the man I was actually fucking said, his words as charged as the action in my mind. As I'd never stopped to think before doing anything to him in bed, I didn't stop to edit my thoughts. I told him what I'd been thinking. He got out of bed, put on his pants and went home" (p. 2).

Friday begins her book with this account of its origin. That sexual encounter, which makes her feel ashamed, unloved, and unnatural for having sexual fantasies, plants the seed for *My Secret Garden*. That intimate pretext repeats itself in a more professional situation. Some years later, happily married to a man who encourages her sexual fantasizing, Friday writes a novel that includes a chapter which narrates a sexual fantasy of the heroine. "[Friday's] editor, a man, was put off. Her fantasies made the heroine sound like some kind of sexual freak, he said" (p. 4). If the sexual encounter of the first pages is the moment of conception of *My Secret Garden*, it is in this confrontation with her editor that the fantasy collection is born. The first incident creates a need to speak her psychic sexuality privately, but the second impels her to bring it out into the world.

My Secret Garden is her retort to these two men, who would prefer her silence because her speech threatens them. She is vulnerable to their rejection, because, as she says, they "hit [her] in that area where women, knowing least about each other's true sexual selves, are most vulnerable" (p. 5). So Friday sets out to learn the truth about women in order to arm herself for the battle of the sexes.

Mangogul brought back his revelations of female truth to Mirzoza as a tactic to arouse her desire. He reports back all the women's lack of constancy. Although Mirzoza persists in her claim that, despite all the damning evidence, women can love faithfully, she refuses to allow him to turn his ring on her, refusing to allow her "jewel" to prove her claim for women's virtue and speak her faithful love. Each report to Mirzoza of an application of the ring is another goad to get her to prove her love by allowing him to make her "jewel" speak that love (allowing him to arouse her desire). Likewise Friday recounts all these women's secret thoughts so that men will consider her a normal, natural woman (so they will desire her). Although this book brings women together as confidantes and sisters, that sorority's function is to enhance their charm for men. Women are to gain liberation and power so as to increase their powers over men. Like Mangogul, as I read him, Friday's ideal heroine would search not for some uncompromising, noncontingent strength but for strategic and defensive powers over the opposite sex.

The Hite Report openly advocates lesbian activity. *My Secret Garden*, while recognizing the importance and prevalence of women's sexual fantasies about other women, would restrict those longings to release in fantasy. Several times Friday is careful to distinguish between the fantasies contributed by "real" lesbians and lesbian fantasies from "regular" women, and to insist that fantasies need not be acted out, that women dreaming of other women are (despite those women's own stated fears and doubts) *not* closet lesbians. The "liberated" author of *My Secret Garden* would prefer lesbian (and all) fantasies to serve the role they do in the following women's testimony: "She licked and sucked my breasts and went down between my legs and performed cunnilingus on me (better than my husband). I could feel her sucking my clitoris, and just to feel her breast was enough to make me come at least twice. I often think of this and then give my husband a good time" (pp. 71–72).

Friday contends that it is not necessary and may not even be desirable to try and make sexual activity more adequately correspond to sexual fantasy. *Garden's* plot for desire is essentially centrifugal. Sexual fantasy portrays scenes that are just beyond acceptable action. As fact would catch up with fictional scenario, ever-bolder fantasies are spun out. Such a model of the human psyche allows for, and expects, the irrational, the mysterious, and the contradictory.

Unlike Hite, who glorifies masturbation, the solitary uncompromised jubilation of the autonomous ego, wherein woman can be strong, free, and exercise a practical, controlled sexuality, Friday advocates an autoerotic schema that is vulnerably intersubjective, rather than the closed godlike circle of individual fulfilling herself. Masturbation in the *Garden* is not a lone woman self-sufficiently and lucidly satisfying her needs in the most efficient way possible. Along with the dry mechanics is a lush fantasy-world peopled (and animaled) with any number of companions, as necessary to the orgasm as the physical sensations themselves.

The prospect of unadorned masturbation throws this articulate writer into defensive tautology: "masturbation doesn't just require fantasy, it demands it. Without fantasy, masturbation would be too lonely, I don't even want to think about it" (p. 68). If there is anyone who believes that thinking need not lead to actualization, it is Nancy Friday; yet she cannot even think about, cannot tolerate the mere fantasy of bare, controlled masturbation. Masturbation might provide better orgasms than shared sex, but Friday is after neither predictable success nor high cardiac rate. She strives for enjoyment, and "it's more fun for two" (p. 295).

Friday might well ask Hite point blank, "If sex is reduced to a test of power, what woman wants to be left all alone, all powerful, playing with herself?" (p. 7). Actually, this rhetorical question appears in the context of Friday's criticism of Women's Liberation—a sympathetic criticism which embraces feminism's goals but regrets the strident tones of its demands for power. *The Hite Report* privileges efficient, reliable sexual stimulation. Yet if sex were fun, would we want to get it over with as quickly as possible?

As we saw in the case of Mangogul and Mirzoza, as long as men and women are jockeying for power, sex must be a battleground. In the scene where Mangogul decides to ask the genie's help in learning about women, we are told that the royal lovers "without loving each other any less, were hardly amusing each other at all" (chapter 3, p. 6). Only when Mirzoza swoons (loses control, loses her ability to speak) and Mangogul gives up his ring can they enjoy their love.

The Hite Report includes the following testimony from a woman for whom sex is irreparably unentertaining: "Unfortunately sex for me is like a fight. I put the penis where I want it; I say 'it feels good there.' He shoves it deep inside and says, 'No, *that's* where it feels good.' This may sound far-fetched, but it's true; God, I wish it weren't. I usually lose the fight" (p. 286). And this is precisely what sex would be like if we were to follow Hite's advice—each partner after her/his own most efficient stimulation, fighting for control. Men, according to Hite, "rub their penises against our vaginal walls so that the same area they stimulate during masturbation is being stimulated during intercourse" (p. 276). Hite urges women to likewise "adapt their masturbatory techniques unabashedly and unashamedly to relations with others" (p. 302).

This superimposition of the "new theory of female sexuality" upon the raw material from which that theory is built draws attention to what is at once the major fault and the greatest contribution of *The Hite Report*. Hite really has broken women's silence and brought their "underground" sexuality out into the open. In the pages of her book, women's voices can be heard in rich diversity. But inasmuch as Hite's science fantasy compels her to organize those voices into a "new theory," which is to say, inasmuch as she wishes to overthrow the old theories and usurp the place of the male sexologist, she necessarily comes to occupy that male place. Hite, the white-coated impartial theoretician, who interprets the confessions, can no longer hear the contradictory cries of the very women she has begged to speak.

So the "new theory" sounds astonishingly like the old: is the mere fact of theorizing a sufficiently powerful common denominator to attenuate any divergent content? Even the elaborate science of the island in *Les Bijoux indiscrets* could not stop infidelity. Is any possibly theory of sexuality doomed to inadequacy because desire must exceed and frustrate logical consistency?

Optimistic about the possibilities for a fresh start, *The Hite Report* begins with a rejection of past contributions in the field: "Researchers, looking for statistical 'norms,' have . . . all too often wound up *telling* women how they should feel rather than asking them how they do feel" (p. 11). (Male) researchers have thrust language upon passive women, whereas Hite's questioning would attentively stimulate women to respond. The model for good sexual research is structurally analogous to the pattern for good sex. Hite asks; women respond. But then Hite tells them what their responses mean. The considerate inquiry reveals itself as pro forma foreplay to Hite's triumphant ejaculation of theory.

What is "wrong" with the *old* theories is that women are made to feel there is something abnormal about their own individual sexual responses. Yet a woman wrote to Hite "after reading *Sexual Honesty* [a preliminarily published version of *The Hite Report*] to ask if she was 'weird' because she *did* have orgasms during intercourse" (p. 271). Hite, admirably, never flinches in reporting this feedback; she simply declares her innocence as logical: "There is certainly no reason for this reverse stereotyping." But four pages later, this champion of women's rights to be heard proudly proclaims that "having an orgasm during intercourse is an adaptation of our bodies. Intercourse was never meant to stimulate women to orgasm" (p. 275). The 30 percent of women who orgasm from intercourse, without additional clitoral stimulation, are a mere aberration.

Male theoreticians (producers of serious, consistent, efficacious discourse) have always dismissed the incoherent protestations of women (which threaten to topple their hypotheses) as lies. Hite called the first version of her report *Sexual Honesty*, because she demanded that women end their dissimulation. When the author of a book called *Sexual Honesty* asks "Do you fake orgasm?" the question just has to be loaded. One woman gave the "right" answer with such vehemence as to expose the moralistic condemnation lurking behind this "new theory of female sexuality": "I never fake orgasm. I am angry with other women who do, because then men can tell me that I am incapable sexually, because I do not have vaginal climaxes, and other women they have slept with do. Since I have never had a vaginal climax, I question their existence . . . and wonder if another woman's faking an orgasm has made it harder for me when I am honest" (p. 257). Angry at all those women who lie, cheat, and deceive, this woman has adopted a candid, straightforward mode of discourse, become a masculine speaker, which means opposed on principle to coy chatter. This does not mean she speaks as real men do. Men too can fake orgasm, thus becoming feminine speakers.[21]

There is at least one example in *The Hite Report* of a woman who fakes orgasm with women lovers (p. 263). Women don't just lie to men; they don't just lie to their lovers. Women may deceive sexual researchers, even female researchers. Sexologists and lovers ask women for the same thing: a true testimonial of the woman's desire.

Hite would like to believe that the mere fact of being a female sexologist should be sufficient grounds for her subjects' trust. This is analogous to the belief/fantasy, recorded in both Friday's and Hite's books, that a female lover is inevitably more sensitive to a woman's need than a male lover. To the extent that this belief about lesbianism is based upon masturbation as the paradigmatic sex act, it implies the sexist assumption that all women are alike. The difference between the sexes would be the only sexual difference that mattered. That assumption is embedded in the very word "homosexuality"— same sexuality. Another woman would know instinctively just how to touch me, because she is just like me. Sex with another woman would thus have all the advantages of masturbation (efficiency, reliability) with the pleasant addition of companionship. Yet one of the things Hite's report documents in groundbreaking detail is the variety of women's masturbatory techniques. If we learn the report's lesson of the diversity of women's sexuality, then we can no longer assume that a sexual encounter between two women would be between two bodies with the same sexuality, that another woman would know immediately (without the mediation of some sort of language) what I want because she is just like me.

With all her talk about loving and sharing between women, Hite simply does not like certain of the women who answer her questionnaire. She dislikes them because they do not fit her notion of the ideal woman: free, level-headed, self-sufficient. Hite waxes highly unscientific as she considers these women who threaten to deflate her theoretical construction. Two pages before the section of the book entitled "Do you ever fake orgasms?" Hite writes: "Of course, the thirty percent of women who said they *could* orgasm regularly during intercourse often bragged about it" (p. 255). *The American Heritage Dictionary* distinguishes between "brag" and its various synonyms thus: "*Brag*, used in more informal contexts, implies exaggerated claims, blatancy, and often an air of insolence" (p. 146). It is not far from an accusation of bragging to a charge of lying (two pages later the woman quoted above makes that charge by "questioning the existence of vaginal climax"). Hite's final put-down is to call these women old-fashioned and unliberated: "Like the competition among women fifty years ago as to who made the best pies, we're still competing for male approval and haven't yet come into our own" (p. 255).

For all Hite's dogma about female solidarity, there is a noticeable mistrust of characteristics and attitudes that are traditionally feminine: passivity, self-sacrifice, passionate illogic. Nancy Friday complains that "the naked power cry of Women's Lib . . . put too many women off" (p. 7). Hite's new theory of female sexuality is likely to alienate those women (whom she would dismiss) whose desire is tied up with the traditional sexual patterns she is working to undo. In the wake of the broad-based rejection of "Women's Lib" style feminism by women, it would be useful to consider the possibility that a certain "feminism" might have substituted one ideal of woman for another. If the old theory of femininity made one sort of woman feel excluded, monstrous, and angry, the new theory could have the same effect on a different sort of woman.

In the statistical table appended to *The Hite Report,* in the very place where mathematics (cold, objective truth) should reign supreme, there appears an alarming note of intersubjective doubt which threatens to erode the scientific edifice. In presenting the percentages for orgasm from various types of stimulation, Hite feels compelled to warn us that the figure 30 percent for orgasm from intercourse "may be slightly high . . . beause women are under such great pressure to have orgasm during intercourse, both from others and from themselves, that in cases of doubt they may very well have said yes" (p. 612).

Although Hite would like to speak from an impartial position, high above any unscientific influences, she cannot. The very fantasies which energize her for the tremendous task of "a nationwide study of female sexuality" prejudice her in favor of certain findings. She wants to ground her theory in Experience, but the only way to gain access to, interpret, and communicate women's experience is through language. Once dealing with and in language, it is no longer simply a question of gathering scientific data. The researcher, rather than immune in some metalinguistic ether, is embroiled in the middle of an interpersonal situation, where what is said always has in view a desired response from the interlocutor. The speaker does not merely convey information; she wants to please, irritate, arouse, or deceive the listener.

Hite is sorely tempted to have recourse to a natural female sexuality ("masturbation provides a source of almost pure biological feedback—it is one of the few forms of instinctive behavior to which we have access" [p. 59]) which has been deformed by an artificial, overlaid culture whose main agent is language. But she is dissuaded from the biological model because that is precisely the tactic of the old, repressive, male theory of female sexuality, which posits a natural, reproductive femininity that has fallen into dysfunction through the decadence and neurosis of modern culture. Eschewing the naturalistic paradigm, she arrives at a philosophy of free will: "Sex and all physical relations are something we create: they are cultural forms, not biological forms" (p. 432).

Do *we* create cultural forms? Clearly we have not in the past—woman's sexuality has been patterned by already existing forms. One might argue that men created those self-serving patterns, and now it is time for women to do likewise. However, autonomous, solitary individuals (male and female) cannot create cultural forms ex nihilo according to whim, any more than one can communicate by making up words. Sexuality, like language, is inescapably intersubjective. If one monadic psyche wanted to structure a sexual exchange according to her caprice, she would need an already understandable means of communicating the new form. The attempt to pattern sexual intercourse after masturbation runs up against the same barrier as the effort to express one's own peculiarity in language.

Fortunately, people do not formulate propositions (sexual or otherwise) merely from the wish to impose their autonomous will upon the passivity of others. Inasmuch as sexuality and language always include a need to elicit a response from an other, they can only be adequately understood in relation to that response. To try to isolate the truth of desire by reducing it to the well-defined, straightforward purity of masturbation produces an image as deceptively simple as words in a dictionary—devoid of irony, rhetoric, and contextual connotation. Meaning ascertained outside of context is of course clearer, crisper, and more easily manipulated; but it is naïvely innocent of the intersubjective desire which determines all worldly intercourse.

The major discrepancy between Hite and her subjects is that she, in search of scientific data, favors strong, clear, calculable responses whereas they, in quest of love and happiness, even power, are interested in diverse, less clearly measurable factors. This distinction determines a dynamic tension played out in *The Report* between the Woman whose voice Hite longs to hear and the women who actually speak. Hite, focusing on the orgasm (a discrete, countable unit, a standard of success or failure) finds that "the physical intensity of orgasm per se is greater for most women when intercourse is not in progress, and especially during self-stimulation. *Despite this*, a *majority* of women *stated flatly* that *no matter* what the difference in feeling might be, they would always perfer orgasm during intercourse because of the psychological factors of sharing with and being loved by another person, the warmth of touching all over, body to body" (p. 194, emphasis added).

For Shere Hite, the new theory is superior to the old because its application will produce *stronger* orgasms. In all matters Hite opts for strength and power over other advantages. However, if the "majority of women" are not interested in physical intensity, there is no longer any standard by which to judge the new theory an improvement over the old.

Oblivious to this conclusion which would undercut its entire theoretical edifice, *The Hite Report* is nonetheless a substantial contribution to an understanding of woman's sexuality, because it quotes women's responses at length, without suppressing those which contradict the theory. My undoing of Hite's interpretation would not have been possible were it not for the sincerity of her effort to let women really speak for themselves. The flaws in Hite's theory do not detract from the success of her report. She set out to let women speak, and accomplishes that goal admirably.

Hite succeeds in getting women to testify because of her evident desire for their testimony. "One of the most striking points about the answers received to the questionnaires was how frequently, *even though it was not specifically asked*, women brought up the fact that they might be interested in having sexual relations with another woman" (p. 397, emphasis Hite's). Women gave more than the questionnaires asked for; and that more was a sexual response (rather than a response *about* their sexuality). Women reacted as is customary when urged to talk about sex; they got aroused ("I like the questionnaire. I've been doing it at work for the past week and have hurried home at five o'clock every day horny horny horny," p. 50). They feel desired and return that desire. Women were volunteering interest in sex with other women, because a woman (researcher) was expressing an interest in their sexuality.

There is no sexual metalanguage; hence the impossibility of an objective "scientific" sexual theory. Seduction is often carried on by means of erotic talk. Talk about sex (as disinterested as it might pretend to be) is sexy. Hard- and soft-core pornography often poses in the (transparent) guise of a scientific study. (*My Secret Garden* runs dangerously close to this genre.) *The Hite Report* does not just register women's sexual habits; it acts upon them. One woman wrote in: "Masturbation has not been important to me until last night when I masturbated for the first time, after reading several confessions in *Sexual Honesty*" (p. 69). Writing and reading confessions is stimulating enough to produce feelings and acts worthy of another confession.

Having exposed her desires to the powerful sexual expert, a woman craves some proof of the researcher's love, some response beyond impressive science. One woman, getting personal if not explicitly sexual, wrote "I like these questions very much. Filling them out I *got the desire to know you* in person, and continue our questions and answers" (Hite, p. 524, emphasis added). Continued in person these questions and answers would be more embarrassing, and all the more exciting. As another woman put it, "I haven't had sex with another woman, except verbally—I think women often make love by talking a certain way, at least I do" (Hite, p. 399).

The Report's dream-woman is strong, proud, free, and masturbating. Yet Hite does not desire self-enclosed solitude any more than does Friday. By reaching out to all these women, by asking them to masturbate for her, she expresses her desire for them. She even uses Friday's word, "sharing," as she boasts of the love and honesty women have exchanged in her project (p. 12). Nonorgasmic women complained that the questionnaire was oriented to the orgasmic woman (p. 205). Hite wants her women to come; she wants definitive proof (no faking, please) of their desire. And it is this insistence upon getting a response that makes Hite (her questionnaire and her book) so seductive.

More attuned to fantasy and sexuality beyond the narrow limits of physical sensation, Friday explicitly acknowledges (in her dedication) that her book is the fulfillment of a fantasy. I do not want to reduce a scientific study, and its very real contribution to knowledge about women's sexuality, to a mere sublimation. But no sexology can be above the sexual register, or else it would lose its validity as a contact with the truth of sex. I would like to suggest a certain resemblance between the fantasy which inspires Hite's nonetheless valuable and legitimate effort and a letter sent to Friday by a militant young French feminist (p. 88), who wrote: "I had a love affair with a girl . . . The pleasure of one worked on the other and vice versa.

"I could write more, but the fact that I don't know you really limits my pleasure in writing. Although it *is* a kind of trip to send some intimate sensations to an unknown girl (that I could eventually seduce? who knows.)

"Je m'aventure à te donner un baiser, ma douce inconnue. [I'll take the risk of sending you a kiss, my sweet stranger.]"

Recalling Conversations

The last half of this text was almost entirely deleted from the version published in *Women and Language in Literature and Society* (1980). As I understand it, the readers for a university press found it both unscholarly and too much about sex rather than language. In particular, most of the lesbian stuff was left out. If the libidinal fantasies fueling feminist studies—behind collectivity, collaboration, and feminist teaching—are lesbian, they must be suppressed in other to prove the seriousness, objectivity, and legitimacy of feminist studies.

When I decided to compile the present book, I wanted to include what had been censored, but I discovered that I had somehow lost the original paper. I phoned everyone I remembered giving a copy in 1977: the editors of the anthology, friends and colleagues from that period, my mother. No one had a copy anymore. I gave up, with great regret. Then, six months later, while editing the essays, I recalled having given it to a man I was, in those days, trying to seduce. I got up the nerve to phone; he still had his copy.

I had completely forgotten the image of the "French feminist" on which the paper ends. That image of writing (to a stranger) as seduction became in the next three years—up through the writing of *The Daughter's Seduction*, which both makes it explicit and tries to work it through—the governing fantasy of my writing. Although the original paper ends with a quotation, I came to take that other woman's place, to speak from her place. Unearthing Friday's "French feminist" in 1987, I felt I had uncovered the model for my "French feminist" period in an image of "French feminism" found in American popular culture.

The attempt to study American popular culture in this piece shares in the elitism of the Frankfurt school model of mass culture critique. A look at a European classic will expose the ideology embedded but not manifest in American mass culture. Whereas the reading of Diderot need only recount the manifest surface, the plot, the reading of Hite and Friday would bring out the text's unconscious. This reading presumes Diderot, but not Hite and Friday, to know. An American becoming a professor of French, I was in search of high culture, *necessarily not* my own. Yet I was also seeking to understand myself and my world. The split between high and popular culture was, for me, mapped onto the difference between France and America: high culture mispronounced as *haute couture*.

In this paper the "French feminist" provides a "happy ending" resolving the difference between Hite (male-identified feminist) and Friday (traditionally feminine). The "French feminist" of the conclusion is also a displacement of the unspoken name of Irigaray whose influence shaped this piece (note 14 was written in 1987).

The beginning of the paper is presented as myth. Like any myth, this one covers over the dynamics of an origin, covering over my theoretical influences. I can, at this remove, recall Irigaray, Lacan, and Foucault, but there is a whole debt to feminist and deconstructionist theory that I cannot repay and, a decade ago, chose simply to erase. I was just out of graduate school, unemployed and broke, living back home with my parents. I wrote this paper in my adolescent bedroom, trying to block out both my literal and my intellectual parents in order to think.

There is one buried reference to Lacan in this text. Not noted in the original or the 1980 published version, it has become note 18. His thinking is very much behind the attack on the monadic self and the insistence on the intersubjectivity of language and sexuality. In Lacanian fashion, the original version of this paper attacked the ego per se. At the time I was unaware of the sort of theses Nancy Chodorow and Carol Gilligan[22] would put forth as to the differences between a male and a female ego. Whatever problems I have with simple sexual differentiation (boys are . . . girls are . . .), I respond to the idea of alternative ego structures. The masculinist ego in search of objective knowledge portrayed in this paper corresponds to the ego behind scientist ideology described by Evelyn Fox Keller in *Reflections on Gender and Science*.[23] Critical of the epistemology based in that sort of ego, it never occurred to the orthodox Lacanian that I was that such an ego might not be the only possible sort. So I attacked the ego per se. I cannot, however, imagine that the solution is some sort of Deleuzian or Buddhist transcendence of ego. That selflessness has been the Christian ideology intended to pacify women and other disenfranchised people by celebrating their powerlessness.

There are at least buried or displaced allusions to Irigaray and Lacan in this paper, and I have written extensively about my relations to those two figures elsewhere. Much more profoundly silenced is the influence of Michel Foucault, never explicitly mentioned in any of my work. In the winter of 1977 I read *La Volonté de savoir*, the first volume of *L'Histoire de la sexualité*.[24] Foucault mentions *Les Bijoux indiscrets* in relation to sexual research. Soon after, I started dipping into *The Hite Report* and then read Friday's *My Secret Garden*. Foucault had clearly given me the idea of bringing contemporary sexology together with Diderot's novel, yet I was loath to mention him, and in fact forgot (foreclosed) the father of this text for a long time, only recently remembering the scene of its conception.

My rationalization for this omission was that I was writing in a feminist context and that those theoretical names would alienate my readers. In relation to the lesbian fantasy, I think that means that I must suppress my heterosexuality, my commerce with men (thinkers) in order to seduce women. Or in an oedipal model, I must deny my desire for the father in order to please the mother.

What I did include in the original were references not to fathers or mothers but to siblings/collaterals/colleagues/friends. The original text had six notes: three to the three texts studied; three to private conversations with friends—Alex Argyros, James Creech, Peggy Kamuf. The reference to "private conversation" is particularly equivocal in the context of this text. The editors asked that I cut out those three unprofessional notes. Kamuf (the one woman of the three) was incorporated into the text; Creech and Argyros were completely suppressed. Those three young scholars were my graduate school friends. Those three notes inscribed me in a certain intersubjective context. All three relations operated in a confusion of registers: intellectual, social, sexual. All three were close friends, objects of desire, true colleagues. Later I would dedicate published texts to each of them, putting them in the appropriate place for friendship in a scholarly, objective publication. I had wanted to footnote them, to transgress the boundaries between authorities and friends, between texts and real people. If the text of "Snatches" is about the way we respond to texts as if they were real people, those footnotes were about the way real people can also function as texts.

Sometimes the generalized text of deconstruction (the enterprise we were all four students of, colleagues in) is understood as a universal formalism which makes nothing real, nothing matter. But at its most powerful it could mean everything matters; everything is real *and* everything is textual, mediated, interpretable.

Notes

1. See Claude Lévi-Strauss, *The Elementary Structures of Kinship*, trans. James Harle Bell et al. (Boston: Beacon Press, 1969).
2. All references to *La Nouvelle Justine* and *L'Histoire de Juliette* are taken from vols. 15–24 of D.A.F. de Sade, *Oeuvres complètes* (Paris: Pauvert, 1968). All translations from Sade mine.
3. Sade, *120 Journées de Sodome* (Paris: Pauvert, 1972), p. 53.
4. Gilbert Lély, *Vie de Sade* (Paris: Gallimard, 1958), 2:333.
5. Sigmund Freud, "Some Psychical Consequences of the Anatomical Distinction Between the Sexes" in *The Standard Edition of the Complete Psychological Works*, ed. James Strachey (London: Hogarth, 1953–74), 19:248–58.
6. Freud, "Female Sexuality," in *Standard Edition*, 21:235.
7. Jacques Lacan, "La Signification du phallus," in *Ecrits* (Paris: Seuil, 1966), p. 692.
8. Sade, *Aline et Valcour* (Paris: Union Générale d'Editions, 1971), 2:469.
9. Unless otherwise noted, references to the letters are taken from Sade, *Lettres choisies* (Paris: Pauvert, 1963).
10. Paul Bourdin, *Correspondence inédite du Marquis de Sade, de ses proches et de ses familiers* (Paris: Librairie de France, 1929), p. 98.
11. Letter of October 21, 1780, found in Lély, *Vie de Sade*, p. 173.
12. Freud, *The Interpretation of Dreams*, in *Standard Edition*, 5:448.
13. Sade, "Idées sur les romans," in *Les Crimes de l'amour* (Paris: Union Générale d'Editions, 1971), pp. 42–43.
14. The structuring imagery of this opening passage derives (I recognize in retrospect) from Luce Irigaray, "The 'Mechanics' of Fluids," in *This Sex Which Is Not One*, trans. Catherine Porter (Ithaca: Cornell University Press, 1985). At the time of writing this article I had read it in *L'Arc* (1974), vol. 58, where it was originally published.
15. Shere Hite, *The Hite Report* (New York: Dell, 1976).
16. Nancy Friday, *My Secret Garden* (New York: Pocket Books, 1974).
17. Denis Diderot, *Les Bijoux indiscrets*, in *Oeuvres romanesques* (Paris: Garnier, 1962). Translations mine.
18. See Jacques Lacan, "Kant avec Sade," in *Ecrits* (Paris: Seuil, 1966).
19. Private conversation, 1977.
20. James Creech, private conversation, 1977.
21. Alex Argyros, private conversation, 1977.
22. Nancy Chodorow, *The Reproduction of Mothering: Psychoanalysis and the Sociology of Gender* (Berkeley: University of California Press, 1978) and Carol Gilligan, *In a Different Voice: Psychological Theory and Women's Development* (Cambridge, Mass.: Harvard University Press, 1982).
23. Evelyn Fox Keller, *Reflections on Gender and Science* (New Haven: Yale University Press, 1985).
24. Michel Foucault, *La Volonté de savoir*, in *L'Histoire de la sexualité I* (Paris: Gallimard, 1976).

5.

The Body Politic

Dressing Anxiety

The following paper was originally presented at the Sixth International Poetics Colloquium, Columbia University, November 19, 1982, presided over by Michael Riffaterre. This was my first invitation to speak at a colloquium in French studies which I considered prestigious. The Poetics Colloquium signified the world in which as a graduate student I had longed to make it. I was the only feminist speaker at the colloquium.

In the original paper I talk about the "American feminist" and her investment in the clitoris. If I am distancing myself from that, it is both masturbatory guilt and more general embarrassment with the celebration of self. The attack on the American celebration of self is part of what by 1982 has become stock discourse contrasting "American and French feminism." Yet who am I when I say that? The attack on the American feminist takes on particular meaning in the context of the *colloque* at the Maison Française. Encoding the guilty as American acts out an identification with "the French woman" and an aggressive distancing from the "American feminist."

The paper's original title was "Quand nos lèvres s'écrivent," the only title I ever wrote in French. For the first time since graduate school I found myself liberally sprinkling my writing with French phrases as well as quoting in French. I was trying to prove my legitimacy within the discipline of French by proving I knew French. In fact my French was not up to the "near–native speaker" standard of the discipline. Yet it was particularly words for the genitals that seemed easiest to say in French. Clearly that is where I felt the need for mediation, the need to cover.

Writing this paper, I tried to make it possible to speak where the men were speaking, despite my body, but also in my body. Since I experienced my inability to transcend the body, where women were trapped, I had to think a way that the body was already "poetic," which is to say, belonged in the realm of high literary theory where I aspired to be.

Delivering that talk felt like an enormous triumph, for it seemed I had not only overcome my own sense of illegitimacy but had moved the body (my body?) from an embarrassment to a source of power. In less dramatic form, those were the stakes of all my performances, to pull off being there as a body, but as a thinking body, one neither whose thought nor whose body could be dismissed. Somehow, explicitly talking about my anxiety, although in a very stylized way, produced that triumph.

"Talking about my anxiety, although in a very stylized way": containing anxiety by style recalls the visual aspect of my performance. I dressed in a manner that bespoke the body as style, stylized sexuality. I wore spike heels, seamed hose, a fitted black forties dress and a large black hat. I was dressed as a woman, but as another woman. If my speech signaled an identification with a woman of another place, my clothes bespoke an identification with a woman of another time. I was in drag. My clothing drew attention to my body but at the same time stylized it, creating a stylized body, what in the paper I called a poiesis of the body. The fit between the paper and the look, the text and the performance, was articulated unconsciously, and it worked.

Lip Service

No utterance, I believe, ever occurs outside some interlocution. For example, this paper is written in response to a short text which served as title for the colloquium where it was originally presented: "Poétique du corps." That three-word heading triggered an anxiety focused upon a tension between the first and last words. "Body," I was immediately comfortable with, at home in. I have plenty to say about bodies and find great pleasure in conversing thereupon. But *poétique* troubles me. I associate it with the most sophisticated and rigorous, the most scientific sort of literary study, something which confronts the literarity of literature—what Shoshana Felman calls "the literary thing"[1]—in all its purity. Precisely the fact that I was so comfortable with "body" (immediately translating it into my mother tongue, whereas *poétique* stubbornly remained in that other language) . . .

Precisely the fact that I have so much to say about the body only points to my backwardness, my provinciality: I cannot help but read referentially, read to learn about the world. The attempt to do poetics of the body so easily slips into thematics of the body, or—worse yet— talk about the "body itself," as if it were transparently there in a text, as if there were such a thing as a "body itself," unmediated by textuality.

One way, of course, to explain my anxiety, to reduce and bind it, would be to consider the body as mother, poetics as the Name-of-the-Father. Unable to assume the poetic order, I fear being trapped in some embarrassing, infantile, imaginary relation to the maternal body, totally inappropriate to a professional gathering.

Another analysis of this anxiety points to the politics of identity. I have had various associations, generally happy, with the label feminist. Yet feminist literary criticism, which is to say American feminist literary criticism, represents, in my worst projections, a naïve reduction of literature to an image of the real world, operating a castration of "the literary thing." To the extent that I feel myself associated with feminism, that I wish to associate myself with feminism, here, I am afraid of embodying it as backward, unworthy, and unable to deal with poetics, unsubtle, flat-footed, and literal-minded.

In this anguish, I determined to write about certain texts by Luce Irigaray. And for good reason. Irigaray seems to propose the possibility of a language that can reflect woman's natural specificity, an unalienated language transparently expressing the real: a speech analogous to the female body, that would speak the female body directly. She has been criticized by some for this naturalistic belief in a real, unmediated body available outside the symbolic order. She has been praised by others for essentially the same thing. This supposed referential naïveté resembles my own tendencies to a misprision of the poetics of the body, of the unavoidable poetics of any speaking of the body. I determined to examine, precisely, the poetics of her writing, to discover how she produces the imaginary impression of female analogy. I thus decided to do a careful study of her rhetoric, her writing technique. Yet as I settled in for this studious rereading, I immediately felt the seduction of anatomical reference.

Irigaray published a collection of essays in 1977 under the title *This Sex Which Is Not One*.[2] The female genitals, she complains, have always been perceived according to male parameters, that is, according to "the sex which is one," the singular penis. Insistent on the multiplicity of the female genitalia ("this sex which is not one"), she seems to be referring to anatomy (clitoris, vagina, labia, vulva, cervix, etc.). Not only female genitalia but woman, the female sex, is multiple ("indefinitely other in herself," p. 28). Thus Irigaray develops a notion of female logic which contrasts with the unicity of phallomorphic logic.

"Anatomy is destiny," Freud was foolish enough to say,[3] and Irigaray would seem at first glance to fall into the same folly. She seems to determine women and men, logic and language from genital anatomy. Yet let us beware too literal a reading of Irigarayan anatomy. When she speaks of "the sex which is one," she is not speaking of male genital anatomy but rather of an already phallomorphic conception of male genitals, that actually has only a selective relation to male anatomy. Irigaray, for example, nowhere mentions the testicles. Male genital anatomy does not determine phallomorphic logic, but rather phallomorphic logic determines a certain unitary perception of male genitalia.

Ironically, we might say that Irigaray herself can see the male genitals only according to phallomorphic parameters. But that is a question of the politics of the body. As for its poetics, we can perhaps recognize here that, if phallomorphic logic is not based in anatomy but, on the contrary, reconstructs anatomy in its own image, then Irigaray's vulvomorphic logic is not predestined by anatomy but is already a symbolic interpretation of that anatomy.

Now if I suggest that what Irigaray calls "this multiple of feminine desire and language" (p. 29) is not based in anatomy but constructs it, I can then assert that the Irigarayan poetics of the body is not an expression of the body but a poiesis, a creation of the body.

"I can then assert . . ." Perfect. I set out to explore Irigaray's anatomy not as referential body but as poetics, and I come to find precisely what I was seeking. But in order to perceive the effect of construction, the composition of her anatomy, I make implicit reference to some "reality" of male anatomy which exists outside the text. Which is to say that the reality effect of her text is so powerful that it leads me to refer to some "real experience of bodies" precisely in order to undo the illusion of that very sort of reference. My triumphant assertion of entry into the poetic order is itself made possible through the stickiest of dealings with some extratextual body.

The fact that it is male anatomy which allows me this defense against the seductions of the Irigarayan body is itself noteworthy. Perhaps, just as Irigaray confuses male anatomy and phallomorphism, I produce a symptomatic confusion between (doing) poetics and (having) balls.

Thus do I succeed in registering the multiplicity of the female genitals as a textual production, construing it in accord with our modern conception of writing. In the essay called "This Sex Which Is Not One" Irigaray also poses some explicit questions about the resonance between female sexuality and modern textuality: "Thus woman does not have one sex. . . . Her sexuality, always at least double, is plural still. Like culture wants to be now? Like texts are written now? Without very well knowing what censorship they are evading?" (p. 27).

"Like culture wants to be now?" Culture wants to be plural; female sexuality is plural. Woman is naturally, in her anatomy, (post)-modernist. We might also contrast "still" and "now." ("Her sexuality is plural still." "Like texts are written now?")

The work of Alice Jardine has impressed upon me the urgency of questioning such a relation between women and modernity.[4] If Irigaray's vulvomorphic logic is not based on anatomy but rather organizes the perception of female sexuality, then we must ask if Irigaray's feminine is not merely a product of (post)modernist aesthetics. If Irigaray sees female anatomy through the grid of (post)modernist aesthetics, an aesthetics formulated by men, why is that any different from perceiving according to phallomorphic, metaphysical notions? Especially when we consider that phallomorphic parameters are themselves not based on male anatomy. Yet there is also something wrong with a simple insistence that (post)modernism is male because men have formulated it, since that objection depends on a reference to an author's extratextual anatomy. The tension between a feminist investment in the referential body and an aspiration to poetics has here become acute.

I would propose, however, that the very exacerbation of that tension produced in reading Irigaray—with the combination of obvious (post)modernist poetics and inevitable referential gesture—makes it possible to glimpse a way out.

Modernity generally couples plurality with the credo that language is nonreferential. Polyvalence makes it impossible to know what a sign refers to, in any simple way. In Irigaray's text, however, a referential illusion stubbornly clings to plurality. And illusory though it might be—since this is only a texture of signifiers, as slippery as any—the effect of this illusion is to point the reader outside the text, extending the (post)modernist gesture to a realm normally considered to be at the antipodes of culture, the female genitals. Irigaray's referential illusion dislodges (post)modernism from its privileged station as "culture" into a surprising, vulgar political efficacy. And in the process might just save (post)modernist poetics from the absurd appearance of asserting the nonreferentiality of language and move it into a more complex encounter with the anxiety produced by the absence of any certain access to the referent.

How can an illusion have political efficacy? And how can such a gesture be salutary? In an attempt to answer such questions, let us slip into another realm: the realm of the Father, the realm of the Law, for it is in the realm of the Father's Law that feminist efficacy is most pertinent.

(Post)modernist polyvalence is the assumption, jubilant or otherwise, of what Lacan calls the slippage of the signifier, and that slippage is an accomplice of the bar which forever blocks the passage from signifier to signified. Yet there is a loophole in Lacan's system. In "The Agency of the Letter in the Unconscious," Lacan says, speaking of his algorithm for metaphor, "The + sign here manifesting the crossing of the bar—and the constitutive value of that crossing for the emergence of signification." In metaphor the bar that forever divides signifier from signified is crossed, which produces, in Lacan's words, "a signification effect which is of poetry or of creation."[5]

Operating by analogy, Irigaray thus operates in the metaphoric paradigm. She thus may cross the bar, creating an effect of poetry. Poetics itself is, in this model, a "crossing" and an "emergence," a liberation from the constraints of phallomorphic Law. Vulvomorphic logic, by newly metaphorizing the body, sets it free, if only momentarily. For as soon as the metaphor becomes a proper noun, we no longer have creation, we have paternity.

Vulvomorphic logic, once in place, would be no less oppressive than phallomorphic logic. Each is necessarily, like any logic, alienated from the body, from the real. But in a moment, in a "now"—"Like texts are written now?"—something loosens, something slips, something moves. A glimpse, a spark, "the creative spark of metaphor," says Lacan (p. 507), but Lacan's creation moves too quickly, too willingly into paternity. In Michèle Montrelay's explication of psychoanalysis, "the analyst's discourse is a metaphor of the patient's discourse."[6] That metaphorization frees the patient from her ruts and repetitions, produces movement where there was only stagnant paralysis. Metaphor heals. It is the poiesis of a new body, one that is freed from hysterical paralysis or phallomorphic rigidity. To speak in vulvo-logic, it flows.

In phallo-logic, the female genital is either a clitoris, phallic-same, or a vagina, phallic-opposite, receptacle, castrated hole. This either-or, same or opposite, always seen according to phallic parameters, has constituted the alternatives for the representation of female genital anatomy. The history of feminist sexology reflects the ravages of that either-or alternative. Irigaray's always-at-least-double woman would of course choose both: "In effect, woman's pleasure does not have to choose between clitoral activity and vaginal passivity, for example. The pleasure of the vaginal caress does not have to replace that of the clitoral caress. They both contribute, in an irreplaceable way, to woman's pleasure" (pp. 27–28). Irigaray seems to be advocating a female sexuality that replaces the anxious either-or with a pleasurable both: vagina and clitoris. But Irigaray ultimately chooses *not both but neither*, and the spark of her genital poetics rather comes to light on the lips.

Irigaray introduces the lips, at the beginning of the essay "This Sex Which Is Not One," in the context of woman's autoeroticism. "Woman's autoeroticism is . . . very different from man's. . . . Woman 'touches herself' all the time, and moreover she cannot be forbidden to do so, because her genitals are made of two lips that are continually kissing" (p. 24). It has been, for some time, a common gesture of feminist discourse on sexuality to attempt to separate our female sexuality from its intrication with male sexuality, so as to determine what it is in itself. This gesture, based in an empirical appeal to the reality of women's masturbatory practice, has focused on the clitoris. Since most women manipulate their clitoris and not their vagina in masturbation, it is concluded that unadulterated female sexuality, female sexuality in-itself is clitoral. It is noteworthy that the "in-itself" is assumed to correspond with masturbation, with what one does when alone. To arrive at the pure state of female sexuality, the intersubjective context must be removed. But what appears to be the same gesture in Irigaray's text, the move toward female autoeroticism for a model of female sexuality, lands not on the clitoris but on the labia.

Irigaray is interested in a plurality that is not reducible to a series of singular elements. In the list of female genital parts, only the lips are already plural. "Her genitals are made of two lips. . . . Thus, in herself, she is already two—but not divisible into *un(e)s* [ones]" (p. 24). *Un(e)s:* one word, the plural of one, is itself already two in that it is both *uns* and *unes*, not separable into one or the other. And the lips are bodied forth in those parentheses. Typographically inscribed on the page, the lips are written (*les lèvres s'écrivent*).

The collection *This Sex Which Is Not One* closes with a piece called "When Our Lips Speak Together" (*Quand nos lèvres se parlent*). Later books, *Amante Marine* and *Passions élémentaires*,[7] continue to insist upon the lips. Irigaray's (post)modernist female body comes to synechdochically inhabit the lips. Yet the concrete specificity of anatomical reference, the synechdochical part's availability to manipulation, is here quite elusive. What lips? Labia majora; labia minora. The Latin terms may glitter like constellations in our English skies, but the French *lèvres* is a catachresis which always necessarily also refers to the mouth. *Les lèvres de la vulve* (the lips of the vulva): the proper term for those vulvar parts is already a metaphor, the last figurative meaning for *lèvres* in Robert's dictionary. Irigaray embodies female sexuality in that which, at this moment in the history of the language, is always figurative, can never be simply taken as the thing itself.

Irigaray's inscription of female autoeroticism onto the labia produces a baffling effect if we continue to understand this gesture as referential in some simple way. Irigaray's notion of female autoeroticism does not refer to any experience of masturbation, perhaps because clitoral masturbation is generally considered to be analogous to penile masturbation. Trying to affirm an-other female sexuality, one that is not phallomorphic, she rejects the clitoris, the darling of feminist sexology, and produces an in-itself of female sexuality that is not rooted in anything recognized as female experience. For example, women do not recognize it as autoerotic that their labia minora are continually touching.

Irigaray's position seems so strange if taken referentially, which is, of course, how we tend to take statements about anatomy, even if we are quite sophisticated about the nonreferentiality of language. Discourse about the body seems to represent a point of unusually suggestive tension about the referent. Yet perhaps the most far-reaching effect of her unrealistic stand on the labia is to force the reader to reconsider the status of anatomical referentiality. For if it is true that, as Irigaray contends, "feminine sexuality has always been thought from masculine parameters" (p. 23), or rather if—as I have suggested in my revision of Irigaray's testicular excision—sexual anatomy, female *and male*, has always been thought according to phallomorphic parameters, then any reality to which we might refer—since realities, that is perceptions, are necessarily constructed—will already be phallomorphic. So, for example, when the feminist reaches out to touch woman's experience of her sexuality, she can only find a clitoral masturbation with a history as phallic analogy because autoeroticism itself is defined according to phallomorphic standards, which means not only is that what men recognize as autoerotic but it is also what we women ourselves recognize as our autoeroticism.

Belief in simple referentiality is not only unpoetic but also ultimately politically conservative, because it cannot recognize that the reality to which it appeals is a traditional ideological construction, whether one terms it phallomorphic, or metaphysical, or bourgeois, or something else. The politics of experience is inevitably a conser-vative politics, for it cannot help but conserve traditional ideological constructs which are not recognized as such but are taken for the "real." And a poetics of experience is no poetics at all if we under-stand poetry to be that effect which finds a loophole in the law of the symbolic. But if the poetics of experience is one that aims for a poiesis of experience, that attempts to reconstruct experience itself, to pro-duce a re-metaphorization, then although we cannot embrace simple unquestioned referentiality, neither can we unproblematically deny referentiality. For if Irigaray is not just writing a nonphallomorphic text (a rather common [post]modernist practice) but actually con-structing a nonphallomorphic sexuality, then the gesture of a trou-bled but nonetheless insistent referentiality is essential. The new con-struction, the (post)modernist, multiple body, will not be any more "real" in an essentialistic, noumenal way, but might nevertheless produce a rearrangement in sexual hierarchies, a salutary jolt out of the compulsive repetition of the same. And if we would create a new body, one no longer nearly paralysed by the alternative phallic and castrated, but a different body, our best hope, our most efficacious politics would be a practice I have tried to outline here which we might call poetics of the body.

The Question of Style

In this text I speak of modernism rather than modernity, as Jardine does, rather than postmodernism. In 1982 I was not very aware of or interested in "postmodernism," which had not had a lot of play in French studies. Revising this text, I tried to decide whether this plu-ral textuality is modernist or postmodernist and I find myself unsure. It seems postmodernist as that usually gets defined, but I remain suspicious of the gesture that proposes to be beyond a modernism that is too embarrassingly masculinist, empire-building, and sacred. At least in the literary academy, we still live under the reign of mod-ernist aesthetics. My anxiety about "the poetic order," about being aesthetic enough or formalist enough is, in any case, a recognizably modernist anxiety. Although my anxiety about being "aesthetic enough" seems modernist, the aesthetics in question seem postmod-ernist. I am having a modernist reaction to postmodernism. This seems anachronistic and in error, which reinforces my anxiety about being out of it. It might also be a clue that postmodernism continues to function like modernism, as a high-culture aesthetic that makes peo-ple anxious for not being sufficiently up-to-date.

I recall a very bright young man telling me that feminism was the last modernism. I immediately felt dowdy and old-fashioned. Yet if feminist criticism along with other politically engaged criticisms has been the most effective challenge to the academic hold of modernist/ formalist aesthetics, postmodernism seems to be a blithe, cynical attempt to go beyond modernism without really questioning the cordoning off of the aesthetic realm. Postmodernism dephallicizes modernism so men can claim to be current. If modernism, as Gilbert and Gubar have so convincingly shown,[8] is itself a defense against feminism and the rise of women writers, postmodernism is a more subtle defense, erected when modernism would no longer hold.

Postmodernist thinkers are defending against the downfall of patriarchy by trying to be not male. In drag, they are aping the feminine rather than thinking their place as men in an obsolescent patriarchy.[9] The female postmodernist thinker finds herself in the dilemma of trying to be like Daddy who is trying to be a woman. The double-cross is intriguing and even fun, but also troubling if one suspects that it is the father's last ruse to seduce the daughter and retain her respect, the very respect that legitimized the father's rule.

In *Spurs*, Jacques Derrida celebrates Nietzsche's "femininity" while attacking feminists' "masculinity."[10] This male champion of the attack on the phallus is still too busy attacking feminists for being phallic. Being antiphallic becomes the new phallus, which women come up lacking once again.

In 1978, Elaine Showalter saw feminist critics as "Annie Hall," women in "men's ill-fitting hand-me-downs."[11] In 1983, she saw male feminists as "Tootsie," men in women's clothing.[12] But what about the post-structural feminist who is wearing the hand-me-downs of men-in-drag, writing a feminine which has become a male transvestite style? What is double-crossdressing? My own sartorial style, in particular the Joan Crawford dress, seamed hose, and spike heels that I wore to deliver this paper, was literally influenced by male homosexual fascination with a certain feminine style. Charles Bernheimer, to my delight, once compared me to Bette Midler, a woman whose career began in homosexual bathhouses. What is the position of the woman who identifies with men who identify with women?

The Perverse Body

In 1973 Roland Barthes, the foremost practitioner of structuralist literary criticism, published a book entitled *The Pleasure of the Text*.[13] It is an attempt to elaborate a theory of the text based on a notion of pleasure rather than structure or cognition or ideology. According to Barthes, pleasure has been radically excluded from criticism, from scientific, serious studies or theories of the text. His own work included, presumably.

The title of the book—*The Pleasure of the Text*—has in fact a subtly double meaning. Grammatically "of the text" (*du texte*, in French) is both objective and subjective genitive; the text is both object and subject of pleasure. The title means both the text's pleasure (the pleasure that is in the text) and our pleasure (the pleasure the text affords). It is, to be sure, difficult to imagine how we might separate the pleasure that is in the text from that which the text gives us. The double meaning points to a difficulty in separating subject and object within the realm of textual pleasure. Barthes writes: "On the stage (in the scene) of the text . . . there is not a subject and an object. The text outdates grammatical attitudes" (p. 29).

The Pleasure of the Text represented something like a break with Barthes's previous writings, inaugurating what would be the last phase of his work. Previously Barthes had been engaged in more or less scientific study of literature as well as leftist-leaning ideological analyses of culture. Whether engaged in disclosing the workings of ideology or trying to formulate a scientific theory of the text, Barthes had been above all a "serious" writer. And that seriousness devolved from his writing stance. Often ironic, highly logical and systematic, sometimes bitingly polemical, Barthes wrote with appropriate critical objectivity about whatever object he was studying.

The object of this book is pleasure, but a new object would not constitute an epistemological break in Barthes's *oeuvre* since throughout his career he had considered widely varying objects. What is new about this book is reflected in the duplicity of the title, in the fact that the object of this book (pleasure) is not simply an object. If in the realm of textual pleasure it is difficult to separate subject from object, that dilemma might render it impossible to write objectively on the subject.

Pleasure is not simply an object in the text but is something that happens to the reader. Whereas structure, for example, would pretend to be immanent in the text where it could be studied and verified once and for all for any possible reading (hence affording structuralism a scientific status), pleasure depends on the individual reading and is thus uncertain. "Everyone can testify," Barthes writes, thus grounding his statement not in objective fact but in subjective experience, "that the pleasure of the text is not sure: nothing can say that this same text will please us a second time: it's a friable pleasure,

crumbled by mood, habit, circumstance; it's a precarious pleasure"
(p. 83).

Pleasure is, we might say, a subjective effect. And certainly what
is new in the book and will intensify in Barthes's later works is the
explicit subjectivity of his writing position. Yet he would not call this
stance subjectivity, since it is not based on a unified, enduring subject
but is related to things like "mood, habit, circumstance," not to whom
the reader is in any substantial, essential way but to the specific historical conjunction of reader and text, to the circumstances of the
scene (the "stage," the performance) of reading.

Barthes's change of style has provoked passionate response, both
negative and positive. The polarity of response could be represented
by two books on Barthes published in the wake of his death in 1980,
each by an author long familiar with and committed to his work.
Their respective titles reflect the divergence in viewpoints on the break
with structuralist science and embrace of pleasure. Annette Lavers
calls her book *Roland Barthes: Structuralism and After*.[14] Although a
study of Barthes's work, it is also equally a book on structuralism,
an introduction to structuralism. The last phase of his career, from
The Pleasure of the Text to his death in 1980, is treated as mere aftermath, an epilogue to the story of structuralism. The book allots only
one of its fifteen chapters to all four books of Barthes's last phase.
That chapter, the last of the book, vigorously condemns Barthes for
betraying his contestatory position as critical intellectual and taking
on the bourgeois image of the writer. Lavers even attempts psychoanalytic explanations of Barthes's fall into weakness, his sacrifice of intellectual and political rigor for the sake of bourgeois acceptance.
Steven Ungar, on the other hand, entitles his book *Roland Barthes:
The Professor of Desire*,[15] a title which makes it clear that for Ungar
the essential Barthes is that of the post-structuralist phase when pleasure and desire became central to his theorizing. Ungar's book treats
the entirety of Barthes's prestructuralist and structuralist work in the
first of its four sections, as a prehistory to the hero of the title, the
professor of desire. For Ungar the 1973 book marks the moment Barthes
came into his own and began doing something really radical, calling
into question his own authority, the authority of objective scientific
criticism.

It is noteworthy that both positions—the attack and the celebration—make explicit connections between Barthes's work and left-wing
politics. Lavers: "Barthes takes refuge in passivity and the pleasure
identified with the mother. But still, they are in his mind impossible
to reconcile with socialism, and therefore guilty" (p. 212). Guilty

pleasure, guilty in relation to Barthes's "socialism." Ungar: "Never a Marxist in an orthodox sense [Barthes's] sensitivity to the use and misuse of authority has often suggested a sympathy to left-wing politics" (pp. xv–xvi).

Lavers considers it the responsibility of the intellectual to challenge the dominant ideology, that is, bourgeois values and myths. Ungar believes we should challenge the power and authority that is masked as scientific objectivity, which itself functions as a very powerful ideology. Both critics judge Barthes from what is in one way or another a leftist, contestatory point of view and come to opposite conclusions about *The Pleasure of the Text*. Certainly this is where the passion comes from.

Passion and politics; politics and pleasure; leftist standards; a book on pleasure. "An entire little mythology," Barthes writes, "tends to make us think that pleasure is an idea of the right. The right, in one swoop, relegates to the left everything that is abstract, boring, political and keeps pleasure for itself. . . . And the left, out of moralism, suspects, disdains any 'residue of hedonism'" (p. 38). "An entire little mythology," writes Barthes. *Mythologies* is the title of one of Barthes's first books, prestructuralism, where he analyzed the workings of ideology in mass culture. That book was translated by Annette Lavers.[16] The quotation above from *The Pleasure of the Text* is a rare use of the word "mythology" in this sense in the last phase of Barthes's work. We thus momentarily return to the language of cultural criticism in order to question the ideological segregation of politics and pleasure, which locates politics as a leftist value and pleasure on the right. At the same time this passage foretells the negative reaction to his own move toward pleasure, correctly imagining the left, morally outraged rejection of his hedonism, and presuming to analyze the ideological underpinnings of that rejection before it even occurs.

Christopher Norris, who in his review of *The Pleasure of the Text* decries Barthes's hedonism from an explicitly Marxist perspective, writes that "the sensitive place in Barthes's exposition is plainly the suasive piece about 'right' and 'left' conceptions of literature."[17] Norris feels that "the little mythology" is "*plainly* the sensitive place." This is obviously the crux; the book clearly, certainly, self-evidently hinges on the question of left and right. By the expression "the sensitive place" Norris means the weak point, the vulnerable spot in the argument, but in the context of Barthes's theory of textual pleasure we could also hear "the sensitive place" as "the erogenous zone." This is the point where the critic can get Barthes, but the attack takes on erotic connotations.

Connotations reinforced by Norris' overheated prose. Norris calls Barthes's last mythology a "suasive piece." According to Barthes, "a word can be erotic . . . if it is unexpected, succulent in its novelty (in certain texts, words *glitter*, they are distractive, incongruous apparitions—it matters little that they are pedantic)" (p. 68). For me, Norris' "suasive" is such a word, a word that sends me scurrying to the dictionary where I learn that "suasive" is the adjectival form of "suasion" which means persuasion and is "used chiefly in the phrase moral suasion." In this "sensitive place" Barthes is using seductive rhetoric, working on the moral sense of his reader. In the "little mythology," we remember, the moral sense is implicated in the left's suspicion of pleasure.

Plainly, "suasive" marks a "sensitive place" in Norris' exposition. Echoes of morality, seduction, and eros, here at the juncture of pleasure and politics, the passionately moral question of left or right. And in *The Pleasure of the Text*, "the sensitive place," the place of passion where the text suddenly gives itself over to the reader's inquisitive touch, turns out to be—in keeping with Barthes's notion of the erotic as the unexpected—not the explicitly sexual ideas and images but this discussion of the politics of pleasure.

The Pleasure of the Text does not seem to be a political text. In fact pleasure is there valued because it is beyond the conflictual positions of ideological struggle. Yet despite a certain impression of apolitical hedonism, politics and ideology are questions running throughout the book. If we try to read *The Pleasure of the Text* apolitically, banishing politics, embracing pleasure, then we have fallen into the reactionary side of the mythology. The right covers over political questions with aesthetic questions of pleasure; the left masks its pleasures with political positions. The book must be read, has been read, will be read within and against this "little mythology." We must think politics and pleasure together. What are the politics of pleasure? What the pleasures of politics?

Barthes writes of a form of ecstasy (intensest, most disruptive mode of pleasure, which he calls "jouissance") that "consists in depoliticizing what is apparently political, and in politicizing what apparently is not" (p. 71). One of the disturbing but also pleasurable effects of this book may be this radical shuffling of the place of the political so that it is not where we expect it and only appears when unexpected. Yes, indeed, the book is a depoliticization—reactionary gesture, Lavers' complaint; it flees serious ideological struggle and escapes to the self-indulgent realm of pleasure. But it seems also, at least in its effects, to make pleasure a serious political question (leftist gesture).

Immediately after the sentence "another ecstasy . . . consists in depoliticizing what is apparently political and in politicizing what apparently is not," there is a dash like those marking another voice in dialogue, and we read, "But no, see here, one politicizes what *ought* to be and that's it." Immediately after positing another, more pleasurable relation to politics, one that is outside "the little mythology," another voice speaks, a critical, impatient voice from within the text that would call Barthes back into line, back to moral obligation. The word "ought" ("one politicizes what *ought* to be") is in italics. This is the voice of the orthodox left for which there is a moral obligation to politicize everything. Any depoliticization shirks that responsibility. The voice could be Lavers', but it is coming from within Barthes's text. As Lavers says: "[Barthes's pleasures] are in his mind impossible to reconcile with socialism and therefore guilty" (p. 212). The question of Barthes's complacency and cooptation by reactionary values is unavoidable, precisely because the book is literally in dialogue with that question.

Barthes's critics debate the politics of his hedonist gesture. So does his text. What is the politics of pleasure? That will be one of our questions here, a question I ask in the light of feminism.

Feminism has gone a long way toward "politicizing what apparently is not," or perhaps I should say, "toward politicizing what *ought* to be." "The personal is the political" is now an overly familiar feminist slogan. And we are indebted to feminism for the most cogent political analyses of sexuality, just as we must thank an early feminist literary critic, Kate Millett, for the phrase *sexual politics*. In Barthes's little book pleasure is always strongly tied to sexual pleasure. Is feminist sexual politics a politics of pleasure? Or does pleasure remain, for feminism, a suspicious depoliticization of the sexual?

Barthes and feminism, strange bedfellows? To my knowledge Barthes never discusses feminism, anywhere: *The Pleasure of the Text* never even mentions sexual difference, although both sexuality and difference are central themes. Lavers implies that feminists are, with good reason, hostile to Barthes, although her sentence about it is more than usually obscure—obscured, no doubt, by passion (p. 208). Lavers cites Claudine Herrmann's book of feminist literary criticism, *Les Voleuses de langue*, as her example of the feminist critique of Barthes. Herrmann uses a passage from *The Pleasure of the Text* to show that for Barthes both bad writing and its reader are feminine, not of course explicitly but in the imagery. For Herrmann, Barthes is only one of an entire tradition of male writers who associate denigration and femininity.[18]

Even Ungar, Barthes's champion, can only say, "Barthes is certainly something less (or other) than a feminist" (p. 90). Writing from a 1980s American progressive point of view, Ungar characterizes Barthes as "less than a feminist." Not to be a feminist in this age is to be lacking, inadequate. But in parentheses he adds "or other," hoping to free Barthes and himself from this moral responsibility, from an oppressive standard into some sort of alterity. Ungar's gesture takes on a disturbing irony when we recall that the history of phallocentric thought has considered woman "less than man"—inferior, castrated—and feminists have argued that we are not "less" but "other."

For Ungar's Barthes the tables are turned, and if this inversion seems suspect or glib, it might also point to some common ground between Barthes's project and feminism. Both, we might say, attempt to rethink what is traditionally "less than" as "other." Barthes writes: "The pleasure of the text is always possible as the exercise of a different physiology" (p. 49). In that valorization of "a different physiology," in the insistence on a positive reading of difference in the body, I hear something potentially friendly to feminism.

The politics of Barthes's book is a sexual politics as well as a politics of sexual difference, but "sexual" there refers not to the sexes but to eroticism, and sexual difference is individual difference, perversion, rather than the difference between the sexes. Textual pleasure and its wilder cousin textual ecstasy are presented not only as bodily and erotic but as specifically perverse. Perversion is here defined as "pleasure without function" (p. 31), just as perverse sexuality, according to Barthes, "removes ecstasy (orgasm) from the finality of reproduction" (p. 40). Pleasure is perverse when it is not subjugated to any function, such as reproduction. Textual pleasure is not only perverse sexually (by not serving the reproduction of the species), but also without any higher function such as instruction, communication, or ideological stance. Or rather, I would say, it is not that the latter functions do not obtain, but that the pleasure of the text is not subordinate to them in any predictable way.

If the pleasure of literature is "an idea of the right," sexual perversion is not. Thus by insistently sexualizing pleasure, Barthes breaks up the mythological solidarity of aesthetics and conservative values. By laying bare the perversion of aesthetic pleasure, he renders textual pleasure unacceptable to the right although it remains condemnable to the left as decadent "hedonism."

What is the relation between sexualizing pleasure and politicizing pleasure? According to Barthes "there are few [writers] who fight against both ideological repression and libidinal repression" (p. 58). The politicizers and the sexualizers are, on the whole, different. Yet, as I have suggested, feminism is at least nominally the place of sexual politics: explicitly sexual explicitly politics. Perversion, however, is a thorny problem for feminism.

If perversion is defined as the liberation of sexuality from reproductive ends, then many of the central issues of feminism would find common cause there. Abortion, contraception, lesbianism, clitoridectomy all involve questions of the right to nonreproductive sexual pleasure. Indeed the central gesture in modern feminist sexology, the displacement of the primary female sexual organ from vagina to clitoris, can be understood as a move from an organ of reproduction to an organ of pleasure which does not serve reproduction. This displacement might then itself be considered a perversion, in Barthes's sense of "removing orgasm from the finality of reproduction."

Feminism has expressed continual solidarity with the gay liberation movement and thus defended that "perversion." But it should be added, of course, that the usual feminist move is not to embrace perversion, as Barthes does, but rather to challenge the notion of homosexuality as perverse. If classically the clitoral woman, whether homo- or heterosexual, is considered perverted, the politics of feminism has been to challenge the classification and redefine the clitoris and lesbianism as normal.

Thus, in fact, feminism has not embraced perversion but has defined it differently than Barthes does. And indeed, large sectors of the feminist movement stand in violent opposition to perversion which is understood to be male. The pervert—child molester, rapist, porno fan, fetishist, voyeur, exhibitionist, sadist, masochist, etc.—is seen as symptom of an aggressive, male sexuality that is inherently perverted and a primary enemy of feminism.

In its effort to reclaim the clitoris and the lesbian from the realm of perversion, feminism has instituted another standard for normal sexuality. The norm for feminist sexuality is an egalitarian relation of tenderness and caring where each partner is considered as a "whole person" rather than as an object of sexual fantasy. This norm clearly devolves from feminist critiques of patriarchal, phallocentric sexuality. Since relations between the sexes are, in a feminist analysis, considered the equivalent of relations between class enemies, the egalitarian standard renders questionable whether any heterosexual relation (at least at this point in history) can be "normal."

Normal feminist sexuality is thus lesbian. If this seems in some way absurd, since the vast majority of feminists are still practicing heterosexuals, let us remember that likewise, according to Barthes's biologico-psychoanalytico-Catholic definition of normal sexuality as subordinate to reproduction, only a small portion of sexual activity could be considered normal. Whatever the standard, few people seem to be sexually normal. When thinking about the functioning of sexual norms, we should bear in mind that, especially in the realm of the sexual, a norm is not a mean but an ideal.

In an excellent article on pleasure, sexuality, and feminism, Cora Kaplan, a feminist literary critic, notes that since both radical and revolutionary feminism "have located the universal truth of gender oppression in a sadistic and insatiable male sexuality, which is empowered to humiliate and punish [a]ny pleasure that accrues to women who take part in heterosexual acts is . . . necessarily tainted." If male sexuality is sadistic, female heterosexual pleasure must necessarily be masochistic. Tainted pleasure, bad, sick, masochistic: perversion. Liberated from subjection to biologico-Christian standards, pleasure must now be politically correct. Kaplan continues: "at the extreme end of this position, women who 'go with men' are considered collaborators."[19]

My point, let me be clear, is not to complain that lesbians oppress their heterosexual sisters. Lesbians are an oppressed minority group who do not have the power to enforce their own hierarchies even if they wished to. My point rather is that there is a standard of normal sexuality in feminist thought, of politically correct sexuality which functions as morality and condemns pleasure that is not subordinate to it. Witness the scandal created within feminism by the "coming out" of lesbian sadomasochists.

Heterosexual feminists may experience their sexuality as a disturbing contradiction to their political stance. Within feminism heterosexual desire has only been theorized negatively. For example, penetration enacts the subjugation of women by men; women's attraction to men reinforces phallocentrism and women's sense of their own inferiority. In such models there is little place for pleasure, which then becomes perverse, rebellious, insubordinate to political reason. Lesbian pleasure, to be sure, has been celebrated in feminist writing: theoretical, fictional, poetic, but the pleasure celebrated is respectably subordinate to correct politics. Pleasure is put in its place, reinforcing sisterhood.

Some years ago, Elaine Marks, an important feminist critic and at that time director of the substantial Women's Studies Program at the University of Wisconsin, gave a talk in which she confessed that she loved to read Proust even though she did not know how Proust fit in with her position as a feminist. Marks is confessing a guilty pleasure, a pleasure insubordinate to feminism. What is the relation between

Proust and feminism? Neither antagonism nor solidarity? Indifference? Barthes: "[Pleasure] is a drift, something . . . that cannot be taken care of by any collectivity. . . . Something *neutral?* It is evident that the pleasure of the text is scandalous: not because it is immoral, but because it is *atopic*" (p. 39). "Atopic": strange word, formed on the model of utopic. Barthes italicizes it as he does "neutral" before it. *Neutral: ne-uter*, neither one nor the other; *atopic:* not of a place, neither here nor there. Indifference? Or simply difference? Proust "is certainly something less (or other) than a feminist." Proust and feminism, strange bedfellows? Perversion?

Proust has a special place in *The Pleasure of the Text.* Barthes writes: "I understand that Proust's work is, at least for me, the reference work . . . the *mandala* of the entire literary cosmogony . . . that does not at all mean that I am a Proust 'specialist': Proust is what comes to me, it is not what I call; it is not an 'authority'" (p. 59). Barthes is not a Proust specialist; he is not supposed to write on Proust; he does not seek and research Proust; but Proust comes to him. Not an "authority," like Freud or Nietzsche, Proust is something personal, individual, perverse, "*at least for me*, the reference work." Proust accompanies Barthes, his companion in textual pleasure.

Marks confesses that she loves reading Proust but does not know how to align this with her feminism. Barthes is writing what is in certain ways a manifesto for postmodernist texts—Sollers, Robbe-Grillet, Severo Sarduy—but Proust is what comes to him unsolicited. I confess that I love reading Barthes but do not know how to align this with my feminism, although that indeed is the project of this paper. When I assigned myself the title "Feminist Criticism and the Pleasure of the Text," my wish was to take this book which is a source of great pleasure to me and reduce the scandal of its atopicality by subordinating my pleasure to some feminist idea.

In the first phase of feminist criticism, literary critics schooled in the tradition of male authors turned on that male canon to show how the great authors were sexist pigs, that is to say, that the images of women in literature by men were distorting stereotypes that contributed to women's oppression and our alienation from self. Male literature had given us inhuman binary roles: madonna vs. whore, child-woman vs. bitch. Like the analysis of heterosex, the analysis of male literature taught us to see subjugation and alienation in place of romance and beauty. Yet women readers had experienced pleasure in reading Rousseau or D. H. Lawrence, had enjoyed identifying with virgins and whores. The analysis showed us that our pleasure was "tainted."

In a second phase, feminists turned to women writers—the few already in the canon, the rediscovery of lost women writers from the past, and contemporary literary progeny of the women's movement. Feminist criticism moved from negation to affirmation, and suddenly there was a place for joy. Legitimate textual pleasure. A feminist can enjoy her identification with the heroine of Kate Chopin's *The Awakening* or Virginia Woolf's *Orlando*. It is politically correct to find women's writing gratifying. Normal pleasure, pleasure properly subservient to political principle.

These two phases are obviously schematic and the neat bipolarities betray a sinister distortion. I should add, of course, that many feminist critics devote themselves to proving various male authors (from Shakespeare to Lacan) sympathetic proto- or crypto-feminists just as other feminist critics exert themselves in vehement critique of diverse women writers. The actuality and plurality of feminist criticism has a tapestried complexity that makes my tight binary scheme of attacking male pigs and celebrating female identity what Barthes might call a "little mythology." Yet my point might be that "an entire little mythology" *makes us think* that feminists *should* critique and demystify male writing and find pleasure in female writing. Feminist ideology produces a morality that could condemn as deviant any pleasure that does not serve the enhancement of female identity.

Elaine Marks, whose credentials as a feminist are good and strong, avows that she loves Proust. To be sure, Proust is not one of the enemies of feminism: no Henry Miller or Norman Mailer, he. But neither is he one of its heroines. Indifferent, atopic, neutral. For Barthes, the wonderful thing about textual pleasure is that, in a world of raging ideologies, in the war of discourses, textual pleasure can be neutral. And Proust is Barthes's point of reference in the pleasure of the text.

One might remark that both Proust and Barthes were male homosexuals. And that male homosexuality may figure as the exemplary thorn in feminism's thorny relation to perversion. We must affirm the normality of homosexuality in order to celebrate lesbianism, yet male homosexuality is also highly phallocentric male sexuality and partakes of all the perversions of male heterosexuality: rape, pornography, child molesting, etc. In practice the allegiance between lesbians and gay males is always problematic. Male homosexuality can neither be condemned nor celebrated. In the highly polarized world of feminism, male homosexuality might be *ne-uter*, neither one nor the other.

But I am not prepared here to explain Proust and Barthes as male homosexual authors. For I do not know how to articulate the relation between their lived homosexuality and their writing. Not that it is irrelevant. Proust functions as a model for the late Barthes in that in Proust there is an unusually profound intrication of text and life. Homosexuality and biography are explicitly important questions in both Proust and (late) Barthes. But it is not clear to me what constitutes the homosexuality of their texts.

In contemplating a feminist reading of *The Pleasure of the Text* I felt discouraged by the lack of markers of sexual difference there, those markers that the feminist critic grabs onto in her intercourse with the text. For example, Barthes never uses the words "masculine" or "feminine." Although there is much talk of sexual activity, the object of erotic desire is sexually indifferent. When Barthes writes, "the most erotic place on a body is it not *there where clothing gapes?"* he lists as his examples of intermittence: "the skin that glistens between two pieces (pants and sweater), between two edges (the half-open shirt, the glove and the sleeve)" (p. 19). The examples seem applicable to either sex; all items of clothing are unisex with the possible exception of the shirt. A faint hint of homosexual desire but set against a general impression of neutrality. Sexual indifference, neutrality in the war between the sexes.

Shortly before writing the present text, I gave a seminar on *The Pleasure of the Text*, a "straight" seminar on the book, no attempt to do a feminist analysis. But I did mention that elsewhere I was trying to work out a feminist reading of the text. Two women spoke out in anticipation of what might be my feminist reading. One asked if I *as a woman* did not find this book offensive. I never found out what she meant, but I can only presume that "as a woman" she found the explicit perversion offensive, since in some analyses perversion is by definition intricated with male sexuality's assaults on women's civil rights. The other woman asked what I made of the word "neuter" in the text. I was surprised since I hadn't known Barthes used the word. I was reading the French text and they were reading the English translation. The word *neutre*, which I had always understood as "neutral," has been translated as "neuter."

The word *neutre* appears three times in this book. Each time I would translate it as "neutral," for it refers to pleasure's atopicality, its status outside the war of values. I am puzzled by the fact that the translator chose to use "neuter," and at first dismiss it as carelessness. Yet in my frustration with the lack of sexual difference in Barthes's erotics, I find myself returning again and again to the word "neuter" as if it shed new light on Barthes's neutrality. On all three appearances of *neutre* in *The Pleasure of the Text*, the word is in italics, as if one should remark something about it, as if the meaning were somehow changed without becoming another word, as if the word had become foreign. Five of the six meanings given for *neutre* in the dictionary could be translated by the English word "neutral." But the other meaning of the word, which is used in linguistics, is "belonging to a grammatical category in which are grouped the nouns . . . that do not present the characteristics of masculine and feminine," in other words, what we in English call neuter nouns. In French, of course, there are no neuter nouns; the neuter is there exotic, atopic perhaps. And it is noteworthy that *neutre* as neuter refers to linguistic gender, to sexual difference as it operates within language, within the text.

A few days after the seminar, I came across an example of Barthes using the word *neutre* in this linguistic meaning. In 1977, in his *Inaugural Lesson at the College de France*, Barthes stated: "I am forced always to choose between the masculine and the feminine; the neuter [*le neutre*] or the complex are forbidden me." I found this sentence in an analysis by Danielle Schwartz of the relation between language and power in Barthes's thought.[20] Schwartz notes that Barthes talks about language in terms of the dichotomy constraint/freedom. In this example, Barthes is constrained to choose either masculine or feminine; he is not free to choose the neuter (neither masculine nor feminine) or the complex (presumably some combination of the two).

Barthes is here talking about the linguistic notion of selection. According to Schwartz, "The notion of selection designates the work peculiar to the speaking subject, consisting in choosing a signifier in an entire paradigmatic chain. This notion, which in Jakobson, for example, is a scientific description, is here taken up and psychologized on the model of the alienating choice. The existential problematic of choice comes and grafts itself on the linguistic notion, thus giving the mechanisms of language a predestination that prepares his political version." Barthes is, according to Schwartz, in the process of recasting the laws of language, and our place under those laws, as a political dilemma. And with the example of the obligation of feminine or masculine, the prohibition of the neuter, one can imagine that the politics of language could become and might already be a sexual politics, or rather truly a politics of gender, not as we have come to use the word "gender," meaning biological sex, but in its dictionary meaning as sexual differentiation within language, textual sexuality.

Schwartz concludes her analysis of this sentence thus: "Implicitly in Barthes's text are manifested the regret and the wish for a counterlanguage, for an emancipation from constraints." And part of Barthes's liberated language, linguistic utopia would be access to the *neutre*,

sexual neutrality. Feminism too has decried our compulsory, either-
or masculine or feminine, created words like chairperson, spokesper-
son. Feminism too has longed for a freedom to be neuter or complex.
Yet beyond the masculine/feminine dichotomy is the realm of perversion. Homosexuals used to be called the third sex. This utopic italicized *neutre* may be a sensitive zone of Barthes's homotextuality. It
certainly is part of a wish to escape the constraints of bipolar gender
differentiation. And so perhaps he shares in feminism's liberatory
project.

And yet I am suspicious of neutrality, suspicious of the wish to deny
sexual difference. Women have historically been associated with sexual difference, have been sexually differentiated from the generic so-
called mankind. The wish to escape sexual difference might be but
another mode of denying women. I distrust male homosexuals because they choose men over women just as do our social and political
institutions, but they too share in the struggle against bipolar gender
constraints, against the compulsory choice of masculine or feminine.

Barthes edges toward an escape from that compulsory choice into
something he calls *neutre:* neutral, neuter, sexually indifferent, outside the ideological war of the sexes. The *neutre* may be emancipatory
but it is not free from eroticism. The *neutre* is reached through perversion and pleasure. Near the end of his book Barthes writes: "Pleasure
is a *neutre* (the most perverse form of the demoniacal)" (p. 102). The
neutral here is far from innocent. Neuter sexuality, outside the dichotomy necessary for reproduction. Neuter, but not asexual, neither
one sex nor the other, but not asexual.

Complex, perhaps. Near the beginning of the book Barthes imag-
ines: "Fiction of an individual who would abolish in himself barriers,
classes, exclusion . . . by simple riddance of that old specter: logical
contradiction. . . . Now this counter-hero exists: It's the text reader,
in the moment when he takes his pleasure" (pp. 9–10). In textual
pleasure one is rid of either-or, momentarily. Including, guiltily enough,
feminine or masculine, and worse yet, feminist or sexist.

The pleasure of Proust. A guilty pleasure. On the question of feminism: *neutre.* The pleasure of Barthes, but what about feminism? What
is Barthes's position on women? He never takes a position on women.
(Out of homosexuality perhaps? Neutrality? Exclusion?) A possible
exception: the word "woman" occurs *once* in *The Pleasure of the Text.*

In a section of the book called "War," Barthes opposes pleasure to
"the warrior *value*," lauds pleasure's atopicality in ideological conflict. At the end of the section, however, he specifies that the text is
not, nor does he want it to be, devoid of ideology. He writes that

"Some people want a text (art, painting) without a shadow, cut off
from 'the dominant ideology'; but that is to want a text without fecundity, without productivity, a sterile text (see the myth of The
Woman Without a Shadow). The text needs its shadow: this shadow,
it's *a bit* of ideology" (p. 53). "The Woman Without a Shadow" is a
story by Hofmannsthal about a woman who could not bear children
because she had no shadow. By speaking of a text without a shadow
he is equating text and woman. Susan Gubar, well-known feminist
critic, in fact cites this passage from Barthes as yet another example
of the longstanding masculinist tradition of woman as text, as art
object rather than artist.[21] Yes, but . . . that is not where I connect
to this passage, which has, I believe, a certain homosexual specificity.

I am interested in the association between fertility and dominant
ideology. Barthes specifies later that there is only dominant ideology,
no such thing as dominated ideology, that ideology is the idea inasmuch as it dominates. Fecundity and ideology, both are shadows, outside the light of reason, the lightness of atopic pleasure. Normal sexuality for Barthes, as we have seen, is fertile, reproductive sexuality.
That is also the dominant ideology of sex. Perversion is pleasure without reproduction, without ideology, without shadow. Yet in this passage he is instead asserting the necessity for a bit of reproduction.
The totally perverse text is sterile. And at the moment he would affirm "a bit" of reproductive sexuality, he writes the word "Woman."

The word is capitalized, refers to another text ("The Woman Without a Shadow") and not to some extratextual being. The woman he
mentions is in fact nonreproductive, that is, perverse. Yet in order to
propose a negative image of nonreproductive sexuality, an image of
sterility rather than perversion, the woman appears, for the first and
only time in the book. Perversion, pleasure, the neuter are positive
images throughout: nonreproductive sexuality is glorified. But suddenly when Barthes needs to counter this by showing nonreproductive pleasure in a negative light, woman appears. As if nonreproductive sexuality were glorious for men (male homotextuality) but a sterile
woman were still a shame, a failure, less than rather than other.

Is woman for Barthes intricated with dominant ideology, normal
reproductive sexuality, all that he is writing and struggling against?
Pleasure has traditionally been associated with woman, particularly
in its erotic sense. In the male heterosexual tradition, subversive pleasure that lures one away from productive duty is female. Women have
thus been suspicious of pleasure because it relegates us to the nonserious, nonproductive, nonwarrior side of things. In a male homosexual tradition woman may be on the other side, allied with duty,
productivity, and ideology. This tradition is hardly restricted to overt

liberal much more than men (the famous "gender gap") because the ideological place for woman is to offset the rapacious appropriations of unfettered capitalist man.

"Snatches" was written in 1977; "The Perverse Body" in 1984. In the early seventies women attempted to obtain the benefits accruing to the male position in this double standard. We gave up moral superiority, motherhood, and the church in quest of worldly power. In the late seventies a new direction in feminism returned to and revalorized the traditionally female, morally superior sphere. I find myself first writing against individualism and then in turn against moralism in feminism. If I counter both of these polarized positions, it is because the opposition and secret complementarity between them is fundamental to capitalist sexual, political, and economic ideology. Feminist analyses of that ideology have exposed how the separation and secret collusion between individualism and moralism allow the individualism of the few to prosper at the expense of the many.

"The Perverse Body" tries to think differently the relation between individualism (perversion) and moralism (political responsibility). It comes to no new resolution but does at least get beyond the separation into spheres (right and left, male and female). We must rethink that relation and come up with a new solution to the very real contradiction between the individual and morality. Or for now, for me, I must live in that contradiction.

Notes

1. See, for example, Shoshana Felman, *La Folie et la chose littéraire* (Paris: Seuil, 1978).

2. Luce Irigaray, *Ce Sexe qui n'en est pas un* (Paris: Seuil, 1977). Translations mine. An English translation by Catherine Porter, *This Sex Which Is Not One*, was published by Cornell University Press in 1985.

3. Sigmund Freud, "The Dissolution of the Oedipus Complex," in *The Standard Edition of the Complete Psychological Works*, ed. James Strachey (London: Hogarth, 1953–74); vol. 19.

4. Alice Jardine, *Gynesis: Configurations of Woman and Modernity* (Ithaca: Cornell University Press, 1985).

5. Jacques Lacan, "L'Instance de la lettre dans l'inconscient ou la raison depuis Freud," in *Ecrits* (Paris: Seuil, 1966), p. 515.

6. Michèle Montrelay, *L'Ombre et le nom* (Paris: Minuit, 1977), p. 76.

7. Luce Irigaray, *Amante marine* (Paris: Minuit, 1980) and *Passions élémentaires* (Paris: Minuit, 1982).

8. Sandra M. Gilbert and Susan Gubar, "Tradition and the Female Talent," in *The Poetics of Gender*, ed. Nancy K. Miller (New York: Columbia University Press, 1986), pp. 183–207.

9. Elaine Showalter, "Critical Cross-Dressing: Male Feminists and the Woman of the Year," in *Men in Feminism,* ed. Alice Jardine and Paul Smith (New York: Methuen, 1987), pp. 116–32. This whole anthology is relevant to the present discussion.

10. Jacques Derrida, *Spurs* (Chicago: University of Chicago Press, 1979). Originally published as "La Question du style," in *Nietzsche aujourd'hui?* (Paris: Union Générale d'Editions, 1973).

11. Elaine Showalter, "Toward a Feminist Poetics," in *The New Feminist Criticism: Essays in Women, Literature, and Theory,* (New York: Pantheon, 1985), p. 139.

12. Showalter, "Critical Cross-Dressing."

13. Roland Barthes, *Le Plaisir du texte* (Paris: Seuil, 1973). All translations mine. The book has been translated by Richard Miller as *The Pleasure of the Text* (New York: Hill and Wang, 1975).

14. Annette Lavers, *Roland Barthes: Structuralism and After* (Cambridge, Mass.: Harvard University Press, 1982).

15. Steven Ungar, *Roland Barthes: The Professor of Desire* (Lincoln: University of Nebraska Press, 1983).

16. Roland Barthes, *Mythologies* (Paris: Seuil, 1957). Translated by Annette Lavers as *Mythologies* (New York: Hill and Wang, 1972).

17. Christopher Norris, "Les Plaisirs des clercs: Barthes's Latest Writing," *British Journal of Aesthetics* (1974), 14:253.

18. Claudine Herrmann, *Les Voleuses de langue* (Paris: des femmes, 1976), pp. 16–18.

19. Cora Kaplan, "Wild Nights: Pleasure/Sexuality/Feminism," in *Formations of Pleasure* (London: Routledge and Kegan Paul, 1983), p. 29.

20. Danielle Schwartz, "Barthes, le langage et le pouvoir," *La Nouvelle Critique* (1977), 106:56.

21. Susan Gubar, "'The Blank Page' and the Issues of Female Creativity," in *Writing and Sexual Difference,* ed. Elizabeth Abel (Chicago: University of Chicago Press, 1982), p. 76.

6.

Beyond the Phallus

Beyond the *Jouissance* Principle

"We translate what the American women write, they never translate our texts." This quotation from Hélène Cixous is the opening sentence of *New French Feminisms*, an anthology of translations from the French, the first major effort to translate what the "French women" write. Some pages later, in a footnote to an introduction, the editors, Elaine Marks and Isabelle de Courtivron, tell us: "The verb *jouir* and the substantive *jouissance* occur frequently in the texts of the new French feminisms. We have constantly used the English words 'sexual pleasure' in our translations."[1] Thus, among other things, what the French women write is the word *jouissance*, which the anthology translates, consistently.

In an article subtitled "The Language of French Feminist Criticism," Michèle Richman writes, in a note: "It is impossible to give an adequate translation of *jouissance*."[2] In a footnote to her translation of Julia Kristeva's "Women's Time," Alice Jardine writes: "I have retained *jouissance*—that word for pleasure which defies translation."[3] And, working in a British context, Parveen Adams, in a note to her translation in Michèle Montrelay's "Inquiry into Femininity," bluntly asserts: "The word *jouissance* is impossible to translate."[4] Richman, Jardine, and Adams, as well as many others involved in various ways in the importation of what the French women write, choose not to translate the word *jouissance*, not to assimilate it, but to retain its foreignness.

In a 1982 feminist issue of the journal *Diacritics*, Jardine states that "those American feminists . . . whose reading habits have been deeply changed by contemporary French thought must remain attentive to what are, ultimately, some very complex problems of translation—

in the most literal sense of the word as well as in its broader and more difficult sense, as the intercultural exchange of ideas."[5]

The complaint opening *New French Feminisms* about *our* failure to translate *them* suggests that if we would foster exchange, we must translate. Yet the specific case of *jouissance* leads me to wonder whether translation in the literal sense is always the best means of translation in the broad sense. Because it always poses difficulties for the translator (a translator's note is now practically *de rigueur*, or, as we say in English, de rigueur), *jouissance* may, in fact, now function as a synechdoche for the broader problems of assimilation of what the French women write. And, because it has frequently appeared untranslated in the English-speaking context, *jouissance* may have taken on a new connotation; it has come to serve as an emblem of French feminine theory.

In an article about French women's writing, Ann Rosalind Jones states, in the obligatory footnote, that "the simplest translation" of *jouissance* is the word "pleasure."[6] In her own text, however, she refuses this "simplest" solution: she too leaves *jouissance* in French. Rather than explain this nontranslation, her footnote refers instead to two other jouissance notes: the one in *New French Feminisms*, and Stephen Heath's translator's note to a collection of essays by Roland Barthes. Although quoted in its entirety, the *New French Feminisms* note in no way explains the rejection of "pleasure," the simplest translation. There is, however, an explanation to be found in the other reference, in Heath's note which, in contrast with the feminist note, is not quoted at all. Heath writes: "English lacks a word able to carry the range of meaning in the term *jouissance*. . . . The problem would be less acute were it not that *jouissance* is specifically contrasted to *plaisir* by Barthes in his *Le Plaisir du texte*."[7]

Heath is not here writing in a feminist context, much less so Roland Barthes. It is a commonplace to recognize the importance of Jacques Lacan and Jacques Derrida for French women's theory. Indeed, Lacan is often credited with distinguishing *jouissance* from *plaisir*, credited with rendering the former untranslatable. But the author of the untranslatability of French feminine jouissance is not Lacan—resented but acknowledged patriarch of French feminism—but rather Roland Barthes, whose influence on French feminine writing is rarely if ever mentioned.

Not that Barthes and his *Pleasure of the Text* are not well known. In fact, that book, published in 1973, is so familiar to literary critics that one of the fates of pleasure in recent literary thought is to be diacritically linked with jouissance in the wake of Roland Barthes.

Briefly, Barthes distinguishes between *plaisir*, which is comfortable, ego-assuring, recognized, and legitimated as culture, and *jouissance*, which is shocking, ego-disruptive, and in conflict with the canons of culture. The book repeatedly embellishes upon this opposition which thence becomes its most easily remembered idea. The reader retains this dichotomy as a new conceptual framework for cultural history and criticism.

But from the first, the reader is warned against leaning too heavily on something so precarious as an opposition between sometime synonyms. On the second page of the text, following the first appearance of the word *jouissance*, Barthes inserts a paragraph in parentheses. The paragraph is headed by an italicized *Plaisir/Jouissance*, the classic formula for a binary opposition, and after the binary formula we read: "terminologically, it still vacillates. . . . In any case . . . the distinction will not be a source of decisive, steady classifications."[8]

Notice the word "vacillates." The word returns later in the book when Barthes says that the "text of *jouissance* . . . causes the historical, cultural, psychological foundations of the reader to vacillate" (p. 25). If the binary opposition, plaisir/jouissance, "still vacillates," then the opposition itself is still a site of jouissance, of unsettling, and is not steady enough to serve as a foundation for future classifications.

Notice the future tense in the statement "the distinction will not be a source of decisive, steady classifications." The future is the undoing of jouissance, which does not endure but burns itself out in a "precocious" instant. According to Barthes, "as soon as it is understood . . . [it] becomes ineffective, we must go on to something else" (p. 84).

Jouissance has a power, the power to unsettle foundations and classifications, to shake up ideology. "Yes," says Barthes, "but not if [jouissance] is stated, doctrinal" (p. 71). It is this power to unsettle ideological founding assumptions that is celebrated in the French feminine concept of jouissance. But the refusal to translate jouissance, the importation of it into a scene where it loses its ambiguities, its sometime synonymy with "pleasure," ends the vacillation of the binary paradigm, renders the distinction steady and decisive. In the last decade, at least in an English–speaking context, jouissance has become a doctrinal concept: singular, unambiguous, steady, and de rigueur.

Jouissance is used in English, it is said, because our language lacks an adequate equivalent. Indeed, we might say that whenever a word passes untranslated into another language, it signals some inadequacy in the second language, some plenitude in the first. That sense of inferiority is most explicitly put in Richard Howard's note to the translation of *Le Plaisir du texte*. Howard writes: "The French have a distinguishing advantage . . . the French have a vocabulary of eroticism . . . which smells neither of the laboratory nor of the sewer, which just—attentively, scrupulously—puts the facts."[9] Oh, those French!

Now, in Anglo-Saxon countries the French probably benefit from a long-standing reputation for superior savoir-faire, as we say, in things erotic: a tradition it would be quite interesting to investigate, so as to uncover what sorts of ideological baggage, massive projections, and repressions it carries. As well, perhaps, to understand why some of us become professors of French. But, in this case, the case of jouissance, the advantage lies in a greater correspondence of signifier to signified, of "vocabulary" to "facts." In the context of this word envy, it is gratifying to note a complaint Barthes makes about an inadequacy in the French language: "there is no French word to cover both *plaisir* and *jouissance*. 'Plaisir' is thus sometimes coextensive with *jouissance*, sometimes opposed to it. But I must accommodate myself to this ambiguity . . . because I cannot purify the word 'plaisir' from meanings . . . I do not want: I cannot help the fact that in French 'plaisir' refers to [two different things]."[10]

Barthes must accommodate himself to the limitations of the French language, limitations not unlike those confronted by the translators of *jouissance*. Most of these translators, in the literal and broad senses of that term, choose, however, not to accommodate but to reach out for another language that would be beyond "ambiguity," "purified from meanings [we] do not want."

Claude Lévi-Strauss, in an introduction to the work of Marcel Mauss, notes that at certain key moments Mauss chose to use native words— *mana* and *hau*—as untranslated concepts in his French text. Lévi-Strauss thinks that the function of such words is "to fill in a gap between the signifier and the signified,"[11] gaps which exist because, according to him, there is a "surplus of signification," a surplus which we might translate as "meaning [we] do not want" or "ambiguity."

Lévi-Strauss is criticizing a blind spot in Mauss's theory, a refusal to think something through in symbolic terms rather than simply accept a native explanation. But Lévi-Strauss' critique must be understood in the context of his praise of and admiration for Mauss. He is interested in the blind spot because of what it allows him to see. By reflecting on Mauss's refusal to translate, he better understands what is at work there and thus prolongs rather than detracts from Mauss's work. Although at first Lévi-Strauss says that the function of *mana* is to "fill in a gap," an image that suggests suppression, the sentence continues: "or, more exactly [the function is] to signal the fact that in such a circumstance . . . a relation of inadequation is established between signifier and signified" (ibid.). What at first appears as a gagging, a suppression of a crying inadequation, is finally seen as a signal.

I hope that my meditation on the rigidification of jouissance in English versions of French theory can be taken in the same way. Let me make it clear that I too have, on occasion, proclaimed the untranslatability of *jouissance* and left it in French. Anglo-American thought has benefited from the introduction of this new and alien concept; it can best benefit further by not becoming inured to this outside agitator. If jouissance is celebrated as something that unsettles assumptions, it becomes ineffective when it itself settles into an assumption. If jouissance is "beyond the pleasure principle," it is not because it is beyond pleasure but because it is beyond principle.

When jouissance itself becomes a principle, we must ask what is beyond that principle, what disrupts it or is suppressed by it. In *The Pleasure of the Text*, Barthes asks "why [emotion] should be antipathetic to *jouissance*" and admits that he "mistakenly used to see [emotion] as wholly allied with sentimentality, with moral illusion" (p. 42). He comes to understand that "emotion" is definitely a jouissance but is not recognized as such "because it contradicts the general rule which would give *jouissance* a fixed form: strong, violent, crude: something necessarily muscular, stiff, phallic" (ibid.). When jouissance becomes a "general rule," a "fixed form," a principle, its image is "strong, muscular, and phallic."

When jouissance becomes an emblem of French feminine theory, however, it is specifically identified as nonphallic, beyond the phallus. But even though jouissance is specified as feminine, the tendency to stiffen into a strong, muscular image remains. The difference between jouissance and pleasure is generally understood to be one of degree: jouissance is stronger and so the person who experiences it is stronger, braver, less repressed, less scared. The timid, defensive egos, cautious in their bourgeois comfort, prefer plaisir and shun jouissance, but we brave, feminist, revolutionary, avant-garde . . .

In a chapter called "Fear," Barthes writes: "Proximity (identity?) of *jouissance* and fear. What is repugnant in such a comparison is obviously not the idea that fear is an unpleasant sensation but rather that it is a mediocre and unworthy sensation" (p. 77). A threat to the ego and its founding assumptions is experienced by the subject as fear. The threatened ego feels unworthy and mediocre: a sense of worthiness is inseparable from ego assurance and gratification.

Fear also appears in conjunction with jouissance in an English translation of French feminism, but otherwise. The editors of *New French Feminisms* state, in a footnote, that jouissance "is a word used by Hélène Cixous to refer to that intense, rapturous pleasure which women know and men fear."[12] Here the two are conjoined but divorced: *we* have jouissance, *they* fear it. If jouissance is defined, as it is by Barthes *and* the women, as a loss of self, disruption of comfort, loss of control, it cannot simply be claimed as an ego-gratifying identity but must also frighten those who "know" it.[13] As jouissance becomes a banner and a badge for French feminine writing, the accompanying fear or unworthiness is projected outward and we—militant and bold—lose the ambiguous link to fear and emotion, which are catapulted beyond the jouissance principle where it might even be their momentary fate to take up residence in that mediocre and unworthy word, "pleasure."

The Emperor's New Clothes

Anna Freud was reaching maturity and began to show an interest in her father's work, so Freud gave her some of his writings to read. About a month later he asked her if she had any questions about what she had been reading. "Just one," she replied, "what is a phallus?" Being a man of science, Freud unbuttoned his pants and showed her. "Oh," Anna exclaimed, thus enlightened, "it's like a penis, only smaller!"—A Joke

Phallus/Penis: Same Difference

When the second wave of feminism began in the late sixties, feminists would have no truck with Freud. Through work like Kate Millett's *Sexual Politics*, it became clear that although psychoanalysis might be associated with liberation from Victorian sexual constraints, it was nevertheless but another agent of the oppression of women, prescribing for women their proper place and aiding adjustment to that place. In 1974, Juliet Mitchell's *Psychoanalysis and Feminism* came out. Suddenly a recognized feminist theorist was endorsing Freud without rescinding her feminist position. Mitchell's feminist Freudianism was made possible by the work of the French psychoanalyst Jacques Lacan. Because Lacan's way of reading Freud located sexuality itself in language, that is, in culture, the Lacanian Freud no longer prescribed normality but described the conflicts and discontents of a bisexual animal who must, in order to function in the social world, become a man or a woman—assume an alienated sexual identity. Lacan's work produced a Freud that might be of use to feminism.

But many feminists still find much to resist in Lacan. Lacan's system is explicitly phallocentric, and feminists find that central, transcendental phallus particularly hard to swallow. The debate over Lacan's and, beyond that, psychoanalysis' value for feminism itself centers on the phallus. Yet the *phallus* is a very complicated notion in Lacan, who distinguishes it from the *penis*. The distinction seems, however, to resist clarification. I believe that a certain concentration on this distinction and its discontents is invaluable not only for an evaluation of the relation of psychoanalysis to feminism, but more important, for an understanding of feminism's relation to men. If the phallus is distinct from the penis, then feminism's battle against phallocentrism is not a battle against men. But if it is nearly impossible to keep the distinction phallus/penis clear, that may account for the constant return of the assumption that men are the enemies of feminism.

To understand the Lacanian use of the term *phallus*, it is helpful to refer to the last phase of infantile sexuality, which Freud calls the phallic phase. In the phallic phase, according to Freud, "Only one kind of genital organ comes into account—the male. . . . At the same time the real female genitals never seem to be discovered."[14] The phallic phase is organized by the opposition phallic/castrated (one either has a phallus or one has nothing); adult sexuality, according to Freud, is organized by the distinction masculine/feminine. The phallus thus belongs to a monosexual logic, one that admits to no difference, of no other sex; whereas the penis can be inserted into the realm of adult sexuality, where it can encounter the feminine.

Thus, to distinguish phallus from penis is to separate infantile sexuality from adult sexuality. To distinguish penis from phallus would be to locate some masculinity that does not necessarily obliterate the feminine. Yet it remains an open question whether there truly exists any adult sexuality, whether there is any masculinity that is beyond the phallic phase, that does not need to equate femininity with castration.

The Lacanian phallus is not simply linked to infantile genitality. It is a signifier, which is to say it belongs to what Lacan calls the symbolic order, which is the order of language. It is neither a real nor a fantasized organ but an attribute: a power to generate meaning. Language implies the ability to make meaning. But no speaking subject can, in reality, perform this generative act. And thus we grant this power to an ideal other: Phallic Mother, Primal Father, God. He says what he means and means what he says. This phallic Other is thus presumed to "know," that is, to speak and hear an unalienated language, which is the adequate expression of an integral self. Yet only the Other has the phallus; the subject, *whatever* organ he or she *may* have, is symbolically castrated. Which is to say that the subject can obtain no full satisfaction because the subject can never *know* what he wants because his "wants" are alienated in language.

The Lacanian phallus is thus a linguistic concept. Discourse is phallocentric. Therefore, to have the phallus would mean to be at the center of discourse, to generate meaning, to have mastery of language, to control rather than conform to that which comes from outside, from the Other.

The distinction between *phallus* and *penis* has great bearing on the question of the relation between psychoanalysis and feminism. Feminists complain about our phallocentric culture; Lacanians agree that our culture is phallocentric, but consider this a structural fact of language that need have no relation to oppression of women by men. For Lacanians phallocentrism is not the same as androcentrism, because the phallus is not a penis. Men are no more in possession of the phallus than are women.

Feminists think we must alter the phallocentrism of discourse in order to alter women's lot in society. Lacanians would simply separate the symbolic phallus from the penis. But is this separation possible? Or is it merely a fantasy?

Of course, the signifier *phallus* functions in distinction from the signifier *penis*. It sounds and looks different, produces different associations. *But* it *also* always refers to *penis*. Lacanians might *wish* to polarize the two terms into a neat opposition, but it is hard to polarize synonyms. Such attempts to remake language to one's own theoretical needs, as if language were merely a tool one could use, bespeaks a very un-Lacanian view of language. The Lacanians' desire clearly to separate *phallus* from *penis,* to control the meaning of the signifier *phallus,* is precisely symptomatic of their desire to have the phallus, that is, their desire to be at the center of language, at its origin. And their inability to control the meaning of the word *phallus* is evidence of what Lacan calls symbolic castration.

The question of whether one can separate phallus from penis joins the question of whether one can separate psychoanalysis from politics. The penis is what men have and women do not; the phallus is the attribute of power which neither men nor women have. But as long as the attribute of power is a phallus which can only have meaning by referring to and being confused with a penis, this confusion will support a structure in which it seems reasonable that men have power and women do not. And as long as psychoanalysts maintain the ideal separability of phallus from penis, they can hold on to their phallus in the belief that their phallocentric discourse need have no relation to sexual inequality, no relation to politics.

In my interest in the distinction between phallus and penis, I began to notice that whenever any Lacanian set out to clear up the confusion between phallus and penis, she or he inevitably fell into the same sort of confusion the effort was meant to remedy. I do not pretend to be able to escape this confusion myself. I believe it to be a symptom of the impossibility, at this moment in our history, to think a masculine that is not phallic, a masculine that can couple with a feminine. Yet I consider that very impossibility to be nonetheless an urgent necessity—it is urgently necessary to think a masculine that is not phallic, to think a sexuality that is not arrested in the phallic phase. This double-bind combination of necessity and impossibility produces, I believe, the endless repetition of failed efforts to clearly distinguish phallus and penis.

In an attempt to loosen this double bind, I would like to analyze one of these attempts at distinction, not in order to transcend the confusion but rather to learn what is at stake in the confusion, why this confusion is, at this moment in our history, necessary. My example is taken from a book published in 1976 in the series Lacan directed at Editions de Seuil. That book, *Partage des femmes*, is by a woman Lacanian analyst, Eugénie Lemoine-Luccioni. Although not particularly well known in our American context, her text is central to my investigation because it was there that, for me, this confusion produced the most readable symptom.

One of the major stumbling blocks in the Lacanian notion of the phallus with its reference to Freud is that, in Freud, the woman's version of the castration complex is called *penis envy*. Indeed, as much as it seems *smarter* theory to say that what the woman "really" wants is not the real organ but the symbolic phallus, Freud nonetheless uses the word *penis*. In *Partage des femmes*, Lemoine-Luccioni articulates phallus and penis envy thus: "When by chance, [the girl] was given the opportunity to see a penis, the desire for the phallus was translated by penis envy."[15] For Lemoine-Luccioni, *penis envy* is a "translation" of "desire for the phallus." In other words, one language, accidentally, "by chance," provides us with a "translation," a secondary, contingent form of an original. *Penis envy* is Freud's term; yet here it seems to be considered merely a secondary, accidental translation of a more originary Lacanian formulation.

The Lacanian term *phallus* would thus become a pure origin, self-referential. In just such an attempt to purify the phallus from any contamination with Otherness, that is, in an attempt to phallicize the word *phallus*, the male Lacanian analyst Serge Leclaire writes: "the phallus, *referent* of the unconscious order, cannot be grasped in a concept: . . . it escapes . . . all inscription. That is to say that there exists neither image nor text of the phallus" (emphasis added).[16] Any image or text is but a "translation" of the phallus which is no longer a signifier ("image" or "text"), not even the privileged signifier (which Lacan has called it), but a referent, that which language invokes, always indicates, but which always exceeds language. Now, certainly, when Lacan talks about the "castration" entailed by the subject's being in language, in the symbolic order, a good way to understand that castration is that one is always deprived of signifying the referent, one's language is doomed never to be more than a good translation. But to say that *phallus*, a signifier forming part of our language, is the name of that unreachable, unspeakable referent constitutes phallus as some fundamental, transcendental truth.

Lemoine-Luccioni writes: "If by chance the girl catches sight of a penis—a fact in itself contingent—this latter becomes the sign of the phallus" (p. 45). The penis, through the contingencies of experience, can become the sign of the phallus—sign as opposed to referent. But the phallus does not depend on any contingencies; it is originary, essential, transcendental. Yet *phallus*, the signifier in its specificity, in its letter, not its spirit—which is how any Lacanian ought to take a signifier—is always a reference to *penis*. *Phallus* cannot function as signifier in ignorance of *penis*. *Phallus* is not the original, proper name of some referent that may get translated *contingently* as *penis*. *Phallus* confronts the inadequacy of any name to embody the referent, and is itself emblematic of that inadequacy by its inevitable referent to *penis*.

One of the weaknesses of the Lacanian orthodoxy is to render *phallus* transcendental, an originary name, not dependent on penis and its contingencies. Yet that is not, I would say, the status of the signification of *phallus* at its most interesting in Lacan's work. Lacan indeed tries to rectify this transcendental, metalinguistic notion of phallus in his commentary on Ernest Jones's "Theory of Symbolism." Jones wrote that "if the church tower can symbolize the phallus, never will the phallus symbolize the tower."[17] Jones would make phallus a

final referent, one that does not symbolize anything else but is the
thing itself, self-referential. Lacan calls Jones's remark "fallacious."[18]

The word *fallacious* likewise crops up in Lemoine-Luccioni's writing and again it is linked to the phallus. She refers to the "fallacious
gift" that the daughter awaits from the father (p. 59). This "fallacious
gift" is usually understood psychoanalytically as the phallus the
daughter expects the father to give her. There seems to be some insistent link between *phallic* and *fallacious*, one certainly attributable
to the material similarity between the two signifiers. Somehow to try
to think the "phallus" is to wind up with fallacy.

The daughter awaits the phallacious gift. In the sentence quoted
earlier, Lemoine-Luccioni writes: "When by chance, [the girl] was given
the opportunity to see a penis, the desire for the phallus was translated by penis envy" (p. 20). The girl, "by chance," if she is lucky, is
"*given* the opportunity to see a penis." That opportunity, that sight,
is a "gift," something wondrous, a wonder for the girl. For Lemoine-
Luccioni, for the analyst, for the daughter, the privilege of the phallus
is linked to the wonder of the penis. I quote at length from Lemoine-
Luccioni: "The phallic function is specifically that which also causes
the penis to become erect. Then it becomes soft again: it falls. These
are not metaphors. How is it that this spectacular penis, thus erected,
does not ordinarily become an object of pleasure for itself, but is the
instrument of sexual *jouissance?* And that it finds in penetration of
another body its pleasure?" I want to repeat this quote: "The phallic
function is specifically that which also causes the penis to become
erect. Then it becomes soft again: it falls. These are not metaphors.
How is it that this *spectacular penis*, thus erected, does *not* ordinarily
become an object of pleasure *for itself*, but is the *instrument* of sexual
jouissance? And that it finds in penetration of *another body* its pleasure?" (p. 168, emphases added).

The penis is "spectacular." Yet what is most wondrous to Lemoine-
Luccioni, most incredible ("how is it?" she asks) is that this "spectacular" erection is not an end in itself, is not self-referential, self-
sufficient, "an object of pleasure for itself." What she cannot believe
is that this phallic penis (a pleonasm, to be sure) is an "instrument":
she can barely believe that it wants "another body," needs another
body for its pleasure, its fulfillment. The erect penis, unlike the symbolic phallus, is not monolithic power, but desire, need for another
body. Lemoine-Luccioni finds it *hard* to believe that the erect penis
is not an end in-and-for-itself, because the *phallus*, the Lacanian Phallus, is just that, the attribute of she or he that is whole, not needy of
the other.

Photograph by Dick Blau

Obviously such a phallus cannot be had by anyone. Yet the difficulty in believing that the erect penis is not in-and-for-itself is a symptom of the inevitable confusion between penis and phallus. And rather than see the phallus as a penis, Lemoine-Luccioni prefers to see the penis as a phallus. "These are not metaphors," she writes. When one talks of the *penis*—not even the *phallus* here, but the very contingent penis with its ups and downs—one is no longer dealing with slippery, always metaphorical language. A metaphor is one signifier in the place of another signifier. In a Lacanian view of language a signifier always signifies another signifier; no word is free from metaphoricity. The speaking subject cannot control whether his or her words are metaphors. Yet knowing all this, Lemoine-Luccioni would still believe that in speaking of the wondrous, spectacular penis, one is finally speaking of the referent, of the thing itself.

Now, I would like to read Lemoine-Luccioni's marvel at the penis as more than a mistake to be corrected. I would like to read this passage as a locus of excitement in her text. Speaking from *within* the confusion between penis and phallus, she is speaking her desire. The two questions ("how is it?") at the end of the passage are the mark of something that goes far beyond some filial piety toward Lacan. These questions bespeak a desire for the penis. Not the Paternal nor the Maternal Phallus. A desire that barely dares believe that there is a penis. That barely can see beyond the Phallus. But if there were a penis . . . One that could desire to penetrate another body, one that could want a woman, need a woman, not just a "woman," but more excitingly, an "other" body, not woman as the appropriate and appropriated phallic object, but an "other body" . . . If there were a penis . . .

After Beyond

The institution of heterosexism would have women desire the transcendent Phallus to legitimate them, raise them above their bodies, castrated, mortal, bloody messes. By insisting on the penis, I was looking for some masculine body, some other body, some bodily object of female heterosexual desire, trying to find not just the institution of heterosexism but also the experience of heterosexuality. I cannot disintricate the penis from phallic rule but neither is it totally synonymous with the transcendent phallus. At this point in history I don't think they can be separated, but to insist on bodily masculinity is to work to undo the heterosexist ideology which decrees the body female, to be dominated not by a male body (too disorderly to rule) but by an idealized, transcendent phallus. I want to render that idealization impossible.

While trying to affirm a woman's desire, my tone is also one of laying down the law about a "correct" Lacanian view of language. Lacan's word is still truth, and it is used here to authorize female desire. I could not disentangle the desire for a male body that responds to a female body from desire for what I here call "the Lacanian Phallus." My own desire for Papa Lacan to authorize my desire produces this contradiction.

In the original version of "Phallus/Penis" there is a sentence that reads: "the subject can obtain no full satisfaction because *one* can never know what *he or she* wants because *our* 'wants' are alienated in language." This pronoun jumble is a pretty good example of "alienation in language." This sentence is written somewhere in between the automatic generic *he* and the assumption of some other solution. The generic *he* supposedly detached from any reference to a masculine subject is the pronominal version of a phallus supposedly detached from the penis. The pronominal confusion bespeaks my difficulty in moving beyond the phallus.

In fixing the sentence up I decided to use the pronoun *he* in this particular sentence, since this is an articulation of "castration." Since I had used *he* for "an ideal other: Phallic Mother, Primal Father, God" I wanted also to use *he* for "the subject" so as to set it up as a contrast between two *he*'s: one phallic, one castrated. The similarity and the difference between those two *he*'s repeats the difference between *phallus* and *penis*—both likewise masculine, one belonging to the ideal other, the other an attribute of an embodied subject.

Locating thinking in a desiring body is also, in another vocabulary, locating thinking in a subject in history. To read for and affirm confusion, contradiction is to insist on thinking in the body in history. Those confusions mark the sites where thinking is literally knotted to the subject's historical and material place.

Notes

1. Elaine Marks and Isabelle de Courtivron, eds., *New French Feminisms: An Anthology* (Amherst: University of Massachusetts Press, 1980), p. 36, *n* 8.

2. Michele Richman, "Sex and Signs: The Language of French Feminist Criticism," *Language and Style* (1980), 13:4:80, *n* 13.

3. Julia Kristeva, "Women's Time," trans. Alice Jardine, *Signs* (1981), 7(1):16, *n* 6.

4. Michèle Montrelay, "Inquiry into Femininity," trans. Parveen Adams, *m/f* (1978), 1:101 *n* i.

5. Alice Jardine, "Gynesis," *Diacritics* (1982), 12:2:55.

6. Ann Rosalind Jones, "Writing and Body: Toward an Understanding of *L'Ecriture Féminine*," *Feminist Studies* (1981), 7:2:261, *n* 2.

7. Stephen Heath, "Translator's Note," in Roland Barthes, *Image-Music-Text* (New York: Hill and Wang 1977), p. 9.

8. Roland Barthes, *Le Plaisir du texte* (Paris: Seuil, 1973), p. 10. All translations mine.

9. Richard Howard, "A Note on the Text," in Roland Barthes, *The Pleasure of the Text*, trans. Richard Miller (New York: Hill and Wang, 1975), p. v.

10. Barthes, *Le Plaisir du texte*, pp. 33–34. It is tantalizing to note that "jouissance" is actually also an English word which once had the range of meanings it does in French, but which has since lost its sexual meaning. See Leon S. Roudiez's "Introduction" in Julia Kristeva, *Desire in Language*, trans. Thomas Gora, Alice Jardine, and Leon S. Roudiez (New York: Columbia University Press, 1980), pp. 14–16, and the *Oxford English Dictionary*.

11. Claude Lévi-Strauss, "Introduction à l'oeuvre de Marcel Mauss," in Marcel Mauss, *Sociologie et anthropologie* (Paris: Presses Universitaires de France, 1950), p. 44. For a discussion of Lévi-Strauss's reading of Mauss, see also Jeffrey Mehlman, *A Structural Study of Autobiography: Proust, Leiris, Sartre, Lévi-Strauss* (Ithaca: Cornell University Press, 1974), pp. 205–16.

12. Marks and Courtivron, *New French Feminisms*, p. 95, *n* 6.

13. After hearing this paper, Margaret Homans reminded me that it is traditionally women who are considered to fear sexual pleasure. I was led to think that the "we have it; they fear it" is a strategic feminist reversal of the tradition that polarizes sexual pleasure into something men want and women fear. Beyond the strategic necessity of the reversal, I am trying to suggest that the polarization is a defense against a powerful ambivalence in which the subject both wants and fears something overwhelming, intense, pleasurable, and ego-threatening. Indeed, one of the functions of polarized sexual roles—the double standard, rake and virgin—may be to defend against the intolerable ambivalence of simultaneously "knowing" and "fearing."

14. Sigmund Freud, "The Infantile Genital Organization," in *The Standard Edition of the Complete Psychological Works*, ed. James Strachey (London: Hogarth, 1953–74); 19:142 and 144.

15. Eugénie Lemoine-Luccioni, *Partage des femmes* (Paris: Seuil, 1976), p. 70.

16. Serge Leclaire, *On tue un enfant* (Paris: Seuil, 1975), pp. 32–33.

17. Ernest Jones, "The Theory of Symbolism," in *Papers on Psycho-analysis* (London: Balliere, Tindal, and Cox, 1948).

18. Jacques Lacan, *Ecrits* (Paris: Seuil, 1966), p. 709.

7.

Carnal Knowledge

A Good Lay

I may say at once that I am no connoisseur in art, but simply a lay-man. I have often observed that the subject matter of works of art has a stronger attraction for me than their formal and technical qual-ities, though to the artist their value lies first and foremost in these latter.

These lines could easily be mine: I am no connoisseur in art and am usually embarrassed to find that what interests me most is cer-tain subject matter, rather than the more artistic values of form and technique. But these sentences are not mine; they are the opening lines from one of the first pieces of psychoanalytic art criticism ever written, Freud's short article "The Moses of Michelangelo."[1]

These opening lines inaugurate a new genre, and from the very be-ginning of the genre, Freud sets out one of the major problems of psychoanalytic art criticism: it reduces art to its subject matter; it interprets away specificities of form or technique or medium to get at psychological themes.

But Freud also begins the genre by stating its illegitimacy. He says "at once" that he is no connoisseur. "Connoisseur" from the French connaître, connoting a certain kind of knowledge, knowledge you can-not just learn by rote or schooling, but which gives its possessor, the connoisseur, a certain aura. The verb connaître, as distinguished from the verb savoir, is most often used for knowing people, not knowing the facts about them but being familiar with them. When used about things, it suggests that one knows them in the way one knows people, suggests familiarity with and understanding through familiarity and interaction. Perhaps this sort of knowing, connoisseurship, is not so very far from the kind of empathic knowledge we tend to ascribe to psychoanalysts. Even when we have every reason (experience, for example) to know better, we tend to think that psychoanalysts have the power to read into the hearts of men and women and discern their secret wishes.

Although not an art critic, in 1984 I was invited to speak on psychoanalytic criticism and feminism at a symposium on art criticism. I decided to read the Freud quotation as my opening line, decided in fact, if only for a moment, to impersonate Freud, in order to calm my own sense of illegitimacy by grounding it in an identification with Freud, legitimating, as it were, my illegitimacy. In fact, every psychoanalytic critic writes in an identification with Freud, whether or not she chooses, as I did, to actually speak his words as if they were her own. To face a work of art, or any other sort of object, with the identity of psychoanalytic critic, is to offset one's sense of uncertainty, ignorance, and insufficient understanding with the authority of a body of knowledge, a history of connoisseurship that traces back to Freud's knowledge.

But when I decided to speak Freud's words as if my own, one of those words, only one, gave me pause. There was one word which made my acted-out identification uncomfortable, and that was the word "layman." Feminism has made me uncomfortable with those supposedly neuter and universal words which actually presume that the universal human being is male. For better or for worse, I can no longer not hear the masculine-sexed being in "layman," and it made my identification an obvious transvestism; the very device that was supposed to assure my legitimacy manifested illegitimacy. To my mind, when I spoke the word "layman" it would give away that these were not my words and spoil the impersonation.

My feminism not only spoiled my identification, it also focused my attention on the word "layman." I looked up the adjective "lay" in my dictionary, and found that the second definition—after its first meaning, in opposition to clergy—is "practicing psychoanalysis but not having a medical degree," which the dictionary follows by the phrase "lay analyst." Psychoanalysis has added its own meaning to "lay." I was thus speaking not only as a layman, or rather, more awkwardly, a laywoman, but as a lay analyst, one who practices psychoanalysis without degree, without medical authority. In general, the American psychoanalytic establishment is opposed to lay analysis, in favor of wedding psychoanalysis to the power and prestige of the American Medical Association and the intimidating authority of the Doctor's knowledge. But even though Freud was a physician, he came out in favor of lay analysis when the International Psychoanalytic

Association was debating the question. If Freud, although a doctor, explicitly writes art criticism as a layman he is perhaps calling into question a certain kind of authoritative and authorized knowledge, the sort exemplified by the AMA but present in any organized, legitimated professional identity. Feminists have been foremost among those challenging the intimidation and mystification of medical authority and even authoritative knowledge in general. My feminism makes me feel great solidarity with the idea of lay opinion and lay analysis, but at the same time it makes me take exception to the word "layman."

It might also be said, of course, that there is a great deal of pride behind Freud's assertion of his lay status. He is challenging established authority and clearly feels he has something to contribute to the understanding of art, something that the "connoisseurs" have not been able to come up with. If he unabashedly proclaims that his is a lay opinion, it is because he considers it an excellent opinion. He is not just any old layman; he prides himself on being a good lay. . . .

Now, everyone knows that psychoanalysis is about sex, that it makes latent sexuality manifest. Psychoanalytic art criticism reveals hidden sexual content—the infamous phallic symbols are the most blatant example. When I told a friend of mine that I was reading Freud's essay on Michelangelo's Moses, he quipped: "Oh, Moses jerking off into his beard!" Certainly more irreverent than Freud's style, but is this not what we would expect Freud to say about that sculpture, with the left hand on the crotch meeting the beard that hangs down into his lap? Would we not expect Freud to uncover some sexual subject matter latent in the sculpture?

Freud, however, does not talk about sex in his interpretation of the sculpture. Sex is nonetheless present in that short article, in unexpected places. For example, in the quotation with which I began, Freud says that "the subject matter of works of art has a *stronger attraction* for me than their formal and technical qualities, though to the artist their value lies . . . in these latter." Freud has a strong attraction to subject matter, and that attraction is in some way forbidden and embarrassing. It is what marks him as a lay rather than a connoisseur. Freud finds himself attracted not to what the artist values but to something else, like when you find yourself strongly attracted to a man's body, even when you are supposed to value him for his mind.

Our education, our culture, teaches us aesthetic values. The proper way to appreciate art, we learn, is to enjoy its formal and technical qualities. But something resists that civilizing education; something continues to respond to subject matter. That attraction becomes, for many of us who have a stake in our cultural sophistication, stupid, naïve, unmentionable. How can we admit our resemblance to the 12-year-old girl who simply loves all pictures of horses, regardless of their formal and technical qualities? Because the attraction to subject matter is in some way forbidden by civilization, that attraction is charged and ambivalent. The common expectation is that in looking at art psychoanalysis finds sexual subject matter, but I would say rather that the psychoanalytic critic finds subject matter sexual. Subject matter is sexual not because it is *about* some experience of sexuality but because we experience the relation to subject matter in art as forbidden, powerful, desiring, and embarrassing.

If the psychoanalytic critic is he who finds himself attracted to subject matter even though such an attraction is not really proper, then we are all, more or less, but nonetheless unavoidably, psychoanalytic critics. And if psychoanalytic criticism is worth talking about, it is not because it is a superior or even perhaps an appropriate way of looking at art, but because no one can help being to some extent, at least unwittingly, a psychoanalytic critic, no matter how illegitimate we think such a relation to be.

I am trying to suggest here that there are two different ways in which psychoanalytic criticism can be linked to sex. The more familiar and the least interesting concerns latent subject matter, but the criticism which interests me, which may in fact be one that barely exists at all, is concerned with something we might call the erotics of engagement, a sexuality that is not in the object, however deeply hidden, but in the encounter. In 1905, Freud wrote a short important book called *Three Essays on the Theory of Sexuality* where he called into question reigning notions of sexuality. One of the principal assumptions he challenged there was the idea that sexual attraction was immanent in the object. This idea is still powerfully present—particularly in the notion that sexiness resides in the woman's body. The viewer looks at provocative images of women and locates the attraction she feels in the represented object: the object, not the experience, is considered to be sexy.

These two alternative definitions of sexuality are deeply intricated in the slang expression "a good lay." When one says that someone is a good lay it implies that person has in him, intrinsically, what it takes to produce a highly satisfying sexual encounter regardless of whom the encounter is with. Yet as we all know, even though we cannot quite ever remember it enough, a good lay is something that happens between people and cannot simply be attributed to an individual's anatomical configuration or technical knowhow.

The psychoanalytic criticism which uncovers sexual content in the object without ever considering the dynamic of encounter with that object shares the mistaken assumption which Freud was challenging when he began his theory of sexuality. Which is not to say that he was immune to such an illusion. It seems to be one that inheres in desire—a wish to locate the arousal, the erotics, in some object rather than in an intersubjective dynamic. Most psychoanalytic criticism, like most sexuality, has been prey to this illusion. But the psychoanalytic criticism which interests me, which may not yet exist, would not be simply an interpretation of the object's sexuality but would be attuned to what in psychoanalysis is called transference, the dialectical situation in which that interpretation is produced.

In "The Moses of Michelangelo," Freud says something quite telling about his drive to interpret the work of art: "Some rationalistic, or perhaps analytic, turn of mind in me rebels against being moved by a thing without knowing why I am thus affected and what it is that affects me. This has brought me to recognize the apparently paradoxical fact that precisely some of the grandest and most overwhelming creations of art are still unsolved riddles to our understanding" (p. 211).

Something in Freud "rebels against being moved by a thing without knowing why." The critic experiences the work of art as "overwhelming," it moves him, has tremendous power over him, and he "rebels against" that power. "Rebels against" suggests a violent challenge to authority, overturning a power hierarchy.

Psychoanalysis, one might say, is the science that aims to understand why we are moved and what moves us precisely when we do not know why we are moved. It is the study of the unconscious causes of our actions and reactions as well as the study of what is most irrational in our sexuality. Freud sets out to understand that which moves us unbeknownst to us. As we can see here, this bold and enormous enterprise of understanding is the result of a rebellion. When he mentions that some of the grandest works of art are riddles, we might recall that he refers to the dream as a rebus—a kind of riddle—and that he sets out to make sense of dreams, to understand why we dream what we dream. Because he cannot tolerate being moved without understanding why, Freud invents psychoanalysis. The psychoanalytic critic is she who cannot bear to be moved without knowing why, cannot bear to be overwhelmed, and would counter the object's power with her understanding.

Yet Freud in this article manages to move quickly from a position of powerlessness to one of a certain superiority over the work of art. The rebellion, extremely successful, not only overturns a hierarchy but reverses it. Less than a page later, he writes: "But why should the artist's intention not be capable of being communicated and comprehended in words like any other fact of mental life? Perhaps where great works of art are concerned this would never be possible without the application of psychoanalysis. . . . It is possible, therefore, that a work of art of this kind *needs interpretation*" (p. 212, emphasis added). The "great work of art" is in some way inadequate, insufficient; it needs psychoanalysis. The great work of art cannot communicate its intentions without the psychoanalytic critic. Freud's rebellion succeeds, and he claims a triumph. No longer overwhelmed, the psychoanalytic critic now presumes a position of superiority.

The analogy between art appreciation and sexual relations gives this "rebellion" some interesting resonances. For Freud, sexual arousal is a state of tension, a disequilibrium in the psyche which generates a drive to reduce that tension. The subject is moved, overwhelmed, experiences something very powerful. He is not in control of the situation because he does not comprehend it. His impulse is to possess the disturbing object so as to reassert command of the situation. The mysterious, desirable woman becomes the poor thing who cannot get along without you. The solution to the experience of desire in which the subject feels he is out of control is to possess the object physically, or legally, or through understanding, and reduce it to dependency through a view of its inadequacy. You marry the enigmatic woman, make her your own, see her not as excruciatingly desirable but as dependent upon you for her place in the world. In Freud's story of the child, the infant first experiences the mother as overwhelming, as powerfully moving in a way that underlines the child's powerlessness, but that child, according to Freud, comes to "perceive" that the mother is "castrated," not powerful but lacking, like the work which is not in itself sufficient and needs the psychoanalytic interpreter to fill in its lack.

Which is not to say that we should give up the rebellion. Anti-intellectual gestures, those that would forgo understanding, are simply another ruse of power, another attempt at control. The appreciator who pretends she has no need to understand is denying what is overwhelming, frighteningly powerful, in what moves her. The naked aggression of Freud's phrase "rebels against" also constitutes a recognition of the force of the work of art: a force that no one can bear simply to submit to. The problem with psychoanalytic criticism is not Freud's rebellion, not the violence or the desire to possess, but that all too often we see only the aftermath of the rebellion, when the critic is instated in his superiority over the needy work of art. In this article Freud calls that moment "interpretation." This is the psychoanalytic critical gesture with which we are most familiar. But what has been forgotten, what has been covered over, is that the interpretive gesture with its assumption of superiority over a mute object is always based upon a prior rebellion against the object's power. It is the aggression and the desire in that rebellion which constitute the most authentic encounter with the object's power, where we experience not only the object's force but equally our own powerful drive to understand, to possess, that which moves us so intensely.

Psychoanalytic criticism necessarily repeats that revolt over and over again, but too often the revolt is covered over, the strong ambivalent attraction is unmentionable. Usually, by the time the critic speaks or writes the rebellion has "succeeded" and the object been reduced to the position of powerlessness where it needs the critic. When the rebellion has succeeded, everything has been lost. The critic has become a connoisseur; he knows what the work of art is about, and once a connoisseur, he is no longer quite so good a lay.

Earlier, through my own identification, I connected Freud's assertion that he is not a connoisseur with a certain legitimation of illegitimacy. When Freud does introduce a connoisseur into his account, it is a connoisseur who challenged the legitimacy, the "name-of-the-father," of various works of art. Freud begins this text by proclaiming "I am no connoisseur in art." The only other appearance of the word "connoisseur" occurs in the opening sentence of the second section of the article, the central section of the piece. In the first section, Freud carefully reviews other people's opinions of the *Moses*, but in the second section he launches into his own analysis. That second section opens thus: "Long before I had any opportunity of hearing about psychoanalysis, I learnt that a Russian art-connoisseur, Ivan Lermolieff, had caused a revolution in the art galleries of Europe by questioning the authorship of many pictures, showing how to distinguish copies from originals with certainty, and constructing hypothetical artists for those works of art whose former authorship had been discredited" (p. 222). Freud is no connoisseur; Lermolieff is. Yet Freud introduces Lermolieff into this essay so as to comment that the art connoisseur's "method of inquiry is closely related to the technique of psychoanalysis." Having established a kinship with the connoisseur, Freud can proceed to analyze the sculpture.

Freud, as we have seen, "rebels against being moved by a thing without knowing why"; his analysis of art works is motivated by a rebellion. Lermolieff "caused a revolution in the art galleries of Europe." Freud's description of Lermolieff's effect on the authorizing institutions of art resonates with his description of his own attitude in considering a work of art: both descriptions connote violent challenges to the legitimacy of authority. Now, of course, these two revolts are completely different, yet in both cases might we not say that a rebellion has broken out in the art gallery?

It may have struck the reader as odd that Freud introduces Lermolieff with the phrase, "long before I had any opportunity of hearing about psychoanalysis." What does it mean for the founder of psychoanalysis to talk about an "opportunity of hearing about psychoanalysis"? A footnote to the text tells us that Lermolieff's "first essays were published in German between 1874 and 1876." Freud did not invent psychoanalysis until the 1890s. Nonetheless Freud is, in fact, the only person who cannot properly say he heard of psychoanalysis, since that implies that it existed before he learned about it. The explanation for this odd phrase is that in this article Freud is not writing as himself, the father of psychoanalysis, but is writing under an assumed identity, writing as somebody else, somebody who could have heard of psychoanalysis.

This article was originally published anonymously in *Imago*, an official psychoanalytic journal, in 1914, where it was prefaced by the following editorial note: "Although this paper does not, strictly speaking, conform to the conditions under which contributions are accepted for publication in this journal, the editors have decided to print it, since the author, who is personally known to them, belongs to psychoanalytical circles, and since his mode of thought has in point of fact a certain resemblance to the methodology of psychoanalysis" (p. 211n).

This article, one of the first pieces of psychoanalytic art criticism ever written, and which therefore in some way serves to define the genre, is shadowed by an insistent suggestion of illegitimacy. The author is no connoisseur in art. The article "does not conform to the conditions under which contributions are accepted for publication in this journal." The author does not even present himself as Freud, the legitimate connoisseur of psychoanalysis, but as an anonymous layman. The illegitimacy of the author's position is perhaps even more likely to alienate the reader because the latter is told that the article was published only because the author was "personally known to the editors."

As puzzling as Freud's adoption of anonymity might be, what is perhaps most odd to read is that "his mode of thought has in point of fact a certain resemblance to the methodology of psychoanalysis." "A certain resemblance" reads as uncanny understatement when we know the author is in fact Freud, whose mode of thought might be said to *be* the methodology of psychoanalysis. But this editorial footnote becomes otherwise suggestive when brought into conjunction with the later statement about Lermolieff, whose "method of inquiry is closely related to the technique of psychoanalysis."

"The Moses of Michelangelo" is not a proper psychoanalytic article, but it can be published because of "a certain resemblance." The psychoanalytic critic is no connoisseur of art, but what he has to say may be worthwhile because there is a close relation between psychoanalysis and the method of the great art connoisseur. A certain legitimacy by association pervades this article, which is neither legitimately psychoanalytic nor art criticism, but resembles both. At the same time that association is accompanied by an oddly militant illegitimacy and a puzzling question about authorship. The art connoisseur caused a revolution by questioning authorship. The founder of psychoanalytic art criticism disguises his authorship, rendering it questionable, as if there were some profound intrication between psychoanalytic art criticism and a radical question about legitimate author-ity.

As we have seen, Freud introduces the connoisseur thus: "Long before I had an opportunity of hearing about psychoanalysis, I learnt that a Russian art-connoisseur, Ivan Lermolieff, had caused a revolution in the art galleries of Europe by questioning the authorship of many pictures." Freud then describes Lermolieff's method, after which he tells us: "I was then greatly interested to learn that the Russian pseudonym concealed the identity of an Italian physician called Morelli who died in 1891 with the rank of Senator of the Kingdom of Italy." Freud inscribes his account of the connoisseur in narrative sequence which preserves for the reader a surprise. First we are told of the Russian named Ivan Lermolieff and are, at that time, given no reason to be suspicious of his identity. Then we are surprised, or at least "greatly interested to learn" that the Russian is actually an Italian named Morelli.

Freud wrote his piece of art criticism as an anonymous layman, concealing his identity as physician and connoisseur of the psyche. Morelli, who is also a physician, likewise disguises his identity, publishing his essays on art not anonymously but under a pseudonym. Having concealed his identity (and his country of origin), he proceeded to call into question the identity of the authors of various works of art. Morelli's assumed identity also disguises his profession of physician and protects the man who will become a senator, a man who will have political power. That powerful man is thus not involved in the "revolution in the art galleries."

Why did Morelli hide his identity as a physician in order to be an art connoisseur? Why did Freud conceal his identity in order to write art criticism? I do not pretend to have the answers to these questions, but do want to suggest that these two puzzles seem to be related. Did Freud, for example, disguise his identity out of identification with the art connoisseur? In any case, I would suggest that we have here a congruence of questionable identities, identifications, concealed authorships, and blatant illegitimacy right at the origin of psychoanalytic art criticism, which serves both to call into question, from the beginning, any effort at a psychoanalytic interpretation of a work of art, and at the same time to legitimate such questionable effort.

This is probably psychoanalytic criticism at its best, this suspect tradition in which an exacerbated illegitimacy militantly proclaims itself. It is in this tradition that the critic feels her identity radically questionable; that very doubt throws her into an identification with some knowledge, some *connaissance* of the frightening erotic force of art, of the desire for and the resistance to meaning. When the identity gels and forgets its dubious founding identification, its imposture, its originary pseudonym, then the psychoanalytic critic who is now secure in her knowledge becomes truly illegitimate, for knowledge that has lost the truth of its roots in desire and aggression is in its very objectivity a lie.

If the psychoanalytic art critic cannot help but write, think, perceive in an identification with Freud, let it not be an identification with Freud's knowledge, with Freud's connoisseurship, with the position that Lacan terms "the subject presumed to know." Lacan criticizes "the subject presumed to know" as the patient's illusory attribution of knowledge to the analyst as an effect of transference. Lacan warns analysts not to fall prey themselves to this illusion, not to believe they are in fact "the subject presumed to know." "The subject presumed to know" would be powerfully superior to the work of art, would have the ability to divine and analyze that which the art work is not able to express.

Let the critic's identification with Freud be rather with Freud's lay status, with his questionable identity, and with his own desiring, symptomatic identification with the Russian art connoisseur who turned out to be an Italian physician. If we willfully identify with Freud in order to triumph in our rebellion against the art work's power, let us remember in our triumph that we are identifying not with legitimate authority but with another rebel, another layman, who felt his own authority shaky, who in his own rebellion felt the need to ally himself with yet another rebel whose connoisseurship might be certain but whose authority is rendered dubious by his assumption of an alias. If there is a rebellion here, an aggression against authority, there is also a crime. I do not presume to know what the crime is, but it has left its trace in this trail of concealed identities. What is so shameful about psychoanalytic art criticism that it must be perpetrated under an assumed identity?

Right after Freud says "I was then greatly interested to learn that the Russian pseudonym concealed the identity of an Italian physician called Morelli," he remarks: "It seems to me that his method of inquiry is closely related to the technique of psychoanalysis." That is, right after Freud discloses the art connoisseur's disguise, he asserts the close kinship between Lermolieff's method and psychoanalysis' (that is, Freud's) technique, which he then proceeds to characterize: "It, too, is accustomed to divine secret and concealed things from unconsidered and unnoticed details, from the rubbish-heap, as it were, of our observations." The technique of psychoanalysis, which it shares with Morelli's method, is to "divine secret and concealed things." Like the "concealed identity of an Italian physician," perhaps. Yet what I am suggesting here is not only that psychoanalysis' technique is involved with uncovering what is secret, but that it is also, at least in its approach to art, involved with concealing, for example, disguising Freud's identity. Both Lermolieff and Freud divine secret and concealed things; but both Morelli and Freud also conceal things.

The technique of connoisseurship, whether of art or of the psyche, involves considering and noticing details which are normally unconsidered and unnoticed, retrieving them from the "rubbish-heap." This is, then, the great tradition of psychoanalytic criticism, the attention to the "insignificant" detail, to what is not "worthy of notice," to trash. There are two things most everybody knows about psychoanalysis: the phallic symbol and the Freudian slip. The latter corresponds to the technique Freud is outlining here. The Freudian slip is some small oddity at the margins of expression that ought to go unnoticed, but which Freud retrieved from the "rubbish-heap" by insisting that it carried meaning. While the phallic symbol represents the worst, most reductive, oppressive sort of knowing psychoanalytic interpretation, the Freudian slip must always be interpreted in context and is not allied to any eternal, archetypal meanings.

The phallic symbol might itself symbolize a certain dominant, reductive form of sexuality—phallocentrism. Freud theorized that children went through a phallic phase of sexuality, a period in which they recognized only the phallic organ and did not know anything about the vagina.[2] That phase may be used to symbolize phallocentrism, a refusal to recognize the force, or the sexuality, of anything outside one's own penetrating desire. The object, in the phallic phase, is simply castrated, lacking. But the "rubbish-heap," the appropriate place for the unconsidered detail, reminds us of another infantile sexual notion: the cloaca. Freud says that because children (in the phallic phase) do not know about, do not notice, the vagina, they imagine a "cloaca" (that is, a sewer) which is both the anus and where babies come from.[3] Thus the overwhelming force of the object (the mother, for example) is relegated to a cloaca, which is beneath our consideration or notice. Female sexuality, or rather the erotic force and power of the object, is not recognized but rather consigned to the cloaca.

Now I am not trying to assert that the "rubbish-heap" is the vagina. That sort of interpretation, which knows where sexuality is located, is always a denial by the knowing subject of her own erotic and aggressive engagement. After all, one always presumes that there is some female equivalent to the phallic symbol, circles, holes, containers or some such. Yet Freud discovered a sexuality that is not genital, or rather is not where we would have it be, is not confined to its place, just as trash should be confined to the "rubbish-heap" and not lifted out for consideration.

Freud says that Lermolieff (aka Morelli) "insist[ed] that attention should be diverted from the general impression and main features of a picture, and he laid stress on the significance of minor details, of things like the drawing of finger-nails . . . and such unconsidered trifles" (p. 222). Freud's account of Lermolieff's technique, the consideration of normally unconsidered fingernails, finds an interesting echo in a recent piece of art criticism. In *The Sexuality of Christ in Renaissance Art and in Modern Oblivion*, Leo Steinberg writes: "We have to consider that Renaissance artists, committed for the first time since the birth of Christianity to naturalistic modes of representation, were the only group within Christendom whose métier required them to plot every inch of Christ's body. They asked intimate questions that do not well translate into words, at least not without disrespect; whether, for instance, Christ clipped his nails short, or let them grow past the fingertips. The irreverent triviality of such inquisition verges on blasphemy."[4]

Steinberg's wonderful book concerns the representation of Christ's genitals in Renaissance art, a representation that has been covered over, either literally or by inattention and denial in modern times. Yet what Steinberg makes clear is that we would be gravely mistaken if we understood Christ's penis to be in any simple way a phallic symbol. Christ's penis is precisely not a symbol of sexuality. However, something else, not explicitly sexual but forbidden, resurfaces in Steinberg's account, not in the genitals, where we would expect forbidden sexuality, but somewhere else, in the fingernails, the same anatomical extremities that were important for Lermolieff's revolutionary technique.

To consider Christ's fingernails is to indulge in "irreverent triviality" which "verges on blasphemy." Such attention to the trivial, to the insignificant parts of the body, to what Steinberg calls "intimate questions" certainly takes on, in Steinberg's language, an air of forbidden, somewhat culpable intimacy. Yet that disrespect, verging on sin, is not exactly immanent in the paintings but happens when we "translate" the artists' intimate questions "into words."

What then is the art critic but he who "translates such intimate questions into words"? That was precisely how Freud saw the task of the psychoanalytic art critic: "But why should the artist's intention not be capable of being *communicated* and comprehended *in words* like any other fact of mental life? Perhaps where great works of art are concerned this would never be possible without the application of psychoanalysis" (p. 212, emphasis added). This translation into words is what Freud calls "interpretation." The work of art needs the psychoanalytic critic so that it can be translated into words. But that translation is precisely what, in Steinberg's view, runs the risk of being disrespectful, irreverent, sinfully intimate. Perhaps this is one of the crimes of the psychoanalytic critic: blasphemy. Blasphemy, not only in a Christian context but in a larger context where it means putting into words something terribly powerful that is demeaned and reduced by being spoken.

Now, let me be clear, I am not arguing for a respectful silence in face of the ineffable nature of art. I am, in fact, not at all opposed to irreverence, disrespect, even blasphemy. But I am trying to point in the direction of what may be an original sin of psychoanalytic criticism, which may have some connection to why the psychoanalytic art critic works under an alias.

Leo Steinberg is not performing psychoanalytic criticism, not at least as we usually think of it. He is not identifying with Freud's knowledge. At the end of the work he specifically says, "It will not have escaped the reader that my discussion has left out of account all psychological considerations" (p. 107). He is in fact writing against the broad tradition called "psychoanalytic," one that presumes to see sexual themes in the work of art. That tradition not only includes the interpreters of Christ's penis as phallic symbol but all those who would cover over that same penis, furious to deny Christ's sexuality because they presume to know what that penis means. Yet in another sense Steinberg's method of inquiry resembles the technique of psychoanalysis (Freud, Lermolieff). He is giving consideration to that which has been deemed unworthy of consideration. He is putting into words "intimate questions," giving attention not to the phallic symbol but to "the rubbish-heap of our observations."

The point is not to claim Steinberg as a psychoanalytic critic, but to argue that the best psychoanalysis has to offer art is attention, erotic and forceful, not to the genitals (except where they have been overlooked, denied, made marginal) but to something as blasphemous as the fingernails. Not to where we presume sexuality to be, but to peripheral, insignificant trivia where it might appear in a way that surprises, embarrasses, and overwhelms the observer. For the potential critic—and everyone who looks at a work of art is potentially a critic—the richest legacy of Freud is not the psychosexual catalogue from which the interpreter supplies meaning to the work of art. Freud's best legacy is his record of the struggle to understand what moves him, a struggle which attests to the critic's violent desire and the object's power, a struggle in which the subject is impelled by a drive that cannot afford to be respectful since the questions raised are disturbingly intimate.

Fingernails

The displacement from the genitals to the fingernails certainly must also refer to a personal action whose meaning escapes me. In graduate school I developed a characteristic, unconscious gesture: I frequently, unwittingly dig my fingernails into the fleshy portion of my thumb. I only know of this because others have pointed it out to me. It is mildly painful and developed shortly after I began to grow my fingernails and paint them, usually blood red, during a semester in Paris in 1974, a semester between my course work and work on my dissertation, a semester I spent reading Lacan's *Ecrits* from cover to cover.

Close Encounters

The preceding essay and the one that follows were originally talks rather than written papers. They took shape in the presence of an audience rather than when I was alone at my desk. They were also my first attempt at speaking to and then writing for a nonacademic audience. Literally constituted in interlocution with an addressee who was not presumed to share my identity, they are about a certain encounter with the other.

I spoke much like I teach, using only a few notes, those mainly quotations from the texts I am studying. The voice is easier, more casual, more open. The audience's response turned me on, juiced me up to think. Most of what I said I had not thought of before I started speaking.

Both essays are on art; both focus not on the individual body but on the sexual relation. This conjunction surely has something to do with the fact that my boyfriend is an artist. But beyond that, art more generally represents an other realm, one I do not identify with (as I have with France or psychoanalysis). For me, to think about art is to encounter an other, a beautiful but unsettling one, over whom I do not have easy mastery.

The Prick of the Object

This paper was delivered in a series sponsored by the School of the Art Institute of Chicago entitled "Sexuality in Art and the Media." I began by talking about the word "in" in the series title. That word "in" implies a relationship of container and contained, a relationship in which sexuality is something interior to—contained within—art or the media, something that is represented. It implies that sexuality is something that is within the work of art. Is that how we want to think about the relation between sexuality and art? Do we want to think about it as something that is represented in art, as something whose image we see in a work of art, or do we want to think about it as somewhere else?

In *The Pleasure of the Text*, in a chapter called "Representation," Roland Barthes writes: "Certainly, it happens very often that representation takes as its object of imitation desire itself; but then, this desire never leaves the frame, the picture [his word is *tableau*, which could also mean scene]; it circulates among the characters; if there is an addressee, this addressee remains interior to the fiction. (. . . Representation is just that: when nothing comes out, when nothing leaps out of the frame: of the picture [or scene], the book, the screen)."[5] Barthes has just asserted that the erotic relation to the text, the pleasure *of* the text, is different from representation, but he, of course,

SEXUALITY IN ART & THE MEDIA

THE SCHOOL OF THE ART INSTITUTE OF CHICAGO, OCTOBER 1-NOVEMBER 24, 1984

Harry Bowers, "Black and White #6"

recognizes that pleasure is often represented. It is noteworthy that this is one of the few places in *The Pleasure of the Text* where Barthes mentions other media besides writing. His formulation implies that the relation of representation works the same for the book, the screen, and the picture. Barthes defines representation as a case in which something remains totally inside.

Barthes is writing *against* representation, which for him is a means of containing and coopting desire, pleasure, sexuality. He defines it as a situation in which nothing comes out, where everything remains inside, where nothing leaps out of the frame. Sex is, of course, the commonest theme of representational art and literature, but it is all contained within. The desire circulates, but it circulates among the characters; it does not come out. It is addressed from one character to another; it is not some relation that might include the artist, that might include the viewer.

I would like to consider Barthes's formulation of an erotics *of* the text rather than *in* the text as that idea shows up in his book on photography, *Camera Lucida*,[6] published seven years after *The Pleasure of the Text*. In that book he defines two elements of the photograph. The first, the *studium*, is what we might call the theme or the subject of the picture, what the photographer is trying to say, but it also has to do with ideas and general culture. According to Barthes, the *studium* can be interesting, significant, and important, but a picture that has only a *studium* is like representation: everything is enclosed within the field of the picture, and nothing comes out. Then there is a "second element" that "comes and breaks up the *studium*" (p. 48). If you think of the *studium* as a kind of enclosure, breaking it up suggests breaking something open, allowing seepage. "This time," he continues, "it's not me who goes after it (as I invest with my sovereign consciousness the field of the *studium*), it's it that goes off from the scene, like an arrow, and comes and pierces me." When Barthes tries to define the other element of the photograph, he refers to something that goes off from the scene, precisely something which is not within representation, not within the frame, within the scene. Barthes refers to this element in striking terms: "it goes off from the scene, like an arrow, and comes and *pierces me*" (emphasis added).

There is a lot of work in film theory on voyeurism—numerous analyses that describe how the gaze is an aggression upon that which is seen.[7] Barthes's consideration of photography does not concur with the notion that the photograph as object of the gaze is passive while the viewer is in an active, even aggressive, relationship to it. In this relationship there is a passive and an aggressive term which are often lined up as female and male, as so often we line up aggressive with male, passive with female. In Barthes something quite different *sometimes* happens, but not all the time. He says, in fact, that a picture which is all *studium* is just a passive object: inert, immobile, lying there. But when there is that second element, the element that breaks up the *studium*, something happens which is quite the opposite of the relationship which occasions complaints about the male gaze and the female object of the gaze. Something happens: the second element goes off from the scene like an arrow and comes and pierces the viewer. There is a reversal: something in the photograph is aggressive and penetrates the viewer.

Barthes has not yet named the second element. He continues: "A word exists in Latin to designate that wound, that prick, that mark made by a pointed instrument . . . I will thus call it *punctum* . . . The *punctum* of a photo, it's that accident which, in it, stings me." He is talking about something that hurts him: wounds, stings, pierces. He mostly uses the Latin word to name it, but when he wants to define the Latin word, the French equivalent he gives it is *piqûre*, which I am amused to find can be translated as "prick." Not, of course, our vulgar word for the male genital, but the word for something that pierces, something that wounds.

Not that it is original to see the viewer as passive. Susan Sontag in her book *On Photography* writes: "One is vulnerable to disturbing events in the form of photographic images in a way that one is not to the real thing. That vulnerability is part of the distinctive passivity of someone who is a spectator twice over, a spectator of events already shaped, first by the participants and second by the image maker."[8] What interests me is the particular kind of passivity that Barthes is talking about. The piercing arrow brings us close to a tradition of a certain mystic discourse in which otherness enters you in some way that is ecstatic. Ecstasy etymologically derives from the Greek *ekstasis*, from *ex-*, "out," plus *histanai*, "to place." Thus, it means something like "placed out." Ecstasy is when you are no longer within your own frame: some sort of going outside takes place. In Barthes's *The Pleasure of the Text*, he talks about the most intense form of pleasure, which he calls *jouissance*, which can be translated as "ecstasy." (Richard Miller translates it as "bliss.") The *punctum* which is not in all photography but is in his favorite photographs, the ones that move him, produces something like a *jouissance*, an ecstasy.

In *Camera Lucida*, the imagery used to describe this ecstasy carries connotations of pain. The arrow recalls Cupid's arrow, a tradition in which love comes from the outside and against your will, attacks you, pierces you, changes you, takes you outside yourself, puts you in a state of passivity that (at least in the European tradition) is seen as a violation of the body, a penetration of the self, something dangerous and threatening and yet at the same time terribly pleasurable, something wonderful.

Later in the book, Barthes once again explains how the *punctum* works, this time by means of a contrast between cinema and photography: "The cinema has a power which at first glance photography has not: the screen (Bazin noted) is not a frame, but a mask; the character who leaves it continues to live" (p. 90). Once again we encounter the notion of something that goes outside the frame, something that is not still, immobile within the frame but that leaves it and continues to live. Barthes continues: " 'A blind field' [Bazin's term] incessantly doubles the partial vision." The idea here is that in photography everything is contained within the photograph, whereas in cinema things continue to live outside the field of vision; and that continuity which we cannot see, Bazin calls the "blind field." Barthes continues: "Now, before thousands of photos, including those that possess a good *studium*, I don't sense any blind field: everything that happens within the frame dies absolutely, once outside that frame." This is Barthes's definition of the bad photograph: it may have a good *studium*, good intentions, good ideas, be well-made, but everything is within the frame and does not continue to live outside the frame. He is talking about a kind of violence; he uses the word "dies." He is not talking about death within the frame, or about the representation of violence; he is using violent imagery for something representation does. He is talking about what happens when a photograph has a good *studium* but no *punctum*. As soon as there is a *punctum*, however, a "blind field" is created or divined. A *punctum* thus does the same thing that cinema does. For my purposes here, it does not matter whether this is how cinema works. What interests me is this contrast between the photograph where everything is contained within the frame and the photograph where things continue to happen outside the frame.

Barthes cites a photograph by James Van der Zee of a black family of three, in which the *punctum* is a necklace one of the women is wearing. "Because of her round necklace, the Negress in her Sunday best has, for me, an entire life outside her portrait." The *punctum*, by breaking open the *studium*, breaks open a sterile impermeable enclosure and allows what Barthes calls "life" to pass through, to permeate the frame.

What Barthes calls "life" has something to do with a kind of eroticism that he valorizes in this book. He has a strong sense of good and bad in eroticism. At various points in *Camera Lucida*, as well as in *The Pleasure of the Text*, he contrasts erotica and pornography to the detriment of the latter. What Barthes valorizes has something to do with the "life" that passes outside the frame. Continuing to talk about this "blind field," he comes to talk specifically about eroticism: "The presence of this blind field is, I believe, what distinguishes the erotic photo from the pornographic photo." For Barthes, pornography is pure *studium* whereas the erotic occurs when there is a *punctum*. "Pornography ordinarily represents the sex-organ, it makes it into an immobile object (a fetish), to which we burn incense, like a god that doesn't leave its niche" (pp. 91–93). This kind of erotic relationship where the sex organ is represented within the frame is sexuality *in* art, and it is described negatively by being likened to religion, by being represented as a god that does not leave its niche, to which we burn incense (in this context, a quite provocative image). For Barthes, pornography is a self-enclosed image: it is sexuality contained, sexuality that does not leave its frame. The viewer can worship it in a kind of masturbatory way but can neither touch it nor be touched by it.

He continues: "For me, no *punctum* in the pornographic image; at most it amuses me (and still, boredom comes fast). The erotic photo, on the contrary (it's its very condition) does not make the sex-organ a central object; it can very well not show it; it draws the spectator out of its frame." That last phrase is ambiguous in French. It could also read: it draws the spectator out of *his* frame. The word would be the same in French. There is a double meaning here: the sense of *two* things coming out of their enclosures. (I do not agree that pornography always makes the sex organ a central object nor that in erotic photography the sex organ is never a central object. I think that is a false distinction as it is based upon what goes on within the frame. I am much more interested in the distinction between pornography as "a god that doesn't leave its niche" and erotica as "drawing the spectator out of the frame").

Barthes continues: "and it's in this way that this photo, I animate it and it animates me." Because of the *punctum*, because the erotic photo draws the spectator out of its frame, out of his frame, out of her frame (all of which are perfectly legitimate translations of Barthes's French), "I animate it and it animates me." Earlier Barthes seemed to define the spectator as passive, as, indeed, a victim of aggression, and yet now his definition seems a lot more complicated, a complex of activity and passivity. There is some sort of reciprocal activity occurring where one is both the subject and the object of the verb "animate," a verb that echoes this notion of life that Barthes talks about. Behind all this is the contrast between that which dies outside the frame and that which continues to live outside the frame, animation as opposed to the inanimate. The erotic photograph is different finally not because of what occurs inside the photograph, not what is represented, but precisely because something occurs between the photograph and the viewer: a relation of reciprocity, if one can imagine a reciprocal relation with a photograph, a relation of mutual animation.

A few pages earlier Barthes writes that the *punctum* is "what I add to the photo and which nonetheless is there already" (p. 89). "What I add to the photo" implies a highly active viewer who puts something there, who is in some way creating the photograph. However, what he is creating is something that is already there, something that is *in* the photograph. In the late sixties, Barthes's great move in literary criticism was his promotion of the notion of active reading as opposed to passive consumption. He called for a kind of reading in which the reader actively contributes to the text, in a sense, writes the text.[9] Yet this is, finally, a subtle activity. He is not talking literally about writing; there is an everyday meaning to writing, and that is not the kind of reading he means.

In relation to photography this means adding to the photograph something which is already there. This suggests a contact we might call "active receptivity," an active viewing in which one contributes to seeing something that is really out there. This "active receptivity" is what he is trying to gesture toward, or at least what I am trying to gesture toward. After all, my reading of his book may be all too actively adding things which I only hope are already there. I would have it that he gestures toward some sort of contact with alterity, some sort of contact with something that is out there in the world already, that is not simply a projection, but that we nevertheless do not just take in as purely passive consumers. That is how I understand the notion of: "I animate it and it animates me."

I am trying to read *Camera Lucida* by means of an analogy between viewing a photograph and some sort of erotic relation to an "other." I am (or he is) trying to think around a way to touch, to contact, to encounter the real of the other. When Barthes talks about the sting and the wound and the arrow that pierces me, he is pointing to a tradition of mysticism. In European thought, mysticism is the great tradition of openness to alterity, of receptivity to being overwhelmed by otherness. But there is something else here beyond a purely passive relation. There is also the relation of the "I animate it and it animates me," the relation of what I add to the photograph which is nonetheless *already* there. In sex the subject must desire, must fantasize, must imagine. Things must come from the mind and cause one to view the other as the object of desire. Yet, at the same time, there is also a wish to encounter the other as something real, out there, beyond one's fantasies, not the god in the niche to whom we burn incense, not the pornographic image, but a relation to some real other. This wish is at play in the notion of the *punctum*: something that leads us outside the frame.

The analogy interests me not simply because I am interested in sex, not simply because sex is the topic of this series, but because it seems a suggestive way to talk about photography. Photography has been said to be a strange hybrid of nature and art or art and the real. Photography is art like sex is fantasy, desire, imagination. It is one's own ideas projected onto the world, shaping and distorting the world, framing the world and making it into an object of art or an object of desire. Photography is also something else. Besides being art, it seems to have some quite special relation to the real.

Photography interests Barthes because of this special relation. He says that the photograph necessarily always takes its referent with it, takes the thing in the world that it refers to with it. Photography is at once representation and yet also some sort of direct registration of the real. According to Barthes: "The photo is literally an emanation of the referent. From a real body, that was there, rays went out that came to touch me, I who am here . . . the light, although impalpable, is certainly here a carnal medium, a skin that I share with him or her who was photographed" (pp. 126–27). For Barthes the photograph is magical because what gets registered on the film actually comes from the real object. I am not sure that this is exactly how photography works, that we are actually looking at a record, or that the object really comes and touches us. Barthes's sense of photography is both very mystical and very naïve.

In the passage just quoted, Barthes uses a number of metaphors related to the body: the skin, touch, the carnal. It seems to be that this body imagery bespeaks his attempt to think some relation to the real, to the body that is really out there, the referent, if you like, to some thing that touches him. He is trying to think some relation to the referent through a notion of erotic contact; hence the difference between the body that touches me and that god in its niche to whom I burn incense without any real contact. There is "a real body," the rays, the light which is a skin that touches me. Yet, this still implies the passivity of the spectator and the activity of either the photograph or the photographic object, its referent. But then there is the last part of the sentence, "the light, a skin that I share with him or her who was photographed." The image of sharing a skin is extraordinary. If you say something touches you, there is a subject and an object of that verb, which has an active and a passive meaning. But if you are sharing a skin, there is another relation.

At the end of the sentence Barthes writes that he shares the skin "with him or her who was photographed." That locution might not sound too unusual to us because nowadays we are all pretty careful to say "he or she," or that sort of thing. But Roland Barthes is an author who never talks about sexual difference, who never sexually differentiates his erotic objects when he describes them. To my knowledge, this is the only place in his work where he sexually differentiates: he actually uses two pronouns, a masculine and a feminine pronoun. The awkwardness of "him or her," of the double pronoun, is not only a recognition of sexual difference, but, I think, also signals an attempt to talk about the real.

I am pursuing the idea of a relation between sexuality and the medium of photography, which is not sexuality *in* photography, but is something like the sexuality *of* photography. In August 1984 I heard Leslie Bellavance, a Milwaukee artist and teacher, make a similar point: "Erotica and photography have what seem to be parallel paradoxes. The erotic paradox is the meeting point of dependence and independence. The photographic paradox is the meeting point of nature and art." Bellavance's paradoxes resemble Barthes's statement that the *punctum* is what I add that is already there. The erotic paradox is this strange combination of dependence and independence. In order to be erotic, the object must depend on the viewer, on the aroused one, on our fantasies, our imagination, our constructs, our framing, and yet, the object must also remain independent, still real, still other. Eroticism itself is a relation to something that is very much part of our imagination, our projection, our desires. Our eroticism is what is most narcissistic or most imperialistic in our relation to the world, and yet, there is also some relation between our desires and something that is really out there, that is independent of our fantasies.

Bellavance defines the photographic paradox as the meeting point of nature and art. Nature is a word we have used for a long time to talk about what is out there, outside culture, outside our constructions, our frames, outside our art. In *On Photography*, Sontag writes that photographs "trade simultaneously on the prestige of art and the magic of the real. They are clouds of fantasy and pellets of information" (p. 69). I would like to provoke you to think toward a relation between sexuality and photography, a relation between two "paradoxes," two contradictory projects, two perhaps impossible projects, in which neither one is contained within the other, a relation of the "of" or the "and," rather than of the "in." I do not want to talk about the representation of sexuality *in* photography. Nor do I want to reduce photography to a manifestation of sexuality. I would rather attempt to think about what it is in the photographic project which uncannily resembles the paradox of sexuality.

In his explanation of the *punctum*, Barthes says: "Certain details could 'sting' me. If they don't, it's undoubtedly because they were put there intentionally by the photographer. . . . the detail that interests me is not, or at least not rigorously, intentional, and probably it must not be; it finds itself in the field of the thing photographed like a supplement at once inevitable and obliging; it does not necessarily attest to the photographer's art" (pp. 79–80).

A lot of photographers would resent that statement, and they would not be wrong. Barthes is interested in that element in the photograph which he does not think the photographer intended. He actually waffles about it; the issue seems pretty complicated for him. He says, "the detail that interests me is not," which sounds like a decisive, negative assertion, but then he adds, "at least not rigorously, intentional, and probably it must not be." Something about the question of the intentionality behind the interesting detail seems to trouble him. The "probably" is in marked contrast to the "undoubtedly" in the preceding sentence. He cannot be certain the detail that pricks him is not intended. He would prefer it not be intended. He would prefer to be stung by the thing rather than the photographer's will. Whatever his fantasies of autonomy, what "stings" him is the "not necessarily" intended detail, the detail where it cannot be "undoubtedly" determined whether or not it was intended. He would like to transform that uncertainty into an indubitable encounter with the unintended, but he cannot "rigorously" do so.

Early in *Camera Lucida*, Barthes states that there are three ways to talk about photography: from the point of view of the photographer, from the point of view of the person photographed, and from the point of view of the viewer. He then says that he will not talk about it from the point of view of the photographer because he is not a photographer. This is consistent with Barthes's larger project, at this stage of his career, that is, the project of a subjective science, a science in which he speaks from his own subjective experience. It stands in marked contrast with Sontag's book *On Photography* in which, although not a photographer either, she writes about photography from her notion of the photographer's point of view.

Sontag may be hard on photographers, constantly talking about their appropriative desire, but Barthes's relation to the photographer is ultimately more subtly aggressive. He is saying: I am interested in *my* relation to the photograph; I am not interested in your relation to the photograph. That is not all: he is most interested in the things that he thinks he adds to the photograph. It may be "already there," but if the photographer did not intend to put it there, it *therefore* constitutes some relation to the real. The erotic relation to the photograph, like so many other erotic relations, may produce a certain kind of rivalry. Thus, Barthes lays claims to the most erotic place in the photograph, the *punctum*. He proclaims: it is mine, it is not the photographer's. I put it there. It is there already, but that is the erotic paradox: what I put there is already there. This could be the less seemly side of Barthes's erotic relation to the photograph, or even the less seemly side of every viewer's relation to the photograph. This is the moment in eroticism when we say: Yes, yes, I am open to otherness; I want to encounter you, but I do not want you to encounter anyone else! This is my relation to you!

As unseemly as it may be, when viewed from this jealous angle, I want to examine further the notion of the questionable intentionality of the *punctum*. The poster for this series, "Sexuality in Art and the Media," is a photograph by Harry Bowers, *Black and White #6*. To discuss its *studium*, it is a photograph of a naked man and a clothed woman, in postures that quote from and reverse Manet's *Déjeuner sur l'herbe*. But for me, finally, the object of greatest fascination, the point which takes me outside the frame and whose intentionality remains uncertain, is neither the man's naked body nor the woman's clothed body. Both these bodies, however attractive, are within the frame of representation. The object that most draws out my imagination is the wedding ring on the man's finger. I find myself wondering whether the photographer wanted it there, or did not realize it was there, or was indifferent. What it does to me bears out Barthes's notion of something that seems to have a "blind field" and lives outside the frame. Because of it, this naked man—coded there as an object for my desire, as an object of my gaze—seems to have a (sexual) life and history outside the frame. Because of it, he is not just an object to whom I burn my incense, but he is also a "real person."

In the passage quoted before in which Barthes defines what happens in the erotic photo, he continues: "The *punctum* is thus a sort of subtle outside-the-field, as if the image flung desire beyond what it offered to view: not only toward 'the rest' of the nudity, not only toward the fantasy of a practice, but toward the absolute excellence of a being, body and soul mingled" (p. 93). I am embarrassed by the phrase "absolute excellence of a being, body and soul mingled." These sorts of words are not in fashion in the post- and antihumanist circles where Barthes is read. "Soul" is not a word intellectuals and critics use much anymore. The embarrassment caused by the phrase "body and soul mingled" is like the embarrassment I feel when I say that the man's wedding ring makes him a "real person." The phrase "real person" is an attempt to indicate that he exists, that he has a life that goes outside the frame. The question is, what is beyond the frame. I think we run into trouble when we start talking about what is beyond the frame. We get into a kind of troubling essentialism and start talking about "souls" and "the absolute excellence of being." I am wary of positing what is outside the frame, because when we posit that, we are once again within a long tradition of ontological and metaphysical projection—projection of what God is, what the real is, what the noumenal world is beyond phenomena. Photography and eroticism both occupy a space that is neither quite outside nor inside the frame, but are rather in some very conflicted and powerfully dynamic relation to inside and outside. In this space we confront the paradoxes of dependence and independence, nature and art, nature and the real, what I add and what is there already, what animates me and what I animate. For me, finally, that is the sexuality *of* art and the medium of photography.

Coming Out

The preceding essay was published in April 1985. In the fall of that year photographers in Houston brought to my attention a picture which was published in the first issue of a tabloid entitled *Theory/Flesh*. Opposite the photograph is an article by Minnette Lehmann entitled "Soft Spots in the Blind Field" in which she quotes Barthes's statement: "ROBERT WILSON, ENDOWED WITH AN UNLOCATABLE PUNCTUM, IS SOMEONE I WANT TO MEET." As I write this in the fall of 1987, I am looking forward to meeting Minnette Lehmann in December when I am in San Francisco (for the MLA Convention).

The Other Woman

In 1981 *Critical Inquiry*, one of the elite American journals of literary criticism and theory, published a feminist issue, edited by Elizabeth Abel. That issue, whose title is "Writing and Sexual Difference," betokens a feminist criticism that is interested not only in feminist so-

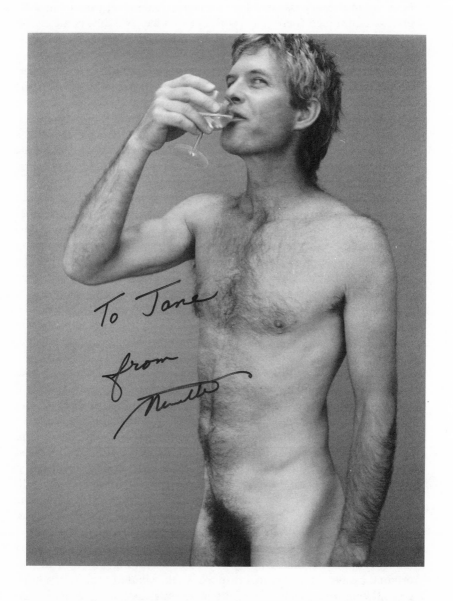

Minnette Lehmann, JANE GALLOP, ENDOWED WITH AN UNLOCAT-ABLE PUNCTUM, IS SOMEONE I WANT TO MEET.

cial, political, and psychological issues but also in "writing," which is to say in literary issues. I first delivered the present paper in 1984 at a colloquium entitled "The Poetics of Gender" which was the eighth in a series of Poetics Colloquia. That colloquium bespeaks the same moment in the history of feminist literary criticism. We might in fact line up "poetics" with "writing" and "gender" with "sexual difference." Yet there is also a specific resonance in Abel's title. "Writing and Sexual Difference" is a revision of Jacques Derrida's *Writing and Difference*, both published by the University of Chicago Press. If "Writing and Sexual Difference" is a feminist revision of Derrida's title, then what is marked is not only feminism's entrance on the stage of high literary theory but that this entrance occurs through the play of something translated from the French.

Things from the French had already fully penetrated the American literary theoretical discussion and had already insinuated themselves into American feminist criticism in a way that, I believe, made possible a feminist issue of *Critical Inquiry*, a certain coming together of literary theory and feminism, of poetics and gender. Conversely the *Colloque* which had always been on *la poétique*, which until recently had been conducted in French, both proceeded in English and had among its speakers a good number of critics from English departments. The new intercourse between literary theory and feminism seems to be concomitant with a permeation of the boundaries separating French and English departments.

"Writing and Sexual Difference" is thus in fact the scene of a double translation: from literary-philosophical terms—"Writing and Difference"—into sexual-feminist ones, as well as from French into English. *L'Ecriture et la différence* becomes *Writing and Sexual Difference*. And yet the two moves may be not simply coincidental but more deeply entwined, one with the other. In English, perhaps the most immediate association to the locution *la différence* is the French expression *Vive la différence*, by which we understand that The Difference, for the French, is sexual difference, and by which we imagine that the French have a peculiarly affirmative and sexy relation to that difference.

In the fall of 1982, the University of Chicago Press republished the feminist issue of *Critical Inquiry* as a book, including—along with the original essays—the "critical responses" that had appeared in a later *Critical Inquiry* as well as two other feminist articles that had been in the journal but outside the special issue. The book, likewise entitled *Writing and Sexual Difference*, is comprised of theoretically sophisticated and yet plainly forceful essays from some of our best feminist critics. Since all the essays in the book were already in the journal and remain unchanged, in some way the most exciting thing about the book when it appeared was the cover, which added a new "text" to the volume, one more striking and more "readable" than most covers.

The color is one of my personal favorites: a color which I, incorrectly, call mauve, one of those colors whose name in English is still in French. Almost pink: that color which is one of our markers of sexual difference and which, unlike its diacritical partner blue, remains—way past the nursery—marked as feminine. If blue, outside the infantile realm, is no longer a particularly masculine color, might not that relate to the phallocentrism which in our culture (as well as in most if not all others) raises the masculine to the universal human, beyond gender, so that the feminine alone must bear the burden of sexual difference? Pink then becomes *the* color of sexual difference, carrying alone within it the diacritical distinction pink/blue. Sexual difference itself becomes feminine, so that *L'Ecriture et la différence* might glide into *l'écriture féminine.*

But, as I said, the cover of Abel's anthology is not quite pink but rather something I call mauve. Not the blatant little-girl color, unseemly in its explicit, infantile femininity but a stylish, sophisticated version of that color, one that bespeaks not the messy, carnal world of the nursery but high culture, high feminine culture, the realms of interior decoration and *haute couture*, and also, of course, things from the French, as suggested by word "mauve." The color suggests that this is a feminine book but a highly cultured one, the feminine, bodily realm of the nursery sublimated through the mediation of Paris.

We may indeed be able to judge this book by its color, but I actually want to draw your attention to two black and white images on the cover. They are both pictures of people writing: on the front a woman, on the back a man. Together they compose a particularly well-articulated illustration of "writing and sexual difference." The woman is writing a letter; the man a book. Women write letters—personal, intimate, in relation; men write books—universal, public, in general circulation. The man in the picture is in fact Erasmus, father of our humanist tradition; the woman, without a name. In the man's background: books. The woman sits against floral wallpaper, echoed in reverse by her patterned dress. Feminine Culture: interior decoration and clothes. Black and white, the writing of flowers. The woman's face is completely smooth; no sense of bones beneath that surface. The man's face is hewn and angular; the skeleton structures his flesh. Perhaps most significantly, the man holds pen to paper and

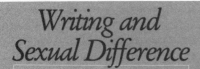

Writing and
Sexual Difference

Edited by Elizabeth Abel

The University of Chicago Press

ISBN: 0-226-00076-1

Quentin Metsys, "Portrait of Erasmus"   Mary Cassatt, "The Letter"

his pen is echoed by the scissors hanging there (on the bookshelves), likewise aiming its sharp point at the smooth white paper. The scissors bring out the incisiveness, penetration, violence of the pen. I would hesitate to associate that threatening point with masculine sexuality—I would not want to jump to a phallic conclusion—were it not so tempting here in proximity to the image of the penless woman literally licking the paper.

Or maybe kissing. In any case, her relation to the paper is not mediated through an instrument but is direct oral contact. Sandra Gilbert and Susan Gubar have suggested that in the masculine tradition the text is a woman, the pen a penis, and writing understood as coitus. In the picture of the woman, her face is as white and smooth as the paper, so that when she brings it to her mouth, like embraces like. Is *écriture féminine* lesbian cunnilingus?

Ecriture féminine: something else from the French. Not only do we supposedly naïve Americans think of the French as having a particular appreciation for sexual difference, but in the slang of our personal ads we refer to oral sex itself as "French" just as we give the French credit for our most seriously sexual sort of kiss. This picture of the woman licking paper is made by Mary Cassatt, an American woman who like many of us went to Paris in pursuit of her art.

Ecriture féminine, not only feminine but somehow French, a switch from the phallic to the oral sexual paradigm. Hélène Cixous, foremost spokeswoman for *écriture féminine,* does not disappoint this expectation. In her 1977 essay "La Venue à l'écriture" (the second word is the feminine past participle of the verb *venir,* to come—I translate the title of this as yet untranslated essay as "Coming to Writing"), Cixous writes: "Texts I ate them, I sucked them, I kissed them." "I caressed [my books]. Page by page, oh beloved, licked." Not only as a reader but as a writer does she affirm the model of writing as oral love: "To write: to love, inseparable. Writing is a gesture of love. . . . Read-me, lick-me, write-me love."[10]

"La Venue à l'écriture" appears in a book by the same title along with essays by two other women: "Le Corps dans l'écriture" ("The Body in Writing") by Madeleine Gagnon and "La Lettre d'amour" ("The Love Letter") by Annie Leclerc. Published in the 10/18 series "Féminine Future," a series directed by Cixous and Catherine Clément, this 1977 volume clearly functions as an important intervention in the politicized discussion of women's writing. And as you can tell from the titles, the three essays, although diverse in many ways, share a continual grounding of writing in the erotic body.

Leclerc's text, "La Lettre d'amour," is in fact, in its own way, a love letter. It contains a second-person addressee, a woman with whom she has just passed a night of lovemaking and to whom, after the morning's parting, Leclerc now wishes to express her love. A lesbian love letter. But of course this is also not a letter but an essay published in a book. Leclerc wishes precisely to heal the split portrayed on the cover of "Writing and Sexual Difference": women write letters, men books.

Love letters have always been written from the body, in connection with love. Leclerc wants all writing to have that connection; she wants love to enter into general circulation, inscribed knowledge, rather than remaining private and secret. "So many love letters [*lettres d'amour*, literally letters of, but also from love], but so few writings, real text, literature, science of/from love. . . . We who were so clever, greedy, and generous in . . . *billets* . . . to the beloved . . . we nonetheless let them say the true and the false . . . if our writings were of/from love, they risked their subversion only across intimacy and discretion. It was up to us, not them, to be philosophers . . . we were the ones who remained in our body, we were in touch with love" (pp. 133–34). We women must continue to write from our loving bodies, but we must break "discretion" and "intimacy" and "risk that subversion" in public, in print, in general circulation. And so Leclerc writes a letter to her lover which is also "real text, literature, science of/from love," philosophy from the body. Leclerc brings the love letter out of the closet and into the public domain.

Leclerc writes with excitement about the "extreme nudity" she experienced with her lover. She speaks of "dawn," of "birth," of "miracle" and one senses that this kind of love is a fresh discovery. In her book *Parole de femme*, published three years earlier, she seemed to write as a heterosexual; in that book the addressee is explicitly male. Only at one point in that earlier, heterosexual work does she mention homosexuality. She has just been affirming the pleasure of difference and then suddenly: "But no I don't spit on homosexual pleasures. I simply refuse to see in them the expression of a lack of sexual differentiation. . . . And what I love in woman is everything that makes her different from you. In truth I only love in the perspective of difference."[11] "But no," she begins, denying something that threatens assertion. For her, love is the celebration of difference, the encounter with difference, which risks sounding heterosexist, but she will not accept the notion that homosexuality is the pleasure of sameness. She wants to affirm difference in homosexuality, however much a contradiction in terms.

After the blatant heterosexuality of *Parole de femme*, we may be surprised that in "La Lettre d'amour" Leclerc writes as a lesbian. But this just-quoted passage does prepare us for the particular quality of Leclerc's lesbianism, an acute sense of the otherness of the other woman. Leclerc's love letter is not an essentialistic affirmation of the universal, anatomically based identity of all women. In its assertion of difference within lesbianism, it in fact recalls for me a crucial point Gayatri Spivak makes in her article "French Feminism in an International Frame": "However unfeasible and inefficient it may sound, I see no way to avoid insisting that there has to be a simultaneous other focus: not merely who am I? But who is the other woman?"[12]

Leclerc's "Love Letter" offers us a different image of woman writing. Whereas on the cover of "Writing and Sexual Difference," the difference was between man writing and woman writing, in Leclerc's picture women's writing takes its place in a tableau of the difference between women. Leclerc's picture? There is no illustration in the text, but the text is invisibly accompanied by a painting to which it continually refers. As she writes her lover, as she writes her text, she comments: "So, here then, she is always near me this Lady Writing a Letter and her Maidservant." The phrase "Lady Writing a Letter and Her Maidservant" [*Dame Ecrivant une Lettre et sa Servante*] is capitalized, and is in fact one of the titles of a painting by Vermeer. I found it under a similar English title—"Lady Writing a Letter, with Her Maid"—but, in the volume I used, it was also listed under the simple title "The Letter."

Leclerc's text is, in fact, a meditation on, an explication of, this painting. Like Cassatt, Vermeer has portrayed a woman writing a letter. She is, however, not simply a woman, but a "Lady" (actually, a *bourgeoise*) and with her is another woman, her servant. The difference between women is here, first of all, a difference of class. Yes, there is a tradition of women writing (writing letters at least), but the women are of a certain class: first the nobility, and then the bourgeoisie. There is a class of women who write and a class who serve those who write. Leclerc writes: "Admit finally that there is in this woman writing, a spoiled woman [*femme gâtée*] . . . a woman for whom the quill came into her fingers without her having to pluck it from the bird's wing" (pp. 138–39). Writing is not just a work of the spirit; there are material requisites. Labor must be done by another so that this woman can write. The labor has historical specificity, as does the scene: in 1667, the presumed date of the Vermeer, someone had to pluck a quill from a bird so a woman could write a letter. Obviously this is no longer literally the case, and yet if Leclerc, three centuries later, writes with a reproduction of this painting in

Vermeer, "The Letter"

the background it is because something about that relation still holds. Women no longer need servants to write letters; but what about the sort of open letters, public love writings Leclerc would write, that we would write? We must know the women of another class whose labor we rely on so that we can write: the women who clean our houses, care for our children, type our manuscripts; cleaning women and secretaries, for example.

Annie Leclerc identifies with the bourgeoise writing and she loves this picture. In fact she says that "the bad reproduction" of it which is in her possession is "the only object for which . . . [she] has . . . an undying attachment, the only object that is nourishment for [her]" (pp. 117–18). Rather than a source of paralyzing guilt, this picture is tremendously enabling for her. She contemplates the difference between these women, and rather than feeling guilt at the difference, rather than feeling pity, she feels desire. She writes: "I love the woman servant . . . oh no, not out of pity, not because I would take up the noble mantle of redressers of wrongs . . . but because I want to touch her, to take her hands, to bury my head in her chest, to smother her cheeks and neck with kisses" (p. 143). Leclerc's position is not the liberal sense that she ought to do something for this poor unfortunate woman. She sees this woman as beautiful, as having something she wants. Leclerc in fact explicitly and repeatedly identifies the maid with the woman to whom she is writing her love letter.

Of course, there is a long phallic tradition of desire for those with less power and privilege (women, for example) and I cannot but wonder about the relation of Leclerc's desire to this tradition. Just as I cannot but be reminded of the romantic and essentially conservative tradition of the happy and beautiful folk, the earthy, free working class. This is certainly a problem. Although Leclerc explicitly associates liberation and joy with socialist revolution, there is, after all, a revolutionary romantic tradition of idealizing the working class. Despite these problems I have with Leclerc's desire for the maid (an erotic attraction to women of another class which I share, I should add), I think it valuable as a powerful account of just that sort of desire, a desire that is frequently hidden under the "mantle of redressers of wrongs." Perhaps this desire gets us no closer than liberal superiority to knowing who the other woman is, but in its explicitness in Leclerc's text it allows us to see more clearly what is usually suppressed, repressed, or sublimated in our relation to the other woman.

Traditionally the maid carried letters between the lady and her beloved, a tradition Vermeer clearly draws on. There is, in fact, a Vermeer painting which Leclerc briefly alludes to which has the same title as her text: "The Love Letter." In yet another Vermeer—entitled "Maid Holding Out a Letter to Her Mistress"—the maid resembles the one in Leclerc's Vermeer. In this tradition the maid serves as go-between; her labor makes possible the love connection, but she is not its recipient. In Leclerc's revision of Vermeer, however, the lady not only would hand the letter to the maid, the maid would be its addressee.

Not only do ladies give letters to maids but they receive letters from them as well. In Leclerc's revision, Vermeer's maid (and the female lover with whom she is identified) is not only the addressee of her writing but also in a certain way its source. Leclerc writes to her lover: "Come . . . my tongue will die if yours doesn't come and bring its warm saliva. Come, I would like so much to tell you the secret that I have from the lady writing, who has it from her maidservant" (pp. 119–20). She cannot speak if her tongue dies. She wants to tell her lover something, but first she must get her lover's saliva. The interlocutor is also an enabling source of speech. Leclerc is writing a chain letter, which carries a secret to her lover, a secret she gets from Vermeer's lady who gets it from her maid. If what women write is not just love but knowledge, the source of the knowledge in "La Lettre d'amour" is not Leclerc the philosopher, not the educated, literate bourgeoise, but the maid.

And where does the maid get this knowledge? According to Leclerc, she "has it from the secret where women we are" (*le secret où femmes nous sommes*, ibid.). The maid gets it from the source, from the secret itself, from some secret feminine space where we are women, where we can be women, where we have been women. The "we" may refer to all women but it is also specifically the writer and her beloved addressee. The "secret where we are" is thus also, for example, the secret space of their loving, that space of discretion and intimacy. But that means it is a space where in the present of writing "we" are not, since she must summon her lover ("Come, my tongue will die"). Likewise it is a space to which her access is twice mediated, by a Lady writing a love letter and by her Maid.

For Leclerc, as for most proponents of *écriture féminine*, women's writing springs from a secret well of immanent femininity. "The secret where women we are" is not even the more grammatically common and predictable "where we are women" (*où nous sommes femmes*): which might imply that here we are women, elsewhere we aren't. "The secret where women we are" (*le secret où femmes nous sommes*)

Vermeer, "The Love Letter"

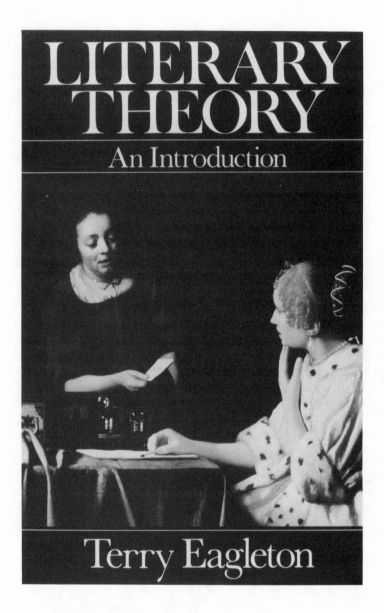

LITERARY THEORY
An Introduction

Terry Eagleton

Vermeer, "Servant Handing a Letter to Her Mistress"

is a space of being, pure and simple (*où nous sommes*), being without attribute. Yet the woman writing has only a mediated relation to that space of feminine being. She is divided from that secret, a division figured by the space between the lady writing and her maid. Leclerc's image of woman writing is an image of the rift between secret feminine knowledge—that is to say, pure feminine being—and writing. There is a space between *écriture* and *féminine*.

"From the woman servant to the woman writing," writes Leclerc, "an all-knowing plenitude is torn open" (p. 136). The woman servant stands in all-knowing plenitude. She is full, present, solid, round, and she knows. Moving from her to the writer, that fullness of knowledge is ruptured. For Leclerc the fullness and the split are morphologically represented in the two women's figures. "Here the curved and rounded arms, the warm and certain closure of the forearms, the hands tenderly linked . . . wedded . . . the splendid repose of a perfectly poised body" (ibid.). The plenitude is figured by the closure of the forearms and hands. She describes the forearms as "tenderly linked . . . wedded" *(épousés)*. Her plenitude is an erotic self-sufficiency. I am reminded here of Luce Irigaray's description of female sexuality as two lips caressing each other as well as of Sarah Kofman's characterization of the narcissistic woman.[13] The maid is narcissistically, pleasurably whole unto herself, hence her desirability.

And then the contrast with her mistress: "Here . . . the closure of the forearms . . . and there, in the foreground, but no longer central, as if displaced . . . leaning . . . and above all those disjoined arms, those separated hands . . . divorced, the left one still woman-servant, curved and mute, and the right one woman-mistress, as if distant from the body" (pp. 136–37). The woman writing is displaced, decentered, removed from the locus of being, as her right arm, her writing arm is removed from her body, from the curve of an embrace. The disjunction between maid and woman writing is repeated as the difference between the mistress's left and right arms. Unlike the maid's erotic self-sufficiency, wedded arms, the mistress' arms are "divorced," erotically bereft, divorced by the very act of writing. The rift in feminine plenitude is at once the space between maid and mistress (the separation of the two female lovers) and repeated as the disjuncture within the woman writer, who partakes of the maid's feminine knowledge but in writing forsakes the maid's mute and perfect curvature, the closure of self-embrace.

Although in her left hand she still partakes of feminine plenitude, "the right one [is] woman-mistress as if distant from the body . . . dare I say it, 'virile'?" (ibid.). The difference between front and back covers of "Writing and Sexual Difference" is in Leclerc's version a difference within the woman writing, embodied in the contrast between her two arms. The right arm, the writing arm, is for Leclerc "virile." Speaking no longer about Vermeer's bourgeoise, but now directly herself, she says: "If you only look at my . . . right hand, you'll see it at a distance from my body, you'll see it independent, abstract, male" (p. 137). In writing, she becomes masculinized—as she puts it, "it's as if I wanted to play the man in wanting to write" (ibid.). Yet the difference between the maid and her is *not* the difference between feminine and masculine women. She is by no means fully masculine: it is only her right hand. Not masculine but split, both in touch with the maid's secret and abstracted from it.

She insists that despite its masculinity, her right hand's "vocation is to formulate, to inscribe on the blank paper what in its shadow [her] wide and soft left hand whispers to it" (p. 138). In the painting, the lady's left hand is in the shadow (more discreet? more secretive?), her right is in the light. Leclerc describes her left hand as if it were a feminine object of desire: "My wide and soft left hand." Leclerc wants her right hand to copy down what the left hand knows. The mistress must write what the maidservant knows.

"She knows. She knows, the woman-servant who greets the babbling of sweet things in the light" (p. 122). The curtain is pulled open to let light in for the mistress' writing, but it is the maid who contentedly gazes into the light. And what she greets, whence the source of her knowledge, is "babbling" (*balbutiement*). *Balbutiement* usually has negative connotions, except when used to describe the speech of infants, and then *balbutiement* can be used tenderly. The reception of the infant's tentative, wondrous efforts is precisely woman's work, domestic work. Leclerc repeatedly and frequently identifies the maid with her mother. The women of another class who serve us recall the mother, recall her attentions to our material needs. The desire for the maid, along with the writer's resemblance to and difference from her, must also be understood in terms of the mother. We need to understand how our relation to the mother colors our relation to women of the class who work for us.

Leclerc's ascription of knowledge to the maid can also be understood as an example of transference, in the psychoanalytic sense. It is not only that Leclerc transfers her relation to her mother (and her lover) onto the maid, but that the maid is for Leclerc "the subject presumed to know," which is Lacan's definition of transference. And as in the case of psychoanalysis proper the transference seems to depend upon the maid's silence, a silence which Leclerc often says hurt her. Leclerc writes: "She knows. . . . And me I want to tell you what she knows. But also what she does not say" (*je veux te dire ce qu'elle sait. Mais ce qu'elle tait aussi;* ibid.). The close resemblance between the verb for "knows" and the verb for "not to speak"—*elle sait* and *elle tait*—enforces a connection between the maid's feminine knowledge and her silence, a silence Leclerc sometimes reads as willful, a complacent unwillingness to speak which abashes Leclerc.

"Whence comes this difficult and delicious will which distinguishes me from her?" (ibid.). The will to write, to write what the maid, the mother, the lover knows but keeps to herself, keeps secret, distinguishes the writer from the other woman. "Are we not, she and I, of the same flesh, same woman servant, woman serving under the same constraint of father, master, and husband?" (ibid.). Are not mother and daughter of the same flesh? Are not all women united in their common oppression? If the husband and master's constraint can be represented by the enclosure of the bourgeois household in which we find the two women, then it is the maidservant whose gaze goes outside, just as, presumably, she will physically carry the letter outside the house. Leclerc writes: "Admit that there is in [the woman writing] an abnegation, a consent to the limits, an adequation to the walls of the house" (p. 139).

The two women are not the same. "How also to want this distance between us and which hurts me so?" Leclerc asks (p. 122). The distance between them hurts Leclerc. But if she loves this picture, if it is the only object to which she is truly attached, it is certainly because it gives her an image of what, in her writing, she is striving for: an acceptance of the distance as well as the proximity between women.

We may well doubt whether the other women here is anything but a projection of a woman who would be truly immanently feminine, who would not be split like the writer. The real woman, the pure being-in-itself, is always the silent woman, always the other woman. And we traditionally project greater integrity of being to those with less power and privilege. And even beyond this big question we might well wonder why a painting by that seventeenth-century man Vermeer would tell us anything we need to know about woman's writing.

These problems with Leclerc's text are undeniable. Yet what I would like to hold on to from Leclerc's identification with Vermeer's Lady is the double image of the difference within *écriture féminine* in the hope of greater future understanding of the relation between these two rifts in an imaginary feminine and feminist plenitude. On the one hand the feminine psychological split: the internal division embodied

La venue à l'écriture

Hélène Cixous
Madeleine Gagnon
Annie Leclerc

Inédit

10|18

in the figure of a right-handed writer who wishes to write precisely what only her left hand knows. On the other hand the feminist socioeconomic rift: the simultaneous proximity and separation, resemblance and difference between the bourgeois woman writer and the other woman who may be our mother, lover, cleaning woman, or secretary. Future understanding not in order to close the divide and reach the space of pure and simple feminine being (*le secret où femmes nous sommes*) but in order precisely to "want this distance between us," in order better to ask the necessarily double and no less urgent questions of feminism: "not merely who am I? But who is the other woman?"

After I read the above paper at the "Poetics of Gender" colloquium, another woman (Nancy Miller to be exact) showed me the cover of *La Venue à l'écriture*, a cover I had never seen since I had worked with a bound library copy of the book. They have deleted the maidservant and left only the single woman writing: this on the cover of the very book wherein Leclerc fairly sings her love for the maid. Thanks to this cover, I realize that the problem of *écriture féminine* is not, as some would have it, its insistence on sexual difference at the expense of some universal humanity but rather, to my mind, its effacement of the difference between women in view of some feminine essence —in this case, the literal effacement of class difference—so as to represent woman alone at her writing table.

The difference between women, the question of the other woman, the rifts in feminist plenitude are extremely difficult to confront and even more difficult to hold on to. The temptation to universalize is powerful, not so much in our texts where difference is allowable, but on the cover, where we would like to encompass difference and get it all together. In our desire to make a book of it—a real book and not just letters—let us not forget the other woman.

Notes

1. Sigmund Freud, "The Moses of Michelangelo," in *The Standard Edition of the Complete Psychological Works*, ed. James Strachey (London: Hogarth, 1953–74), 8:211.

2. See Freud, "The Infantile Genital Organization," in *Standard Edition* (London: Hogarth, 1961), 19:141–45.

3. Freud, "On the Sexual Theories of Children," in *Standard Edition*, 9:215–20.

4. Leo Steinberg, "The Sexuality of Christ in Renaissance Art and in Modern Oblivion," *October* (1983), 25:16.

5. Roland Barthes, *Le Plaisir du texte* (Paris: Seuil, 1973), p. 90. Translations mine. Richard Miller has translated this book as *The Pleasure of the Text* (New York: Hill and Wang, 1975).

6. Roland Barthes, *La Chambre claire: Note sur la photographie* (Paris: Gallimard, Seuil, 1980). Translations mine. Richard Howard has translated it as *Camera Lucida: Reflections on Photography* (New York: Hill and Wang, 1981).

7. The best-known and most influential of these is Laura Mulvey's "Visual Pleasure and Narrative Cinema," *Screen* (1975), 16(3):6–18. My argument here is not with Mulvey's text but with a certain orthodox feminist position which has reified that text. I am aware that much current feminist film criticism is well beyond the simplistic position to which I take exception.

8. Susan Sontag, *On Photography* (New York: Dell, 1977), p. 169.

9. Roland Barthes, *S/Z* (Paris: Seuil, 1970), pp. 10–11. Translated by Richard Miller (New York: Hill and Wang, 1974).

10. Hélène Cixous, "La Venue à l'écriture," in *La Venue à l'écriture*, ed. H. Cixous, M. Gagnon, and A. Leclerc (Paris: Union Générale d'Editions, 1977), pp. 19, 30, 47–48.

11. Annie Leclerc, *Parole de femme* (Paris: Grasset, 1974), p. 80.

12. Gayatri Spivak, "French Feminism in an International Frame," *Yale French Studies* (1981), 62:179.

13. Luce Irigaray, "Ce Sexe qui n'en est pas un," in *Ce Sexe qui n'en est pas un* (Paris: Minuit, 1977), translated by Catherine Porter as *This Sex Which Is Not One* (Ithaca: Cornell University Press, 1985). Sarah Kofman, *L'Enigme de la femme* (Paris: Galilée, 1980), translated by Catherine Porter as *The Enigma of Woman* (Ithaca: Cornell University Press, 1985).

Index